CREATING
A
NATIONALITY

The United Nations Research Institute for Social Development (UNRISD) is an autonomous agency that engages in multi-disciplinary research on the social dimensions of contemporary problems affecting development. Its work is guided by the conviction that for effective development policies to be formulated, an understanding of the social and political context is crucial. The Institute attempts to provide governments, development agencies, grassroots organizations and scholars with a better understanding of how development policies and processes of economic, social and environmental change affect different social groups. Working through an extensive network of national research centres, UNRISD aims to promote original research and strengthen research capacity in developing countries.

Its research themes include Crisis, Adjustment and Social Change; Socio-Economic and Political Consequences of the International Trade in Illicit Drugs; Environment, Sustainable Development and Social Change; Ethnic Conflict and Development; Integrating Gender into Development Policy; Participation and Changes in Property Relations in Communist and Post-Communist Societies; Refugees, Returnees and Local Society; and Political Violence and Social Movements. UNRISD research projects focused on the 1995 World Summit for Social Development included Rethinking Social Development in the 1990s; Economic Restructuring and New Social Policies; Ethnic Diversity and Public Policies; and The War-torn Societies Project.

CREATING
A
NATIONALITY

*The Ramjanmabhumi Movement
and Fear of the Self*

Ashis Nandy
Shikha Trivedy
Shail Mayaram
Achyut Yagnik

DELHI
OXFORD UNIVERSITY PRESS
CALCUTTA CHENNAI MUMBAI
1997

Oxford University Press, Great Clarendon Street, Oxford OX2 6DP

Oxford New York
Athens Auckland Bangkok Calcutta
Cape Town Chennai Dar es Salaam Delhi
Florence Hong Kong Istanbul Karachi
Kuala Lumpur Madrid Melbourne Mexico City
Mumbai Nairobi Paris Singapore
Taipei Tokyo Toronto

and associates in

Berlin Ibadan

First published 1995
Oxford India Paperbacks 1997

ISBN 0 19 564271 6

Typeset by S.J.I. Services, New Delhi 110 024
Printed in India at Pauls Press, New Delhi 110 020
and published by Manzar Khan, Oxford University Press
YMCA Library Building, Jai Singh Road, New Delhi 110 001

PREFACE

This book began as an effort to give, through a partial narration of the Ramjanmabhumi conflict, a glimpse into the political culture of inter-religious or, as the South Asians prefer to call them, communal conflicts. The book, as it has emerged from our hands, seems to stand witness to the cultural and moral resilience of traditional communities in South Asia and their resistance to the assembly-line violence that now characterizes ethnic conflicts globally. That resistance has not always been successful or consistent. It has not even been always a matter of individual or collective volition; it has been rarely if ever heroic. It depends on social inertia and local politics, on the robust commonsense of people living ordinary lives, and on their sheer 'cussed' refusal to change their way of life when under cultural attack.

At Ramjanmabhumi, this resistance faces formidable odds. The following story, which had a happier ending in its earlier tellings, has now a more uncertain ending. Not merely due to the bitter memories of the recent past but also because of the more impersonal political processes taking over the entire public sphere in the subcontinent today. Community life in India may not be facing extinction, but it has obviously become a part of a larger project. That explains why the narrative, despite being in many ways an optimistic essay, is nevertheless tinged with a certain sense of tragic inevitability at times. But it does, we believe, make a case that no analysis of the Ramjanmabhumi movement is possible without reference to the resistance to the impersonal forces of organized mass violence at ground level.

This study of communal violence is actually part of a series on ethnic conflicts. Serious academics tell us that the two are not the same. Usually, the core concept in studies of religious fanaticism is fundamentalism; in studies of ethnicity, it is nationality. Our title hints at how we reconcile this anomaly, which we consider a direct product of western scholarship on the subject. The title represents the awareness that the chain of events we describe is the end-product of a century of effort to convert the Hindus into a 'proper' modern nation and a conventional ethnic majority and it has as its underside the story, which we have not told here, of corresponding efforts to turn the other faiths of the subcontinent into proper ethnic minorities and well-behaved nationalities. To many, these are worthwhile goals but unfortunately, for a world defined by the concepts of progress, development, secularism, national security and the nation-state, these goals have to be achieved in a society where the borderlines of communities and cultures have not been traditionally defined by census operations or electoral rolls and where traditional ideas of community life and inter-community relations survive. For others, therefore, even the partial achievement of these goals is a minor tragedy, for its consequence cannot be anything but ethnocide in the long run. We hope we have captured something of that tragic awareness in the following pages.

South Asia has always been a salad bowl of cultures. For long it has avoided—to the exasperation of modern nationalists and statists of the right and the left—the American-style melting pot model and its individualistic assumptions and anti-communitarian bias. In a salad the ingredients retain their distinctiveness, but each ingredient transcends its individuality through the presence of others. In a melting pot, primordial identities are supposed to melt. Those that do not are expected to survive as coagulates and are called nationalities or minorities; they are expected to dissolve in the long run. Much of the recent violence in South Asia can be traced to the systematic efforts being made to impose the melting-pot model upon time-worn Indian realities.

Not that everyone rues this imposition. Now that the witches' broth has been brewed in South Asia, those committed to the nineteenth-century European concepts of state and nationalism seem happy that old-style conflicts of nationalities have surfaced in Mother India to prove that the savages have entered the modern age and have begun to diligently climb the social evolutionist ladder so thoughtfully gifted to them by the European Enlightenment. To such statists and nationalists, the escalating communal and ethnic violence in South Asia is only an unavoidable by-product of state-building and nation-formation and could be easily handled by the law-and-order machinery of the state, given adequate political will.

What remains unexplored is the way the modern state itself invites the formation of such adversarial nationalities by leaving that as the only effective way of making collective demands on the state and playing the game of numbers in competitive politics. For reasons of space and the limited skills available to us, we have focused here on a part of the story: on how such nation-building has unfolded in the case of the Hindus, the largest and most pervasive religious community in the region, with notoriously ill-defined borders. (As Kumar Suresh Singh's recent work, done for the Anthropological Survey of India shows, about one-sixth of the communities in the landmass called India cannot be clearly identified as belonging to any single religion, as conventionally defined.) We have told the story mainly from the point of view of Hinduism not only because it scaffolds the Indic civilization but also because it is now being pummelled into a standardized religion of a standardized majority, no different from the other religions in the 'advanced' societies that have already become primarily the markers of majorities and minorities in the world of enumerative politics. We hope we have been able to give a flavour of that process of apparently inevitable social progress.

We say 'apparently inevitable' because cultures protest, even if sometimes in silence. As those who speak on behalf of Hindu nationalism froth at the mouth to sustain the fever-pitch pace of the cultural engineering of the Hindus, the lived world of Hinduism has brought into play its own mechanisms of re-reading and cauterizing its traumatic experiences and its even older traditions of social healing. In this tradition of re-reading, cauterizing and healing of social traumata, two crucial psychosocial attributes are: principled forgetfulness (as an antidote to the ravages of modern historical consciousness) and multi-layered primordialities within an open-ended self (as an antidote to the ravages of the impersonality and massification that characterize the modern market, economic as well as political, and have become the underside of modern individualism). No description of inter-religious violence in India is complete unless it takes into account these attributes.

It is also our belief that any description of inter-religious violence in South Asia must take note of the resistance that such violence faces from everyday Hinduism and Islam. That resistance is not noticed because another kind of 'principled' forgetfulness comes into play when modern, secular scholars study religious or ethnic violence. That forgetfulness is not accidental, for to remember such resistance is to deny the importance of one's own categories and the monopoly that one's class has come to claim in the matter of ethnic and religious tolerance. That forgetfulness sanctions the use of state power and statist propaganda for repressing the awareness that the ideologues of religious violence represent the disowned other self of South Asia's modernized middle classes. That is why any interpretation of ethnic and religious violence that defies the categories of the subcontinent's westernized bourgeoisie manages to trigger such immense anxieties; it becomes in effect an attempt to defy the defences that protect oneself from any awareness of that disowned self.

This book, being mainly written from the point of view of Hinduism, makes no attempt to balance its portrayal of Hindu nationalism by a discussion of Islamic revivalism or of the cynical Muslim leaders who have played a significant role in the Ramjanmabhumi issue. Nor is there in the book any discussion of the truth or otherwise of the historical or archaeological evidence adduced by the contending parties. They are important, but not for this narrative. We are primarily concerned here with the living reality of Indian civilization and the fate of its moral vision. This has imposed on us the responsibility of first stating what the Ramjanmabhumi events might mean to a majority of Indians.

Is it all a losing battle against time? Are we chronicling a present that is quickly becoming a past? Does the future lie only in the impersonal checks of institutions and ideas such as the constitution, democratic elections, and human rights? We are reluctant to answer these questions here. Let our story speak for itself. But we are not giving out too much of it if we reveal here that we have been forced to reckon with the tendency in the contending parties to bounce back to what might be called their authentic primordialities once they have even partly extricated themselves from the loving embrace of the cultures of the modern state and nationalism. Ayodhya has often been close to being back to its 'normal', lethargic, easy lifestyle and to its own distinctive mix of the petty and the sublime even while it has waited warily for the next move on the chessboard of national politics. Even today the sacred city is trying to return to its own rhythm: almost all the victims of the riots that followed the traumatic events of December 1992 are back, and the political formation that hoped to ride the Ramjanmabhumi movement to power has been defeated in the state elections of 1993, even in eight out of the nine constituencies in the district of which Ayodhya is a part. That there are still forces resisting this return to Ayodhya's own concept of normal life is part of the same story.

In other words, while this is a simple story simply told, we are aware that the Ramjanmabhumi conflict is part of a larger civilizational encounter, though not in the way it is often made out to be. The conflict *can* be read as another unresolved problem bequeathed to Indian civilization by the imperial West and its vision of a good society, the last frantic assault by nineteenth-century social evolutionism on the core organizing principles of Hinduism, another great proxy battle the modern West has chosen to fight through its brain children in the Southern world. On this plane, the conflict is not the climax in a series of grand crusades between Hindus and Muslims, but one more desperate attempt to make the two communities deserving citizens of a global order built on the values of the European Enlightenment.

That is why in the story we have told there are no villains. We might have slipped here and there, as for instance in chapter 4 where we come close to identifying individuals and groups which systematically stoke communal violence. Usually those who look like villains in our story turn out to be messengers carrying messages they themselves cannot read. For to get behind their slogans, in the words of Ziauddin Sardar and Merryl Wynch Davies, 'is to enter the world of the marginalized and realize that theirs is an invaded, fragmented, destabilized, recreated, modified territory.' To see these unhappy, torn, comic-strip crusaders for Hindutva as great conspirators and bloodthirsty chauvinists is to underwrite the self-congratulatory smugness of India's westernized middle class and deny its complicity in the Ramjanmabhumi stir. But perhaps we are being unfair. Everything said, in both cases we are dealing with a frightened species facing extinction, trying to discover in its own ideology of violence clues to a changing world where neither the definition of a 'proper' state nor that of nationality or nationalism has remained constant.

We are grateful to the United Nations Research Institute of Social Development and its imaginative director, Dharam Ghai, and to Rodolfo Stavenhagen, who co-ordinated the programme, for supporting this venture and providing the comparative intellectual background that frames this study. They are not, of course, responsible in any way for the contents of this book. For all we know, they might violently disagree with some of our interpretations.

Others who have contributed to the book in various capacities are the not-so-anonymous referees of UNRISD, the plethora of political functionaries, activists, religious leaders and plain citizens whom we interviewed in and around Ayodhya. We specially remember with a deep sense of gratitude the help given to us by the chief priest of the Ramjanmabhumi temple, Laldas, who was murdered in 1993 when this book was in press.

Parts of the work were presented at a meeting organized by the UNRISD at Dubrovnik in the summer of 1990 just before that breathtaking medieval city tasted the fruits of another grand venture in state-formation and nation-building that sought to sacrifice the vernacular at the altar of the global and the modern. We have gained much from the comments and suggestions of participants at that meeting. Another part of the work was presented at the Wellfleet Conference in the autumn of 1993 where the participants, especially Robert J. Lifton and his colleagues at the Center for Violence and Human Survival, were a source of rich insights.

This study was done at the Committee for Cultural Choices and Global Futures, a collaborative venture of scholars, activists and thinkers. It has gained much from the criticisms of G. P. Deshpande, Asghar Ali Engineer, Harsh Sethi and Yogendra Yadav, and from the help given by institutions such as the Centre for the Study of Developing Societies (Delhi), Setu (Ahmedabad), Institute of Development Studies (Jaipur), and the Indian People's Front (Colonelgunj, UP). We are especially grateful to Pankaj Chaturvedi for assistance in fieldwork and to Dr Binda for the map used in the section on the Jaipur riot in this book. Vaqqar ul Ahad, Shubh Mathur and Kavita Shrivastava commented on this section and voluntary groups that helped are PUCL, IPTA, Hindusthani Manch, Vishakha, Coordination Committee on Relief and Rehabilitation and Communal Harmony, All India Muslim Women's Welfare Organization, Rajasthan University Women's Associations, Sampradayikata Virodhi Samiti, Prayas, and Mazdoor Kisan Shakti Sangathan. Others to whom we are particularly indebted are Ramkripal Singh, B. N. Das, Bhalubhai Desai, and Ramesh Parmer. But above all, we are beholden to C. V. Subba Rao, gifted human rights activist, for his detailed suggestions and critical comments; many parts of the present version of the book have improved enormously due to his painstaking notes. Subba Rao died when the book was in press. It is to the memory of Laldas and Subba Rao that this work is dedicated.

One final word of apology. This is a collaborative work done by four independent, self-willed persons who differ in significant ways in their approach to the problem handled in this book. These differences are sometimes reflected in the book. We have not tried to hide them in the belief that what binds us together is a common commitment to a more humane society in South Asia, a conviction that professional and academic boundaries will have to be crossed to make sense of the problem, and the belief that the social pathologies in this part of the world will have to be grappled with on the basis of the inner strengths of the civilization as expressed in the ways of life of its living carriers. Our attempt has been to make this a straightforward narrative woven around a reportage on Ayodhya that would allow for a glimpse of the sacred city at three critical moments in its life. It is meant not so much for specialists researching ethnic violence as for intellectuals and activists trying to combat mass violence in the Southern societies unencumbered by the conceptual categories popular in the civilized world.

We are told that there are at least 2,500 potential nationalities in the world waiting to stake their claim to full nationhood. Maybe that is one way of looking at the problem. We have tried to show in the following pages that the idea of such nationhood is not a space-and-time-independent mode of self-affirmation and that it may have to be built, as it has been in the case of India, on the ruins of one's civilizational selfhood. It is too early to say whether the effort will be successful.

For the fastidious reader, we should clarify that for easier reading we have avoided all diacritical marks except ā (as in palm) and ī (as in deep). In the case of proper names, diacritical marks have been done away with altogether (Rath Yatra though otherwise *yātrā*). We have also tried to be faithful to the local languages rather than to Sanskrit. Hence, Rath and not Ratha, Ram and not Rama.

Contents

Seeing Ravan riding a chariot and Ram chariotless, Vibhishan was worried.... Touching Ram's feet, he asked affectionately, 'Lord, chariotless and barefooted, how will you vanquish such a brave and powerful adversary?'

Ram the all-merciful replied, 'Listen friend. The chariot that leads to victory is of another kind. Valour and fortitude are the wheels of the chariot; truthfulness and virtuous conduct are its banner; strength, discretion, self-restraint and benevolence are its four horses, harnessed with the cords of forgiveness, compassion and equanimity....

There is no other way of victory than this. my friend, whoever has this righteous chariot, has no enemy to conquer anywhere.'

—Tulsi, 'Lankākānda', *Ramcharitamānas*

CHAPTER ONE

I. THE BEGINNING

The temple town of Ayodhya is situated on the bank of the river Saryu, some six miles from the city of Faizabad in eastern Uttar Pradesh or UP. Ayodhya is a sacred city. Its name suggests a place where battles cannot or do not take place. Tradition says that it is the birthplace of Lord Ram, an incarnation of Vishnu. According to the 1991 census Ayodhya has about 41,000 residents; it is a part of the Faizabad urban conglomerate which has a population of about 1,77,000. Ayodhya being a pilgrimage town, such estimates can only be rough. The number of its residents constantly fluctuates. It is as difficult to guess the number of temples the city has. Estimates by local residents usually range between three and five thousand, though many mention figures around six thousand and a few mention figures close to ten thousand.

As in a few other temple towns of India, the temples in Ayodhya have been places of residence for its inhabitants. Till some decades ago, it is said, nearly all the inhabitants of the city stayed in these temples. Even now, a huge majority does so. Probably as a result, the style of the city is clearly influenced by its religious status; it is markedly Vaishnava.

Daniel Gold begins his analysis of organized Hinduism with the following comment on the city:

Ayodhya has ... managed to escape the chaotic excitement and hucksterism that comes with the worst excesses of the pilgrim trade. To the jaded researcher of traditional Hindu life, it can seem an unusually peaceful place, with visitors and residents calmly following their customary pursuits in the shops and temples throughout the town. Only once during my several sojourns there in 1980 and 1981 was an attempt made to draw me into a charged religious situation—and this by no traditional pilgrim guide.[1]

[1]Daniel Gold, 'Organized Hinduism: From Vedic Truth to Hindu Nation',

Unlike the famous temples in some other Indian cities, Ayodhya temples are open to all—Hindus and non-Hindus, Brahmans and 'untouchables', believers and non-believers. There are at least two temples that have been constructed by Muslims.[2] One of them is still managed by a Muslim. A fairly large number of temples, according to their priests, have benefited from land grants and tax exemptions given by Ayodhya's erstwhile Shia Nawabs and British rulers and some of the most famous temples have been built on land donated specifically for that purpose by Muslim aristocrats. Many temples enthusiastically show their visitors documents relating to land grants given by Muslim officials during the times of the Nawabs in return for rituals performed by the priests of the temples. Hanumangarhi, for instance, was built with the help of a land grant from Nawab Safdar Jang (1739–54) to the *mahant* or abbot of Nirvani *ākhāda*, Abhayramdas, and Khaki *ākhāda* was established on the basis of another land grant from Nawab Shuja-ud-Daulah.[3] Peter van der Veer goes so far as to say that Ayodhya became an important pilgrimage centre in the eighteenth century not as a result of the removal of interference by the Nawabs but, on the contrary, as a result of the patronage of the court of the Nawabs.[4] According to the belief of some local Hindus, the city of Ayodhya itself was gifted to one Darshan Singh by the Muslim nawab of Lucknow to honour god Shankara. Some priests say that the city was given as a gift by the Emperor Babar to the Acharyas, a Vaishnava sect. And there is at least one instance when a Muslim philanthropist donated his all for the founding of a temple and lived the rest of his life on the food and apparel provided by the temple itself.

There are other forms of interweaving of pieties and communities, too. Even today, despite the bitterness of the last eight years, the flowers offered for worship in the Ayodhya temples are almost all grown by Muslims. The Muslims still weave the garlands used in the temple and produce everything necessary for dressing the icons

---

in Martin E. Marty and R. Scott Appleby (eds), *Fundamentalism Observed* (Chicago: University of Chicago Press, 1991) pp. 531–93; see p. 531.

[2] The sentiments are reciprocated; there still survive in the region *imambadas* owned by Hindus.

[3] Peter van der Veer, *Gods on Earth: The Management of Religious Experience and Identity in a North Indian Pilgrimage Centre* (New Delhi: Oxford University Press, 1989), pp. 143–4.

[4] Ibid., p. 37.

preparatory to worship. Until some years ago, the making of the crowns of the gods was the near-monopoly of Muslim master craftsmen such as Rahmat Sonar and Nannu Sonar; the thrones for the gods are even today made by the likes of Balam Mistri, a highly respected Muslim carpenter.

All this is not strange, some say. After all Ayodhya is located in the cultural region called Avadh, a region that has been remarkably free from communal or inter-religious tension and strife in recent times. There has always been in the high culture of Avadh a certain mix of courtly sophistication, pastoral earthiness and, one might add, an androgynous creative style. To this culture the Nawabs of Avadh, who came into their own during the decline of the Mughal empire, contributed greatly. To them, respect for the faith of the majority of their subjects made both moral and political sense. During their rule the administrative control of Avadh was mostly in the hands of Hindu Khatri and Kayastha families; even the army was dependent on the regiments of Dashanami Nagas and, at times, a majority of the generals were Hindus. Talking of the reign of one of the Nawabs, Asaf-ud-Daulah (1775–93), van der Veer says: 'It is not difficult to conclude that ... the *nawabi* Avadh was as much a Hindu state as it was a Muslim one.'[5]

Most of the older temples of Ayodhya were built in the eighteenth century under the rule of the Nawabs. The last Nawab of Avadh, Wajid Ali Shah (1847–56), is often mentioned as a typical product of the region; many consider him a king only Avadh could have produced. The Nawab was a scholar, musician, poet and dancer deeply influenced by the Vaishnava lifestyle and legends (he himself sometimes danced in the role of Krishna). When he was deposed by Lord Dalhousie in the mid-nineteenth century, these 'unkingly' qualities were used as a justification for his unceremonious dismissal. Many modern Indians, too, saw and—like film director Satyajit Ray in *Shatranj ke Khilari*—continue to see his fall as just desserts for his effeminacy, feudal decadence, and poor grasp of realpolitik.[6]

In such a culture, Ram might not have been a national hero, but he certainly was a cultural hero. Historian Bipan Chandra tells us that in parts of UP the standard greeting used by both Hindus and

---

[5]van der Veer, *Gods on Earth*, p. 144.

[6]Satyajit Ray, *Shatranj ke Khilari* (Calcutta: D. K. Films Enterprise, 1977), producer: Suresh Jindal, script: Satyajit Ray, story: Premchand.

Muslims until the 1920s was '*Jai Ramji*' (victory to Ram). We found that in Ayodhya, even till 1991, despite what had happened during the previous few years, the Muslims continued to use the salutation '*Jai Ramji ki*' or '*Jai Siyā Ram*' (victory to Sita and Ram).

Ayodhya, however, is not all pastoral innocence. There have been Hindu-Muslim conflicts even in the earlier centuries centring on the Ramjanmabhumi, which the Hindus claimed, and Hanumangarhi, which the Muslims did.[7] (These conflicts were obviously interspersed by periods of mutual accommodation. The first European visitor to the place, William Finch, for instance, found that even in the compound of the newly built Babri masjid, Hindu worship was possible between 1608 and 1611).[8] Today, the priests of Ayodhya have their usual proportion of the corrupt and the lecherous. Some of them have also developed criminal connections. The succession of a *mahant* is no longer a simple, peaceful affair. Politics and money play an important part in it.

Electoral politics has also entered Ayodhya in a big way. There have been local elections in the region since the latter part of the nineteenth century but, since 1952, the town has been a part of the Faizabad Parliamentary and Assembly constituencies, where a number of castes have tried over the years to translate their numerical strength into political presence. In the Faizabad Parliamentary constituency and district, Brahmans, Ahirs and the previously untouchable Chamars are numerically the strongest. When the geographically smaller Faizabad *tehsil* or *pargana* is taken into account, political competition seems to involve, apart from these three castes, also the Pasis. In the Ayodhya Assembly constituency though, the Chamars have been much less important. But even in an open polity, political success is not a matter of only numbers; it also depends on local power bases and alliances. The most consistent competition in Ayodhya and the area around it has been between the Brahmans and the Ahirs, but it has crucially involved a number of other communities, notably the Kurmis and the Muslims.[9]

[7]van der Veer, *Gods on Earth*, pp. 38–9.

[8]Ibid.

[9]For a comprehensive account of the politics of the Faizabad district, see Harold Gould, 'Modern Politics in an Indian District: "Natural Selection" and "Selective Co- Optation"', in Richard Sisson and Ramashray Roy (eds), *Diversity and Dominance in Indian Politics* (New Delhi: Sage, 1990), Vol. 1: *Changing Bases of Congress Support*, pp. 217–48.

As a result of this long exposure to competitive politics, the denominational and caste divisions among the priests of the Ayodhya temples have now in many cases acquired political meanings and factionalized even the supporters of individual parties. With politics have come the media, new kinds of entrepreneurs and, in recent years, larger contingents of police and paramilitary forces. To the older divisons and hostilities among sects have been added new divisions and hostilities based on party allegiances, factional alignments and economic interests.

On 30 October 1990, a few thousand men, largely members or sympathizers of ultra-Hindu organizations belonging to the *Sangh parivār* or the Rashtriya Swayamsevak Sangh (RSS) family, mainly the RSS itself, the Vishwa Hindu Parishad (VHP), the Akhil Bharatiya Vidyarthi Parishad (ABVP), Bajrang Dal, and their common electoral face, the Bharatiya Janata Party (BJP) converged here in response to a call given by a militant section of their leadership to liberate the 'real' and 'only' site of Lord Ram's birth. This site, they claimed, was the same on which stood the Babri masjid of Ayodhya and where an ancient Ram temple built by Maharaja Vikramaditya had been desecrated and destroyed in 1528 by Mir Baqi, a noble in the Mughal Emperor Babar's court.

There was, at the time this story begins, a relatively modest temple within the compound of—actually telescoped into— the masjid called the Ramjanmabhumi temple, with its *garbha griha*, sanctum sanctorum, located within a part of the masjid.[10] It co-existed with a number of other temples claiming the same status near about the same place and at least two of them had traditionally competed, more or less on an equal footing, with the now-controversial temple for devotees, offerings, and fame.

[10]Within the compound of the mosque there was also a charming little temple called Sita-ki-Rasoi, Sita's Kitchen, which was conveniently forgotten with the rising tempo of the Ram temple movement and its demand for a big temple and the demolition of the mosque. On the larger meaning of this forgetfulness, see Ramchandra Gandhi's evocative account, written from the point of view of India's spiritual traditions, *Sita's Kitchen: A Testimony of Faith and Inquiry* (New Delhi: Penguin, 1992).

For the moment, we bypass the dishonesty and moral vacuity of the likes of Koenraad Elst (*Ramjanmabhumi vs Babri Masjid: A Case Study in Hindu–Muslim Conflict*, New Delhi: Voice of India, 1990) on this issue. In any case, they have been adequately answered by Gandhi in *Sita's Kitchen*, see esp. pp. 108–9.

To 'liberate' meant to pull down the existing structure of the Babri masjid and perform *kārsevā*, work as service or offering, to construct a Ram temple exactly at the same spot to avenge the injustice done to the Hindus in the past. At 12.02 PM that day, a 300-strong vanguard of *kārsevaks* representing the militant spirit of Hindutva—the early twentieth-century expression for Hindu nationalism or political Hinduism—were marginally successful in their attempt to damage the mosque as thousands more cheered this act of 'vengeance'.[11] Five people were shot dead by the security forces at various spots in Ayodhya during the day. Two days later, on 2 November, another attempt was foiled, resulting in the death of nineteen people. But before we begin to tell that story, a brief digression on what we know about inter-religious strife in contemporary India.

II. THE PAST

The incidence of communal riots has been increasing consistently in India over the last four decades. Available data show that the increase has been more than six-fold between 1954 and 1985 (Table 1). The annual casualties in such riots, too, have increased nearly ten-fold. Given the vagaries of official statistics, both figures are likely to be underestimates; this underestimation probably compensates for the growth in communal violence due to the country's growing population.

These incidents of violence in India are not distributed randomly. A large proportion of them take place in six states—Andhra Pradesh, Bihar, Gujarat, Maharashtra, Rajasthan, and Uttar Pradesh. In four states, they take place infrequently, some would say rarely. In ten other states, virtually no riot ever takes place, not only showing the difficulty of formulating propositions that can have pan-Indian applicability, but also the difficulty of relating such problems to the general contents of faith. After all, most of the ten states that are almost entirely peaceful are inhabited by the

---

[11]*Kārsevaks* are those who offer *kārseva*, worship through work. There is no tradition of *kārseva* in Hinduism. No Hindu temple has ever been built through *kārseva*. In much of Hindu India, the word did not even make any sense till recently. The idea and the term have been borrowed from Sikhism and, as a result, have meaning only for north Indians.

TABLE 1
FREQUENCY AND CASUALTIES OF COMMUNAL INCIDENTS
(1954–85)

Year	Number of incidents	Persons killed	Persons injured
1954	84	34	512
1955	75	24	457
1956	82	35	575
1957	58	12	316
1958	40	7	369
1959	42	41	1344
1960	26	14	262
1961	92	108	593
1962	60	43	348
1963	61	26	489
1964	1,070	1,919	2,053
1965	173	34	758
1966	144	45	467
1967	198	251	880
1968	346	133	1,309
1969	519	673	2,702
1970	528	298	1,607
1971	321	103	1,263
1972	240	69	1,056
1973	242	72	1,318
1974	248	87	1,123
1975	205	33	890
1976	169	39	794
1977	188	36	1,122
1978	230	110	1,853
1979	304	261	2,379
1980	421	372	2,691
1981	319	196	2,631
1982	470	238	3,025
1983	500	1143	3,652
1984	476	445	4,836
1985	525	328	3,665

SOURCE: P. R. Rajgopal, *Communal Violence in India* (New Delhi: Uppal, 1987), pp. 16–17.

FIGURE 1

DECADE-WISE RISE IN RATES OF COMMUNAL
VIOLENCE IN INDIA (CASUALTIES PER 1 MILLION)

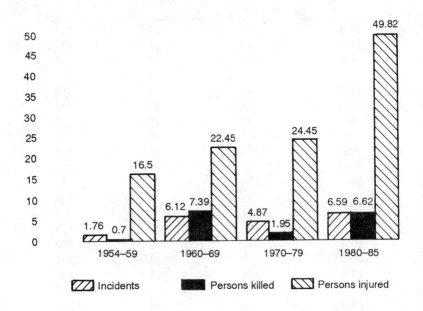

same religious communities, and at least two of them have undergone communal holocausts in 1947 in which nearly one million died.

Within the ten states in which the bulk of riots take place, the great majority of the violent incidents takes place in the cities. According to Gopal Krishna, of the 7,964 incidents of communal violence in the period 1961–70, only 32.55 per cent took place in rural India though roughly 80 per cent of Indians lived in villages at the time (see Table 2).[12] Data for recent years are not available but P. R. Rajagopal says that 46 per cent of communal incidents in 1985 were rural.[13] That may have been an aberrant year; there are indications

[12]Gopal Krishna, 'Communal Violence in India: A Study of Communal Disturbance in Delhi', *Economic and Political Weekly*, 12 January 1985, 20, pp. 62–74; see p. 64.

[13]Rajagopal, *Communal Violence*, p. 20.

that rioting in villages is growing at a much slower rate than in the cities, except probably in eastern India, though it has been increasing, especially in villages close to cities. However, if one goes by the place where riots originate, cities reportedly account for about 90 per cent of the riots even today.

Table 1 and Figure 1 give the reader an idea of the growing scale of communal violence in India. These figures can, however, be read another way. To be fair to the reader and to the Indian experience with inter-religious violence, one must at least mention the alternative, more optimistic interpretation here. The casualty figures mentioned above do not add up to the total number of homicides in a respectable North American metropolitan city.[14] Though in recent times these figures have sometimes risen dramatically—1990 and 1992, for instance, were particularly bad years—the Indian figures still remain remarkably small when viewed in the context of the nearly 900 million who inhabit the country.[15] For instance, the other large, multi-ethnic, open society, the United States, though one-third of India in population, had in 1990 more than 30,000 cases of homicide (about twenty times the number of people killed in communal violence in India).

There is also the possibility that the Indian over-concern with communal violence is at least partly a result of the over-concern with communal violence in the national media, particularly in the publications that cater to the north-Indian audience—so at least one would suspect from the recent exploratory work done by a journalist.[16] We hope that those who would prefer to read the following account as an exercise in qualified optimism will find in it reasons for optimism.

The most influential explanations of communal riots in India are the ones that emphasize communal ideology. Most people are convinced,

[14]We are grateful to Otto Feinstein for bringing this to our notice at a meeting on ethnic conflicts at Dubrovnik (6–10 June 1991).

[15]Even when one looks at the spate of separatist movements in contemporary India—a major source of anxiety for Indian political leaders and the country's well-wishers—the total population involved in such movements turns out to be not more than roughly 25 million out of 900.

[16]Sukumar Muralidharan, 'Mandal, Mandir aur Masjid: "Hindu" Communalism and the Crisis of the State', in K.N. Panikkar, ed., *Comunalism in India: History, Politics and Culture* (New Delhi: Manohar, 1991), pp. 196–218, esp. pp. 206–18. Muralidharan has, however, an entirely different explanation for this difference. That interpretation, derived from his ideological posture, is not relevant here.

TABLE 2

INCIDENTS OF COMMUNAL VIOLENCE IN RURAL AND
URBAN INDIA 1961–70 (PER CENT)

Year	Incidents	Rural (%)	Urban (%)
1961	439	34.9	65.1
1962	211	52.1	47.9
1963	138	49.3	50.7
1964	2,115	41.2	58.8
1965	487	29.0	71.0
1966	573	13.1	86.9
1967	1,471	26.9	73.1
1968	475	25.7	74.3
1969	1,126	22.5	77.5
1970	929	43.4	56.6
Total	7,964	32.5	67.5

SOURCE: Adapted from Krishna, 'Communal Violence in India', p. 64.

like Rajgopal, that 'communalism as an ideology is the ultimate source of all communal riots'.[17] As with some of the major interpretations of racism offered in North America and Europe in the immediate post-World-War-II period, such as the trend-setting work on the authoritarian personality by T. W. Adorno and his associates in the early 1950s,[18] most modern social thinkers and activists in India have used communal ideology, if not as the ultimate source, at least as a major independent variable in their explanations of communal riots. In fact, this is *the* modernist explanation of ethnic violence in the country.[19]

[17]Rajgopal, *Communal Violence*, p. 20.
[18]T.W. Adorno, Else Frenkel-Brunswik, Daniel J. Levenson, and R. Nevitt Sanford, *The Authoritarian Personality* (New York: Norton, 1950).
[19]Some examples are Romila Thapar, Harbans Mukhia, and Bipan Chandra, *Communalism and the Writing of Indian History* (New Delhi: People's Publishing House, 1969); most of the papers included in Asghar Ali Engineer (ed.), *Communal Riots in Post-Independence India* (Hyderabad: Sangam Books, 2nd ed., 1991); and S. Gopal (ed.), *The Anatomy of a Confrontation: The Babri Masjid-Ram Janmabhumi Issue* (New Delhi: Viking, 1991). For even neater examples, see Akhilesh Kumar, *Communal Riots in India: Study of Social and Economic Aspects* (New Delhi: Commonwealth, 1991); and Nirmala Srinivasan, *Prisoners of Faith: A View From Within* (New Delhi: Sage, 1989).

Many of those who use western studies in fascist personality as their theoretical and operational frame are not psychologists. Their practice, therefore, has been to offset this emphasis on ideology against a straightforward socio-economic or class profile of the protagonists and to ignore both the core fantasies and psychological defences behind communal ideology and the cultural links between the ideology and the social background of the ideologue, as if the stress on ideology was not fully acceptable even to those researching the ideology and had to be forgotten as soon as possible.

This ambivalent fascination with communal ideology could have many sources. First, there is the fact that all political parties that have espoused the 'Hindu' or 'Islamic' causes have been heavily ideological parties. For various reasons, they have sought to plead their case primarily on ideological grounds. One reason could be that the stress on ideology makes organized violence against victim communities more palatable to the social sectors having a disproportionate access to, or control over, the state machinery, the judiciary and the media. As a result, those who oppose such ideology have also, over the years, come to concentrate on ideology as the prime mover of communal violence. Even this book, though it tries to break out of the straitjacket, is itself implicitly structured at many places by the ideological concerns of the main protagonists.

Second, communal ideology, though tinged with the language of religion and tradition, is usually crude, offensive and violent. That mix makes excellent copy for the news media and manages to get wide coverage. And when given massive publicity, such ideologies can be used as triggering mechanisms for communal violence. So both the spectators and the organizers of such violence come to acquire a morbid fascination with ideology. What is often purely political or economic is thus given an artificially moral stature, even sanctity.

Also, the emphasis on ideology in this instance gives outsiders, especially perhaps modern scholars, the feeling that they have entered the mind of the actor and attained mastery over the problem posed by the actor. This presumed accessibility, as we shall show later in this book, comes partly from the core concerns that communal ideologies share with the ideologies of modernity, including that of the internal critiques of modernity such as Marxism. Perhaps this is the reason why many interpretations of communal ideologies in India so easily become a play of liminalities and cross-projections and an attempt by modernists to set up as an Other that which is an essential constituent of the self.

Paradoxically, this emphasis on ideology is often the forte of intellectuals who otherwise refuse to view human subjectivity as the prime mover of social behaviour in other areas of life, and who see communalism as part of a historical process, moving through social evolutionary stages. The emphasis on ideology often sits uneasily upon the presumption that societies are like biological species, moving from a more primitive stage encoded in tradition towards a modern, secular humanism that would de-ethnicize all communities.[20] Such evolutionism sees communalism as defining an earlier stage of social development or as a throwback or regression to such a stage. The expectation is that with the forces of secular individualism gaining ground, communalism will die an unnatural but deserved death. Communal ideology will then enter the textbooks of history and politics as a marker of a transient historical stage in which Indian society was once caught.[21]

It is against this background that one must examine the secularist consensus that modern India has built and brought to bear upon the communal problem. This is a consensus which now extends beyond the boundaries of the country. Much of the work on communalism in South Asia is contextualized by the ideology of secularism.

[20]For a recent example, see Tapan Basu, Pradip Datta, Sumit Sarkar, Tanika Sarkar and Sambuddha Sen, *Khaki Shorts Saffron Flags* (New Delhi: Orient Longman, 1993).

[21]This attitude is only an internalized version of the secular evolutionalism that defines western attitudes towards the non-West.

> Secularism once gave Western man and woman an assurance about their past that legitimated the extension of political and economic control over all traditional cultures and societies. The patterns of life of all traditional societies represented stages of human social development the West had transcended in its history.... All that the secular outlook admitted was a distinction in the form of domination: naked force as in chattel slavery: or benign upliftment of the inferior according to the dictates of the master.

> — Ziauddin Sardar and Merryl Wyn Davies, *Distorted Imagination: Lessons from the Rushdie Affair* (London: Grey Seal and Kuala Lumpur: Berita, 1990), p. 243.

In recent years, though, some have critiqued the intellectual and cultural limits of such an approach to ethnic violence. Empirically, too, the approach has not fared well.[22] As the reader might have noticed, the data presented at the beginning of this section are not compatible with secularist dogmas. Indeed, they seem to support the proposition that as the modernization and secularization of India has progressed, communal violence too has increased. It is in fact a major paradox for the secular Indian that religious and ethnic riots have now become one of the most secularized areas of Indian life; money, politics and organized interests play a much more important part in them than do religious passions.[23] Communal violence in India varies with geographical areas; it tends to be concentrated in cities and, within cities, in industrial areas, where modern values are more conspicuous and dominant. As Asghar Ali Engineer in a moment of absent-mindedness puts it, communalism is an urban phenomenon, whose roots may be traced to the middle and lower classes; peasants, workers, and upper class élites are seldom affected by com-

[22]T. N. Madan, 'Secularism in its Place', *The Journal of Asian Studies*, 1987, 46(4), pp. 747–59; and 'Whither Indian Secularism?', *Modern Asian Studies*, July 1993, 27(3), pp. 667-97; Ashis Nandy, 'An Anti-Secularist Manifesto', *Seminar*, October 1985, (314), pp. 14–24; and 'The Politics of Secularism and the Recovery of Religious Tolerance', *Alternatives*, 1988, 13(3), pp. 177–94; and Don Miller, 'Religion, Politics and its Sacred State', *The Reason of Metaphor: A Study in Politics* (New Delhi: Sage, 1992), pp. 159–80. Also, less directly, K. Raghavendra Rao, 'Secularism, Communalism and Democracy in India: Some Theoretical Issues', in Bidyut Chakrabarty (ed.), *Secularism and Indian Polity* (New Delhi: Segment Book, 1990), pp. 40–7; Gyanendra Pandey, *The Construction of Communalism in Colonial North India* (New Delhi: Oxford University Press, 1990); and Rustom Barucha, *A Question of Faith* (New Delhi: Orient Longman, 1992).

For a critique of this position, see Prakash Chandra Upadhyay, 'The Politics of Indian Secularism: Its Practitioners, Defenders and Critics', *Occasional Papers on Perspectives on Indian Development 11* (New Delhi: Nehru Memorial Museum and Library, 1990), mimeo; and 'The Politics of Indian Secularism', *Modern Asian Studies*, 1992, 26(4), pp. 815–53. A spirited, if conservative, constitutionalist reply to the criticisms of secularism has been given by Upendra Baxi, 'The Struggle for the Redefinition of Secularism in India: Some Preliminary Reflections', *Social Action*, January–March 1994, 44(1), pp. 13–30.

[23]Nandy, 'The Politics of Secularism and the Recovery of Religious Tolerance'.

TABLE 3

CAUSES OF COMMUNAL VIOLENCE IN INDIA, 1961–70 (N= 841)

Causes of Violence	Per Cent
Religious causes	
Festivity/celebrations	26.75
Cow slaughter	14.39
Desecration of religious places	4.04
Disputes over graveyards	2.14
Subtotal	47.32
Secular causes	
Private property disputes	19.26
Quarrels over women	16.89
Personal transactions, enmities, etc.	16.53
Subtotal	52.68
Total	100.00

SOURCE: Adapted from Krishna, 'Communal Violence in India', p. 66.

munalism.[24] Though recent experience confutes Engineer's engaging faith in workers, on the whole his formulation holds.

As telling are the causes of communal violence between 1961 and 1970 identified by the Home Ministry, Government of India. They show that the majority of riots during the period were triggered not by religious but by secular conflicts (Table 3). If one excludes from consideration Bihar—a state chronically prone to rural violence, where 33.17 per cent of the riots over religious matters took place, almost all of them in villages—the trend becomes even clearer.

In contrast to those who emphasize communal ideology, there are the scholars and human rights activists who emphasize structural

[24] Asghar Ali Engineer, 'The Ideological Background of Communal Riots', quoted in Hussain Shaheen, 'Software and Hardware of Communalism' in Ashghar Ali Engineer and Moin Shakir (eds), *Communalism in India* (Delhi: Ajanta, 1985), pp. 82–7, see p. 85.

Actually, Bipan Chandra in his *Communalism in Modern India* (New Delhi: Vikas, 1984) was one of the first to draw attention to the modern connection of communal violence but, caught in the progressivist discourse, failed to recognize or pursue the implications of his own formulation.

TABLE 4

PROPORTION OF MUSLIMS IN RIOT-PRONE STATES

State	Proportion of Muslims
Andhra Pradesh	8.5
Bihar	14.1
Gujarat	8.5
Maharashtra	9.2
Rajasthan	7.3
Uttar Pradesh	15.9
India	11.4

SOURCE: *Census of India: Household Population by Religion of Head of Household* (New Delhi: Registrar General and Census Commissioner, India, 1984), pp. 2–5.

factors such as the human geography of Hindu–Muslim violence. The focus is usually on the spatial concentration of Muslims. (In recent times, some Hindu chauvinist elements, too, have adopted this argument about the concentration of Muslims being a major cause of communal clashes.)

Muslims are the largest religious minority in India; they form roughly 11 per cent of the Indian population and constitute the world's second largest Muslim community. Even Pakistan, which claims to be the home of all subcontinental Muslims, houses fewer Muslims. Only Indonesia, with 153 million Muslims, boasts of a larger settlement of Muslims. However, they are not distributed randomly in India.

At the state level, this does not make a difference. The concentration of Muslims in the six riot-prone states of India is not above the national mean (see Table 4). But the relationship changes when one moves from the level of the state to that of the city where more than 90 per cent of the riots still reportedly originate. Table 5 suggests that cities which have a higher rate of communal violence tend to have larger proportions of Muslims.

One possibility is that the places where the Muslims are numerically strong, and can take advantage of competitive democratic politics to assert their rights, are more prone to communal violence. In such places, it is probably possible to mobilize larger sections of the

TABLE 5

PERCENTAGE OF HINDUS AND MUSLIMS IN SOME CHRONICAL-
LY RIOT-PRONE CITIES[25]

Cities	Hindus	Muslims
Hyderabad	59.9	36.9
Bhiwandi	41.5	52.4
Moradabad	51.2	47.4
Aligarh	63.8	34.5
Ahmedabad	78.2	15.3
Nalanda (Biharsharif)	61.1	38.7
Urban India	76.5	16.3

majority community against the 'uppity' minorities, and to use
the stereotype of socio-economically aggressive ethnic groups
taking advantage of their political clout to pose a threat to the social
order 'naturally' dominated by the majority.[26] There is scattered support
for such a formulation in the reports on riots in places like
Moradabad, Aligarh, Ahmedabad, Etawah and now Bombay. Often
riots in such cities do not remain confined to random acts of violence
and end up in heavily damaging the socio-economic life-support systems of the Muslims.[27]

The structural factors involved in communal violence do not
negate the role of stereotypes, folk sociologies, and subjective
justifications for communal violence at the community level. The two
kinds of predisposing factors often feed on each other. For example,
in some metropolitan cities where Muslims form a sizeable proportion
of the population, large sections of Muslim youth are unemployed or

[25] Adapted from Rajgopal, *Communal Violence*, p. 19. As can be seen from
Tables 3 and 4, while Muslims are roughly 11.4 per cent of the Indian population, they are about 16.3 per cent of urban India.

[26] See the *Pioneer* editorial quoted in Section IV for a neat example of this
strand of consciousness.

[27] See for instance Ajay Singh, 'Mafia Politics led to Etah Violence', *The
Times of India*, 9 December 1990; and Asghar Ali Engineer, *Delhi-Meerut
Riots*. Also Radhika Ramaseshan, 'A Date with Destiny', *The Pioneer*, 23
March 1992. In 1986 at Ahmedabad, for the first time, the Akhil Hind Sanatan
Samaj gave a call to boycott Muslim shops; some pamphlets openly suggested
that the Muslims should be 'killed' economically. See chapter 4.

underemployed either due to poor access to modern skills, including modern education (borne out by available data) or due to social discrimination (more difficult to document for low-paid jobs and self-employed people). Many of these youth, therefore, are easy recruits for criminal gangs and 'vocations' such as smuggling, illicit distillation, extortion and drug-pushing. This allows negative stereotypes of the minorities fuller play in such cities, and the fear and anger against urban crime strengthen communal hostilities. In many instances, criminals from Muslim communities precipitate riots by the very nature of their activities as well as by their attempts to redeem themselves in the eyes of their community by aggressively taking up the community's cause. There is some indirect support for the proposition in Krishna's data which show that as much as 52.68 per cent of cases of communal riots are directly triggered by personal conflicts of various kinds (Table 3).

While such formulations are seen as politically incorrect and have not been explored by scholars and human rights activists fearful of compromising their secular credentials, they have been systematically used by grass roots workers of Hindu nationalist parties and organizations. The stereotype of Muslim aggressiveness, the alleged tendency of fanatic lumpen proletariat elements among the Muslims to precipitate communal clashes, and their disproportionate involvement in urban crime (often because of their lesser access to the usual channels of employment), are all popular themes in the mobilization that precedes a communal riot and in the *post facto* justifications offered for the consumption of the newspaper-reading public.

The mobilization that precedes communal violence is also important because it is now a part of 'normal' politics. Few social processes have contributed as handsomely to communal violence as the demands of competitive mass politics. These demands have turned communal violence into another form of organized politics. After all, communal attitudes by themselves do not lead to violence in a politically ill-organized society. The violence has to be specifically organized by groups keen to politically cash in on the fall out of such violence. Those who organize the violence or encash it politically are not necessarily communal. They can even be fully secular in their calculations and are often even in league with politicians of the victim communities.As Engineer graphically comments, 'the politicians are the principal and anti-social elements, at their beck and call, the subsidiary agents in promoting and inciting communal violence.'[28] As we have already said, communal riots have become over the years one of the most secularized aspects of Indian public life.

Though it does have support in Indian experience, one must hasten to add that, for long, one variant of this interpretation has served as a staple of mainstream Indian nationalism and has also heavily influenced left-wing political theory. The main consumers of official nationalism and mainstream left politics have been the urban middle class, which is increasingly ambivalent towards the mass politics threatening to marginalize the class. Any interpretation that even partially hides the complicity of the middle class in communal violence has a natural appeal for the Indian nationalists and radicals. Starting as the widespread belief that communal clashes were the direct or indirect products of the colonial policy of 'divide and rule', this interpretation has acquired a new slant in independent India due to the middle-class hostility to competitive, democratic, mass politics. Instead of the colonial power, it is now the interests of competing political parties, factions, or local leadership which are seen to create communal vote banks and, in the process, to mobilize communal sentiments and contribute to communal violence.[29] Some analysts see a few communal parties as the main culprits; others see all parties as responsible to a greater or lesser degree, for all of them now have to compete to win or maintain unstable vote banks.[30]

Surely one of the root causes of ethnic violence in a diverse society like India is the entry of large sections of the population into what political theorist Sudipta Kaviraj calls an enumerative world

[28]Asghar Ali Engineer, 'Bombay–Bhiwandi Riots—A National Perspective', in Engineer and Shakir, *Communalism in India*, pp. 205–14, see p. 205. Also Dilip Simeon, 'Power at any Price is Communalism's Worst Legacy', *The Times of India*, 26 March 1990; and A. D. Bhogle, 'Communal Violence as a Political Weapon', *The Independent*, 14 December 1990.

[29]It is said that the internal party report of the Communist Party of India on the great Partition riots, 1946–7, represented this line of argument. Interestingly the BJP's position on communal violence is the same. Only it paints the Hindus as the victims of political parties exploiting religion for partisan purposes. The BJP calls such exploitation 'minorityism'.

[30]A recent analysis of this part of the story is in Rajni Kothari, 'Challenge Before Nation: Dealing with Rabid Populism', *The Times of India*, 22 January 1993.

where numbers matter. The entry itself expands the scope for communal politics. Earlier in Indian society everyone was in a 'minority' and no one's status as a member of a minority was 'fixed', in that one was invariably a member of more than one minority. Now, with the borders of many communities getting less permeable, the expression 'minority' is acquiring a clear-cut and rigid meaning. We shall see in this essay that this formulation has some relevance for the present narrative.

Finally, there is a growing belief that the changing contours of Indian nationalism and the concept of nation-state have contributed heavily to the growth of communal hostilities in the country. This belief is sustained by the clear difference between the standardized concepts of nationalism and nation-state—which nineteenth century India borrowed from Europe and which, since 1947, its modernist élite has applied uncritically to all situations—and the traditional Indian concepts of allegiance to one's soil and the traditional view of the state as a protector of a social order that is expected to elicit different levels of allegiance from different sections of the people.

The modern ideas of nationalism and state have sanctioned the concept of a 'mainstream national culture' that is fearful of diversities, intolerant of dissent unless it is cast in the language of the mainstream, and panicky about any self-assertion or search for autonomy by ethnic groups. This culture promotes a vision of India that is culturally unitary and a belief that the legitimacy of the modern state can be maintained only on the basis of a steamrolling concept of nationalism that promises to eliminate all fundamental cultural differences within the polity.[31] Occasionally, modern nationalism and the modern state can make compromises with ethnicity or religion on political grounds, but that is seen as only a temporary compromise.

[31] A succinct discussion of this part of the story is in Tariq Banuri, 'Official Nationalism, Ethnic Conflict and Collective Violence', Symposium on Nationalism Revisited, Goethe Institute, Colombo, 1994, mimeo. See a discussion of the culture of the state within which this belief is located in Ashis Nandy, 'Culture, State, and the Rediscovery of Indian Politics', in Iqbal Khan (ed.), *Fresh Perspectives on India and Pakistan: Essays on Economics, Politics and Culture* (Oxford: Bougainvillaea Books, 1985, and Lahore: Book Traders, 1987), pp. 304–18; and 'The State', in Wolfgang Sachs (ed.), *The Development Dictionary: A Guide to Knowledge as Power* (London: Zed, 1992), pp. 264-74.

For both these institutions are essentially secular in their ideological thrust. It is in this context that one must read the proposition of Ziauddin Sardar and Merryl Wyn Davies that fundamentalism is a direct creation of secularism—'the last refuge from the abuse and ridicule of the secular mind' and 'a grotesque projection of the worst nightmares of secularism on the world stage'.[32]

Both these ideas of state and nationalism have as their model the pre-war European colonial state, as it is remembered by large sections of the Indian élite. That remembered state underwrites the idea of an imperial, native state that would act as the ultimate arbiter among 'traditionally warring' communities in the country and ruthlessly suppress religious and ethnic separatism.[33] A case can, however, be made that while in India these concepts of state and nationalism were underwritten by imperialism, the colonial state itself was, in its actual style of governance, more open-ended on communal and ethnic issues and often borrowed much from the traditional Indian concepts of statecraft and Indian style of configuring political loyalties. The need to survive in an alien environment forced the British-Indian state to compromise its European principles and grant greater play to the surviving memories and expectations from the state in India. The successor regime did not feel pressed to make such qualifications.

Those who consider the ideas of nation-state and nationalism themselves to be major contributory factors in communal violence believe that the ideas have, over the years, reduced the range of options within Indian public life and made it more difficult to accommodate or cope with the grievances, demands, and anxieties of the different ethnic groups. First, if all ethnicity is seen as dangerous and all ethnic demands are seen as falling outside the range of normal politics, they are naturally sought to be contained with the aid of the coercive power of the state. This in turn leads to deeper communal divides and to the perception of the state as essentialy hostile to the interests of the aggrieved communities. Also, the state itself often

[32]Sardar and Davies, *Distorted Imagination*, p. 242.
[33]Rabindranath Tagore, one of the major builders of Indian and Bangladeshi national self-consciousness, was also one of the first to draw attention to the problems associated with such uncritical import of categories. His novel, *Ghare Bāire* specifically relates communal violence to the adoption of the European ideas of state and nationality. See Ashis Nandy, *The Illegitimacy of Nationalism: Rabindranath Tagore and the Politics of Self* (New Delhi: Oxford University Press, 1994).

becomes partisan in communal conflicts, not necessarily because of communal considerations—even though that also sometimes happens—but because of electoral and other secular considerations. In either case, the state is unable to prevent such violence.[34] Those given to this way of looking at the communal situation in India emphasize political processes, both within and outside the state sector, as vital linkages between contesting religious communities, and between such communities and the state. They are convinced that communal problems can be contained primarily through politics.[35] For democratic politics allows the resistance to communal violence that exists at the level of communities to assert itself. From such a perspective Indian secularism, given its strong statist connections, is itself a part of the disease.

In the contemporary world, the ideology of the state and official nationalism are not isolated entities. They are embedded in a world-view that systematically fosters the breakdown of traditional community ties and the traditional socio-economic and cultural interdependence of communities. Inter-community ties in societies like India have come to be increasingly mediated through distant, highly centralized, impersonal administrative and political structures, through new consumption patterns and priorities set up by the process of development, and through reordered traditional gender relationships and ideologies which now conform more and more to the needs of a centralized market system and the needs of the masculinized culture of the modern state. These issues have remained mostly unexplored in existing works on ethnic violence in India. Only from

[34]Random recent examples are People's Union of Democratic Rights and People's Union of Civil Liberties, *Who are the Guilty?: Report of a Joint Inquiry into the Causes and Impact of the Riots in Delhi from 31 October to 10 November* (Delhi: PUDR and PUCL, 1984); *Vikalp* (published by the Sampradayikata Virodhi Andolan), January–March 1985; Asghar Ali Engineer, *Delhi-Meerut Riots: Analysis, Compilation and Documentation* (Delhi: Ajanta, 1988); and Hemlata Prabhu, *PUCL Investigation Report: Jaipur Communal Riots* (Jaipur: Rajasthan PUCL, n.d.); Ghanshyam Shah, 'The 1969 Communal Riots in Ahmedabad: A Case Study', in Engineer, *Communal Riots*, pp. 175–208.

[35]Rajni Kothari, 'Culture, Ethnicity and the State', *The Thatched Patio*, April 1989, 2(2), pp. 22–6; and 'Communalism: The New Face of Indian Democracy', *The State Against Democracy: In Search of Humane Governance* (Delhi: Ajanta, 1988), pp. 240-53; Ashis Nandy, 'The Discreet Charms of Indian Terrorism', *Journal of Commonwealth and Comparative Politics*, March 1990, 28(1), pp. 25–43; and 'Terrorism—Indian Style: The Birth of a Political Issue in a Populist Democracy', *Hull Papers in Politics* (Hull: University of Hull, 1991).

the intermittent attention paid to such issues by such writers as Vandana Shiva and Helena Norberg-Hodge would one suspect that they have become tragically relevant to our times.[36]

The reasons for this scholarly blindness are not clear, but there are clues in works such as Tapan Raychaudhuri's recent autobiographical essay.[37] Raychaudhuri, a professional historian fully committed to the dominant ideology of the state backed by the ideologies of progress and secularization, has to set up a formidable anti-self, part-comic and part-serious, through which only can he articulate, in quasi-anecdotal style, his powerful insights into the religious 'divide' in South Asia and its complex relationship with community life. Presumably these insights his professional self has to disown—as irrational, non-secular, ahistorical compromises with native categories. He defends the enterprise, as the title of his book indicates, as the memoirs of a senile gossip.[38]

We shall try in the next section to briefly narrate the build-up, course, organization, and ideology of the most important communal conflict in India today, the one centring on the Ramjanmabhumi, with reference to these broad formulations. However, the narrative will be guided by the implicit, as yet inadequately explored perspective that sees communal violence as a direct product of three processes: (1) the breakdown of traditional social and cultural ties crossing religious

[36]Vandana Shiva, *The Violence of Green Revolution* (Penang: Consumers Association of Penang, 1990); Helena Norberg-Hodge, *Ancient Futures: Learning from Ladakh* (San Francisco: Sierra Club Books, 1991), pp. 122–30.

[37]Tapan Raychaudhuri, *Romanthan athabā Bhūmratiprāptar Paracharitacharchā* (Calcutta: Ananda Publishers, 1993); see esp. pp. 56–99.

[38]Such defensiveness is not unique to the social sciences. A similar defensive structure, based not on professionalism but on radical and modernist rhetoric, forces the famous film-maker Ritwik Ghatak to disown the 'hermeneutic self' projected into his films that identifies the breakdown of communities and loss of culture as the crucial issue in communal divide. Only a few such as Sadaat Hassan Manto, the Urdu writer, seem to have escaped, through a tremendous effort of will, this defensiveness of modern India.

On the complicity of history as discipline in the growth of communal divide, see Vinay Lal, 'The Discourse of History and the Crisis at Ayodhya: Reflections on the Production of Knowledge, Freedom, and the Future of India', 1994, unpublished MS; and Ashis Nandy, 'History's Forgotten Doubles', *History and Theory, Studies in the Philosophy of History*, 34(2), 1995, pp. 44–66.

boundaries, as these boundaries are conventionally defined within the modern sector; (2) the emergence of a modern, massified, and paradoxically élitist version of religion that acts as a political ideology but also compensates for the deculturation, rootlessness, and loss of faith in the massified sections of the urban population; and (3) the emergence of a politicized modern and semi-modern middle class that seeks to have access to political power disproportionate to its size on grounds other than numbers and its need for an ideology of state that would legitimize that access.

CHAPTER TWO

III. THE BATTLE FOR THE BIRTHPLACE

L et us now get back to our story. Behind the bald statement of facts in chapter 1 lie contending strands of consciousness and contending constructions of the past and the present. Some of them will become clearer from the following narration of the events of 30 October 1990, as witnessed by one of us, and some random reactions to the events.

The first clash between the police and the *kārsevak*s took place at the crack of dawn, on the two-kilometre long Saryu bridge linking Ayodhya with the neighbouring district, Gonda. A crowd of 2,000-odd people, intent on forcing their way into Ayodhya, were being pushed back slowly and with restraint by a small police contingent under the command of a tall, well-built Sikh whose identification badge had been removed but who belonged to the Central Reserve Police Force (CRPF). Brandishing their sticks in the air and rarely striking anyone, they successfully thwarted this first attempt by the *kārsevak*s to overrun the bridge. There were a few casualties, none of them serious.

The crowd was a mix of those who had come to Ayodhya specifically to participate in the *kārsevā* and others who had come to perform the yearly *panch kosi parikramā* (a five-kilometre ritual perambulation that takes place before the *kārtik purnimā* fair in Ayodhya every winter). They were largely elderly men who were unaware of anything else happening in Ayodhya that day, and stood around totally confused and helpless, begging the police to let them go back to their homes.

The determination of the *kārsevak*s to cross into Ayodhya remained unaffected despite this reverse. Those who avoided arrest, mainly students, spilled on to the left bank of the river, where they stood raising slogans, ranging from their anthem of the previous few weeks, '*Ramlallā hum āyenge, mandir wahin banāyenge*' (Dear Ram, we will come and build your temple right there), to the plea to the security forces obstructing their path, '*Hindu Hindu bhāi bhāi, bīch mein vardi kahān se āyi*' (All Hindus are brothers; how has a uniform come between them?).

The police were not taken in, but a large number of them were unhappy with the duty they had to perform. This was evident from the half-hearted manner in which they had pushed the crowd back earlier. In fact, one of the policemen burst into tears in the middle of the operation, saying that he could no longer carry on. He was immediately surrounded by his concerned colleagues and seniors. They did not admonish him; they pleaded with him to keep his emotions in check and concentrate on his work. Meanwhile, the ranks of *kārsevaks* began to swell rapidly as hundreds more, who had spent the night among the tall grass on the river bank or in villages nearby, started to come out of hiding.

Back in Ayodhya town, the situation at first appeared to be under control. Small groups of *kārsevaks* could be seen squatting harmlessly in the many lanes and bylanes leading to the disputed site, chanting '*Jai Shri Ram*' and '*Bacchā bacchā Ram kā, Janmabhumi ke kām kā*' (Every child is Ram's, all serve his birth place) It was around mid-morning that things began to go wrong, as a few thousand *kārsevaks* suddenly materialized in the streets of curfew-bound Ayodhya, despite the district administration's claims of 'water-tight security arrangements'. These arrangements had been in effect for weeks to prevent these very people from entering Ayodhya. Once again, it was clear where the sympathy of a section of the security forces and administration lay. For the *kārsevaks* could not have reached the town without their connivance, as they themselves admitted freely.

In no time at all, all roads leading to the Babri masjid were swarming with sadhus in saffron, red and white, ash and vermilion smeared on their foreheads and chests; with men, young and old, drawn from different parts of the country, different professions, and different castes (though a majority of the *kārsevaks* interviewed were found to belong to the upper castes).[1] The party workers were, of course,

---

[1]Another observer, Nilanjan Mukhopadhyay, found that while volunteers came from all states except Jammu and Kashmir and north-east India, most of them were from the Hindi-speaking states. Also, roughly three-fourths were from urban India, mainly from small towns. Pradip K. Datta, 'VHP's Ram at Ayodhya: Reincarnation through Ideology and Organization', *Economic and Political Weekly*, 2 November 1991, 36(44), pp. 2517–26. This is a useful essay based on observations made soon after the events of 1990.

present in full force, along with some of their leaders such as Vinay
Katiyar, the head of the Bajrang Dal, and K. Narendra, Vice President
of the BJP in Andhra Pradesh. They were joined later on by Ashok
Singhal, General Secretary of the VHP, and Shrish Chand Dikshit, a
former DIG of the UP police who was, at the time of these events,
the vice-president of the VHP.

Some of the *kārsevaks* carried tridents, sticks and pick-axes, but
otherwise were largely unarmed. But they had a fearsome resolve to
demolish 'this symbol of national shame'. As a group of traders coming from Lucknow put it, 'Today, we have the blessings of Lord Ram
on us. Hence, no force can stop us from wiping out from this sacred
earth all signs of the masjid of these sinning Muslims. We shall kill
or be killed, but we shall complete the task.' A large proportion of
the crowd was what some commentators in India have begun to call
elements of the lumpen proletariat—jobless, ill-educated, partly massified, urban youth, waiting to be mobilized for any cause that would
give them some sense of solidarity, purpose, and adventure, preferably of the violent kind.[2]

By now, all movement of traffic in the area had come to a
standstill. As a result, most of the state government buses loaded
with arrested *kārsevaks* could not move at all. It was the hijacking
of one such bus, full of frenzied *kārsevaks* near the Hanumangarhi
temple by one of its priests, that helped pave the way for what was
to come later on. The security personnel, on duty in the area, were
caught unawares as the bus veered around dramatically and roared
down one of the roads—which eventually lead to the mosque some
one and a half miles away—at a wild speed. Later, it could be seen
clearly that of the several iron checkposts the bus encountered on its
flight, only one was slightly dented, not broken. Either the bus had
hit the checkpost and the fastening had come loose and opened on
its own, or the checkpost was deliberately opened. The second was

---

[2]The massification and criminalization of some sections of Hindu youth
in north India is a relatively new phenomenon. Although some elements in
the RSS family had been allegedly trying for decades to link up with this
process, they had failed time and again, till taking a leaf out of Shiv Sena
head Bal Thackeray's book, sections of the family, especially some closely
associated with the VHP, began organizing the urban, upper caste, jobless
youth, frustrated and angry against the establishment, on the pattern of his
Sena in Bombay. Apparently, the Bajrang Dal in north India has more or less
the same profile as the Sena.

more likely because there was no sign of any damage to the remaining checkposts. They were simply not fastened. The bus was ultimately stopped, just a few feet away from the disputed site, and the hijackers arrested.

This incident made it clear to those leading the *kārsevaks* that the security arrangements were not impregnable. Either the administration had not expected and, therefore, was not prepared to handle such a massive turnout, or some of the security personnel were more than willing to oblige the *kārsevaks*. Emboldened by this awareness, the *kārsevaks* began to get more aggressive, testing the patience of the police force. As one of the leaders revealed, the idea was to tire out the forces, before reassembling for the final assault. The police were by now barely able to hold the crowd at bay with their sticks. Even the bursting of tear gas shells had little effect. Partly because some of the *kārsevaks* had smeared lime on their faces to nullify the effect of the gas, but mainly because the shells were being used with great discretion just two or three at a time.

A word now on the reactions of the citizens of Ayodhya. Before the incident of 30 October, there was no evidence that Ayodhya felt very strongly on the Ramjanmabhumi issue. This was always a matter of great concern to those leading the movement for the temple. While they could generate passions in many parts of the country and abroad for their cause, Ayodhya itself had remained an island of peace.[3] Now, they felt, was their final chance to involve the people of Ayodhya in their cause.

All this time the citizens of Ayodhya had stayed away, at least physically, from the events of the morning—this, despite being heckled loudly by those among them who had already thrown in their lot with the *kārsevaks*. A young teen-aged boy, the son of a local chemist, was for instance seen running up and down the lane in which his house was located shouting at the closed windows and banging his fists on the locked doors, 'Come out people of the locality. Why are you sitting in your homes wearing bangles? If you are men, come out on the streets.' The local people had hidden the *kārsevaks* in their houses, given them food and shelter, and that, they said, was enough. But now seeing that slowly and steadily the *kārsevaks* were gaining

---

[3]See for instance D. R. Goyal, 'At Peace with Themselves', *The Indian Post*, 12 October 1989.

the upper hand, they got carried away by the excitement and the religious fervour in the air and poured onto the streets. They were joined by a few women as well. But it was the manner in which those who stayed back in their homes and lent their support to the *kārsevak*s, that turned the tide in favour of the latter.

While to begin with they had thrown packets of food from the rooftops to the *kārsevak*s below, they now started pelting the police with stones and bricks, injuring several of them. In one of the main lanes around the corner from Hanumangarhi, the mood turned ugly, when a brick cracked open the head of a senior Sikh officer leading the forces there. As he was carried away bleeding profusely, his men, including the young Sikh CRPF man who had been in command on the bridge in the morning, rushed up to the District Magistrate of Faizabad, Ram Sharan Srivastava, and demanded permission to open fire. The police wanted to open fire not on the *kārsevak*s but on those people who were attacking them from the rooftops, that is, they wanted to shoot in self-defence. The DM refused to give permission and quietly began to walk away from the scene. The policemen ran after him, caught him, and openly threatened to shoot him if he left them there to fend for themselves.

The DM had no choice but to return. However, the police themselves, under attack once again, suddenly seemed to lose their will to continue. One of them bitterly remarked, 'Look at the DM. He has not taken his helmet off since the morning. And look at us; we have not even been provided with helmets. Why should they care if we break our heads.' Thereafter the police contingent positioned there just sat around doing nothing. 'If we cannot shoot, there is little else we can do now,' they said flatly.

In the meantime, the rumour had spread that Ashok Singhal, who had entered the city with the covert help of some senior police and district officials, had been injured in a lathi charge in an adjoining lane. Close on its heels came word of a shoot-out on Saryu bridge in which a second attempt by *kārsevak*s to reach Ayodhya had resulted in 'hundreds' of deaths. (Actually, Ashok Singhal had received minor injuries and the death toll in the shooting on the bridge was two). This news excited the crowds even more.

Just as it looked as if all hell would break loose—now that the police had more or less assumed the role of bystanders—the DM suddenly produced S. C. Dikshit in front of the throng, microphone in hand, and requested him to appeal to the crowds to disperse.

Dikshit, in what later turned out be a clever ploy, asked the *kārsevak*s to turn back: 'You have already performed *kārsevā* by coming to Ayodhya. I am now telling you to leave.'

Dikshit made this speech over and over again, and held repeated parleys with the DM and other officials. It turned out, however, that he was marking time, diverting the attention of the officials from the *kārsevak*s in the neighbouring lanes and bylanes who were closing in on the disputed site. When this particular crowd saw hordes of *kārsevak*s rushing past them at the other end of the lane, up the road leading to the site, they too joined the race in one big surge.

It was about 11.00 AM now. The *kārsevak*s took just fifteen minutes to bring down the first barricade. Faced with an unruly mob and fearing for their own safety (and having personal sympathy for the cause), the security forces proved totally ineffective. Incidentally, the Sikh CRPF man, who till then had done his job efficiently, was suddenly relieved of his duty at the trouble spot. 'I have been assigned another duty' is all that he would say. However, for about an hour, he could still be spotted just hanging around in the area. (Later the VHP showroom, near the place where the foundation for the Ram temple had been laid, put up a poster of a tall helmeted Sikh police officer with a name tag. The officer was turned into an object of hate and contempt by the VHP propaganda machine. He was portrayed as a murderer of innocent *kārsevak*s and had a price on his head, whereas on 30 October he was the one policeman who, unprotected by a helmet, was doing his duty while exercizing restraint at the same time.)

For some distance after this, there was no one and nothing to stop the *kārsevak*s, who on the way set fire to a UP Roadways bus and a jeep. The violence of their slogans more than matched the violence of their actions: '*Katuā jab kātā jāyegā to Ram Ram chillāyegā*' (When the *katuā*—a derogatory term for the circumcised—will be cut into pieces, he will take the name of Ram). The more excited they became, the more violent became their words: '*Katuon ke bas do hi sthān, Pakistan yā Kabristān*' (There are only two places for the circumcised to be in; Pakistan or the graveyard). One song they sang had been popularized in the previous months. It went something like this:

Ao sab mil chalen,
Ram ka mandir bhaiyā banāne ko,
Khun kharābā hotā hai,

To ek bār ho jāne do . . . .
Samajh na pāye bāton se,
Ab lāton se samjhāne do ...

(Let us all get together brother,
to build the temple of Ram,
If there is bloodshed,
then for once let it happen ...
Since our words have not made them see reason,
let us now make them understand by kicking them ...)

If the slogans and the songs were to be taken as a reflection of
the prevailing mood at that point in time, then there was a definite
softening in the *kārsevaks*' attitude towards the police, whom they
now began to recognize as partners in the same enterprise. '*Police
hamārā bhāi hai, inse nahin ladāi hai*' (The police are our brothers;
we have no quarrel with them) was the new slogan. They were not
far from the truth. The police took no notice of the manner in which
residents of the lanes through which the *kārsevaks* were passing, were
egging them on, much in the manner of spectators cheering their
team in a soccer game. Asked why no one was trying to restrain the
residents, a police officer responded, 'It is not a crime to encourage
someone.'

Soon afterwards, just before the crowd reached the last barricade,
the police did fire with plastic bullets on the *kārsevaks*, injuring two
of them. But it was already too late. The police, heavily outnumbered,
could no longer control the thousands pressing forward in a final
desperate attempt to enter the masjid. Now only a single iron gate
stood between them and their objective. Police officials later said
that there was no sense in opening fire at that point on an unarmed
crowd. They were not wrong; all the roads in the vicinity were choked
with people and any such action would have only resulted in a massacre.

Suddenly, at 12.08 PM, before anyone could realize what was happening, the iron gate opened wide enough and long enough for about
300 men to enter the mosque, pull down the fence separating the
Ramchabutra from the structure of the mosque and leave gaping holes
in its walls. They climbed atop the mosque's three domes, and
loosened some stones there with pickaxes to unfurl saffron flags on
each dome.

The police just stood and watched, apart from giving some *kārsevak*s a helping hand over the ledge, and into the grounds of the mosque. For instance, Dikshit—aged, and not very agile, was helped thus when he twice failed to cross the ledge on his own. At 12.20 PM, senior police officers finally swung into action and managed to clear the site of the mob and restore some order.

A carnival-like atmosphere prevailed in Ayodhya following the attack on the mosque. The sound of conch shells and the peal of temple bells filled the air. Sweetmeats were distributed by the residents to the *kārsevak*s, who danced down the streets, chanting '*Ayodhya to bas ek jhānki hai, Mathura, Kashi bāki hai*'—'Ayodhya is only a sample; Kashi and Mathura remain [to be taken]'. Policemen, who till just a little while ago looked tense and wary, were also seen celebrating the occasion with the *kārsevak*s, accepting the *prasād* given to them with folded hands and a '*Jai Shri Ram*' on their lips. They certainly did not look unhappy that they had failed in carrying out their duty.

During the countdown to 30 October the RSS had been saying that the police was going to revolt and not follow the orders of their seniors. As events unfolded, it became clear that the RSS may not have been literally correct, but it had certainly anticipated the police reactions at ground level better than the administration.[4]

IV. CONTENDING REACTIONS

We tried to find out the reactions of a small, randomly chosen group of educated young men who had participated in some of the events at Ayodhya. They said that, at long last, the first step had been taken to avenge the partition of the country and the sell-out to the Muslims by M. K. Gandhi; 'he was no Mahatma, he was a traitor'. However,

[4]The BJP was to field in the 1991 Parliamentary elections S. C. Dikshit and B. P. Singhal, another senior police officer, as party candidates. They contested from Varanasi and Moradabad respectively. Incidentally, during the Moradabad riots in 1980, when the police opened fire on Muslims praying in the Idgah on Id day, Dikshit was the Deputy Inspector General (Intelligence) of UP, and Singhal the DIG of Moradabad Division.

they also seemed horrified by the idea that Gandhi's assassin Nathuram Godse could be their hero. To them Godse was a murderer, even if the murderer of Gandhi. But they did feel that, even in death, Gandhi had cheated the nation. For had he been killed by a Muslim, they said, the Muslims would have been wiped off the face of India a long time ago.

Whom did they regard as national heroes? They mentioned four names—Shivaji, Maharana Pratap, Bhagat Singh and Chandrashekhar Azad. The first two they admired for their relentless fight against the Muslim conquerers of India; and the other two for their bravery in the face of British repression. Probably Bhagat Singh and Azad were singled out from among the freedom fighters because of their militancy, since neither of them had anything to do with a Hindu cause[5.] The youths were unaware that Bhagat Singh was not a Hindu, but a Sikh. Nor did they seem to know that he and Azad were non-believing socialists.

That night Diwali was celebrated in Ayodhya with much pomp and splendour. Many of the residents lit up their houses with earthen oil lamps and sparklers, decked themselves up in their finery, and flocked to the temples where devotional songs were sung late into the night and broadcast from the rooftops. Also seen celebrating Diwali that night were some senior officers of the district administration and journalists. One of the officers—he had been a Maoist in his student days in Bihar—was congratulating the people of Ayodhya for their remarkable behaviour that day. He said that if they had wanted, the people could have done anything in the town that day—looted property, set houses on fire, even killed people, and no one would have been able to do anything because, for a couple of hours, the law and order machinery had completely broken down. But they did nothing; 'they have protected the prestige of Ayodhya today'. 'What else do you expect to happen if you try to swim against the tide of overwhelming public sentiment, if you disregard it and try to crush it?' he asked rhetorically.

[5]Paradoxically, the names of those associated with the birth of political Hinduism—V. D. Savarkar, who did the most to give a political content to the concept of *Hindutva*, is an example—are often avoided in BJP propaganda lest they might give political mileage to other political parties such as the Hindu Mahasabha.

Such statements, though at that time sounded crudely self-congratulatory, did contain a kernel of truth, at least as far as the participants from Ayodhya were concerned. The city might have at first reluctantly given some marginal support to the movement launched by the VHP, but the hamhanded political style of the administration, combined with the propaganda unleashed by the movement, had turned the events into a civil disobedience movement, a *satyāgraha*, for the citizens. It is no accident that Pradip K. Datta, though clearly hostile to the entire Ramjanmabhumi movement, frequently uses the expression *satyāgraha*, with its clear Gandhian associations, to describe the nature of the movement at the grass roots level.[6]

About sixteen months after the event, in February 1992, the chief priest of the Ramjanmabhumi temple, Laldas, otherwise a sworn enemy of the VHP-led movement, was to say with some pride that it was the earthy, traditional sense of decency, tolerance, and restraint of the people of Ayodhya that ensured that the Muslim community of Ayodhya, though about one-fortieth the size of the Hindus, could continue to live in safety and dignity when the outsiders left Ayodhya to itself.

Local journalists were seen distributing offerings from the temples in the streets on the day of the 'great victory', afterwards to be compared by the leaders of the movement to Vijaya Dashami, one of the most sacred days in the Hindu calendar. But this was not the first time that the journalists had participated in the spirit of *kārasevā*. For the real victory of the movement had been in the domain of the local print media. Even before the events of 30 October, two leading Hindi dailies *Dainik Jagran* (published from Kanpur, Lucknow, Jhansi, Gorakhpur, Varanasi, Meerut, Agra and Bareilly in UP and New Delhi) and *Aaj* had already begun their *kārseva*. They had invited their readers—through news reports, editorials and published statements and appeals by just about any Hindu religious leader—to take an open stand on 30 October. A front-page headline in *Aaj* on 30 October enquired whether 'Emergency had been enforced'. It was referring to the precautionary curfews and cancellations of trains to Ayodhya and invoking the fear of the internal emergency imposed by Prime Minister Indira Gandhi during 1975–7 when civil rights were suspended in the entire country. The same day, the paper invited

[6]Datta, 'VHP's Ram'.

its readers 'to decide, once and for all, whether India should become a theocratic state, or remain secular'![7]

Prior to 30 October, these newspapers either accused the security forces of atrocities on the *kārsevaks* or sought to undermine their confidence as agents of law and order. For instance, it was alleged that the police were harassing anyone who publicly took the name of Ram whether it was by way of the traditional greeting '*Ram Ram*' or '*Jai Ramji ki*' or mourners chanting '*Ram nam satya hai*' over a dead body. *Aaj* accused the police of forcing the *kārsevaks* to say 'Mulayam' instead of Ram.[8] Another report in the same paper claimed

---

[7]The reader might have noticed that in the temple agitation and the political subculture the *Sangh parivār* represents, the idiom is often strongly secular and anti-theocratic, even anti-theological. The *parivār's* anti-Muslim sentiments, too, now increasingly find expression in secular arguments, such as the risks to national security, population control policies, and urban law-and-order situation that the Muslims supposedly represent. See on this theme, Ashis Nandy, 'An Anti-Secularist Manifesto', *Seminar*, October 1985, (314), pp. 14-24.

In other words, the BJP's emphasis on genuine as opposed to pseudo-secularism and its continuous attempts to recruit at least a section of the Muslims are no accident. Even assuming these to be a form of tokenism, the fact remains that even symbolic ethnic purity has never been a passion with the leadership of the BJP. At the height of the temple movement, two of the national leaders of the BJP, including Advani, were neither uncomfortable nor secretive when their close relatives married Muslims and the BJP ministries continued to have Muslim cabinet members.

Despite all facile comparisons between fascist movements in the West and the BJP, this remains a crucial difference between the two. This, combined with the party's demonstrated commitment to democratic rights, which it re-reads as only an endorsement of its ruthless majoritarianism, at certain crucial times (as for instance during the Emergency in 1975–77, when civil rights were suspended in India and when some of the most dedicated political enemies of the BJP collaborated with the regime) explains its success in recent years in recruiting a few conspicuous members of the minority communities. See also the memoirs of the secretary to the late Fakhruddin Ali Ahmed, a Congress party stalwart who was the President of India during the Emergency, on the discomfort of the Congress regime and the Congress Muslim leaders at the increasing closeness of the BJP and the Jamat-e-Islami activists in jail. F. A. A. Rehmaney, *My Eleven Years with Fakhruddin Ali Ahmed* (New Delhi: S. Chand, 1979).

[8]*Aaj*, 19 October 1990.

that the police was feeding horse dung to the *kārsevak*s lodged in Mirzapur jail![9]

Paradoxically, and as if to spite those who saw in the supporters of the *Sangh parivar* only Indian versions of European fascists of the 1930s, this crude propaganda often went hand in hand with an almost pathetic attempt to establish the non-sectarian nationalist credentials of the movement. A series of reports in the press around this time also claimed wide Muslim support to the movement. A front-page report in *The Pioneer* of Lucknow claimed that the Muslim driver of L. K. Advani's *rath* was persuading other Muslims to offer *kārsevā*.[10] The same newspaper carried a story headlined 'Five Thousand Muslims to Demolish Masjid', quoting one Mukhbar Abbas Naqvi of Lucknow saying that 'the Babri Masjid will be demolished by a batch of five thousand nationalist Muslims who will reach there on October 29 under their secret plan.'[11] Such stories, untrue though they were, suggest that the partisan press might have been as aware as some of the BJP functionaries of the limits of unqualified majoritarianism. While trying to profit politically from the religious sentiments of the majority community, both consistently felt compelled, for the same political reasons, to demonstrate that it had place within it even for the minority it was attacking.

A front-page story headlined 'Will it be another Operation Bluestar?' was a warning by one Brigadier Dal Singh, President of the Uttar Pradesh Ex-Servicemen's League. He warned against the danger of deploying the army because its personnel, being trained to sacrifice their lives for the cause of the country, were deeply religious.[12] He stressed that it would be highly improper and dangerous to utilize their services for a task that might bring their religious sentiments into conflict with their duty.

Singh's warning was not particularly unthinking or unjust. However, the overall result of such media coverage was the build-up to 30 October, for partisan religious colour began to be given to the most trivial of incidents. For instance, a monkey dropped a burning

[9]Ibid, 25 October 1990.

[10]The BJP made much of the fact that the driver of Advani's chariot was a Muslim, which he indeed was. On the other hand, he had converted to Islam not very long ago, reportedly in order to marry a Muslim girl with whom he had subsequently parted ways.

[11]*The Pioneer* (Lucknow), 25 October 1990.

[12]*The Sunday Pioneer* (Lucknow), 28 October 1990.

log, which it had stolen from some soldiers cooking in an open field, on the nearby DAV college in Azamgarh which got slightly burnt. Some 500 *kārsevaks* were being held in this building. *The Pioneer* of Lucknow carried a front-page report on the incident titled, 'A *Lankādahan!*', drawing a parallel with the burning of the city of Lanka by Hanuman in the Ramayana.

On 30 October, many of the journalists reporting from Ayodhya described their experience as way beyond the normal. The report of the hijacking of the bus at Hanumangarhi, and its moment of entry into the disputed site by *kārsevaks* read something like this in the daily *Dainik Jagran*:

It was a miracle. Here was this bus full of devotees of Ram, who were desolate at the thought of not being allowed to perform *kārsevā* as they had been arrested, when suddenly a priest from the Hanumangarhi temple leapt into the driver's seat from nowhere and drove off as if possessed towards the mandir. It was as if Hanuman himself had appeared to drive the bus. The power of the goddess [presumably Durga] opened each and every barrier on the way just as the bus would approach them. When it finally halted at the gate of the Ram temple, it appeared from the expression on the faces of the devotees that Ramlalla himself had come down from the heavens to applaud their bravery. Much later when the gates opened to let the devotees of Ram in for performing *kārseva*, many believed that it was Ramlalla himself waiting impatiently, who opened the gates and invited them in.[13]

Another report detailed the efforts of a dying *kārsevak* to write *Jai Shri Ram* with his own blood on the street where he had fallen. Apparently he died the second he finished writing.

Almost all newspapers reported that day that *kārsevā* was performed at the Janmabhumi temple and that the construction of the temple had begun—they meant the damage inflicted on the structure of the mosque and the unfurling of saffron flags on its domes. Even the Press Trust of India, one of India's two official news agencies, flashed the news that *kārsevā* had begun at 1.00 PM at the disputed site with an Ayodhya dateline. Later it was discovered that the news had emanated from Delhi, not Ayodhya.

The number of those dead in the shoot-outs was quickly inflated to absurd figures, especially with regard to the firing on 2 November. *Aaj* carried the headline, 'Hours of firing on the unarmed devotees of Ram after surrounding them—200 dead, Ayodhya bathed in blood on Kartik day dip, Jalianwala Bagh episode dwarfed'.[14]

[13]*Dainik Jagran*, 30 October 1990.
[14]*Aaj*, 3 November 1990.

Similarly, *Dainik Jagran* in its special bulletin brought out in the afternoon of 2 November taking advantage of the usual official tendency to under-report casualty figures, claimed that 'Hundreds of *kārsevaks* had died on the spot in the indiscriminate police firing on devotees of Ram'. Next morning the paper itself inexplicably reduced the death toll to thirty-two.[15] The Lucknow edition of *Aaj* spoke of corpses of *kārsevaks* being fished out of the river Saryu. It carried the headline: 'Over a hundred bodies have been thrown into the river Saryu.'[16] The administration denied all such reports.

None of these local papers as much as mentioned that during this period, every day, huge public meetings were being held in Ayodhya outside the Maniram Chavni temple, where the most abusive speeches were made against the Muslims. Neither were reports of the attacks on the homes and properties of Muslims in Ayodhya-Faizabad, specially in the Chunniganj area, carried in the local press.

If the reporting was partisan, the editorials were no better. One simply said, 'They did it.' Another in *The Pioneer* was grandiloquent:

It was bound to happen. People's power at its extreme. Everyone knew it except our wooden headed government. For the next 1,000 years, this day will be remembered for what honest, simple religious folks wanted to do out of devotion and faith, and how many obstacles were put in their path by a state machinery determined at every stage to stop their march to Ayodhya. Mulayam Singh will have to answer before the bar of the people and that of history. Because of this short-sightedness, in gaining a few votes, he has lost sight of the basic tenet of democracy—that is, it is the rule of the majority—the minority is heard, respected and given equal time, but it is the majority that forms the government.[17]

Some rather fantastic stories continued to make headlines in the regional press till many days later. This was not particularly surprising, given that, in the case of some newspapers, the local stringers were partisan priests of local temples in Ayodhya and the editors VHP sympathizers. For instance, *Dainik Jagran* carried a news item based on an anonymous letter which claimed that at least 1,000 police and army men who were devotees of Ram were quitting their jobs to support the activities of the newly formed Shriram Kranti Brigade, the first task of which would be to cut off the hands and feet of Mulayam Singh Yadav.[18]

[15]*Dainik Jagran*, 3 November 1990
[16]*Aaj*, 2 November 1990.
[17]*The Pioneer* (Lucknow), 31 October 1990.
[18]*Dainik Jagran*, 18 November 1990.

The Course of the Movement

Since India's independence few issues have aroused such violent emotions as the Ramjanmabhumi–Babri masjid controversy. The polarization of public sentiments over it has been associated with a number of communal riots, two of which we have briefly covered in chapter 5.

At the forefront of the temple movement has been the VHP, backed by the RSS, the BJP, and their youth fronts, Bajrang Dal and Durga Vahini. (We provide thumb-nail sketches of the four major organizations involved in the movement later in this book.) The VHP had by the early 1950s launched their agitation for the construction of the Ram mandir in Ayodhya with the slogan, '*Āke bolo, jor se bolo, Janmabhumi kā tālā kholo.*' (Come and loudly ask for the lock on the Janmabhumi to be opened.) More than thirty years later, in 1986, the Congress (I) regime, apparently trying to appear impartial after a section of Muslim religious and political leadership had forced its hand in the Shah Bano case, allowed the lock on the disputed shrine to be opened, and thus gave VHP the hope that its dreams might be realized. We say 'apparently' because the aim of the Congress was no different from that of the *Sangh parivār*;—to build a vote bank that would undercut the support base of the Hindu nationalists. Prime Minister Rajiv Gandhi had then not only unlocked the disputed shrine, but had sought to take electoral advantage of it. As a BJP leader, Atal Behari Vajpayee, told one of us:

It was not the BJP which made Ayodhya into a burning issue. It was the Congress which did that. It was they who allowed the *shilānyās* ceremony. It was Rajiv Gandhi who went to Faizabad to start his election campaign and he solicited votes on the promise of ushering in *Ramrajya* [literally the kingdom of Ram but, connotatively, an ideal polity]. The BJP had to respond to the situation.[19]

[19]This is one of the few issues on which Vajpayee and Syed Shahabuddin, the Janata Dal MP and leader of the Babri Masjid Action Committee, agree. The latter, as alert as Vajpayee to the politics of nationalities, said to us in an interview in October 1990: 'Rajiv Gandhi played his cards very badly. Mrs Gandhi from 1979 onwards indirectly helped the Hindu communal and chauvinistic forces. I don't say that she was communal in a strategic sense. But in her quest for power she could take help from Hindu communalism as a tactical measure. It was she who really reopened the Babri Masjid issue. ....And of course, her son was the beneficiary. He inherited this. And in 1986

But once the issue became live, the VHP was better equipped to take political advantage of it. Emboldened by the unlocking, the VHP intensified its campaign for the liberation of the *Janmasthan* and its posture became increasingly aggressive. '*Jab tak mandir nahin banegā, tab tak yeh sangharsh chalegā*' (We will continue our struggle, till the temple is constructed) was their new war cry. However, despite its determination, the VHP did not think it was going to be either an easy or a short struggle. But electoral politics made things easy for them. In 1989, the Congress (I), trying to win over the Hindus, once again acquiesced with the demands of the VHP and allowed the foundation-laying ceremony of the temple to take place near the disputed site. The foundation stone had been laid, the VHP claimed, not only for the proposed Ram temple but also for a Hindu *rāshtra* in the hearts of the people.

Without losing any time, the VHP announced their next programme of *kārseva*, borrowing a term normally used in connection with the building of Sikh places of worship. In this instance, the term had more to do with destroying rather than building a place of worship. It was a small step from the more tentative 'we shall struggle till a temple is built' to the assertive, 'we will build the temple only here'.

In other words the aim was to break the mosque[s] to humiliate the Muslims and to affirm 'Hindu' potency and pride. Syed Shahabuddin recognizes this. In an interview with us he conceded that

in the eyes of the Shariat only about the three mosques at Mecca, at Medina and Jerusalem can one make a distinction, if at all. Otherwise all mosques have equal sanctity in the eyes of the Shariat. After all you worship the same Allah in every mosque. You don't worship Babar in the Babri mosque or the structure of the Babri Masjid. In fact, the structure of the Babri Masjid is not important at all. You can demolish it. You can completely replace it. After all, the holiest of the holy mosques in Islam have been built and rebuilt many times. But the fact is that the Babri Masjid has been made by the Hindu chauvinists into a symbol of assertion and the Muslims are on the defensive.

---

on February 1, when the lock was opened, there is no doubt in my mind that the order of the district judge of Faizabad was a contrived order. The entire scenario was written by the government. It was done as a matter of state policy. Thus a monster was raised which grew and grew and has come to the present stage.'

The countdown to 30 October began the day the BJP President, Advani, set out on his Rath Yatra on 25 September, 1990—literally a journey on a chariot—which was to take him from Somnath in the state of Gujarat in western India to Ayodhya in UP, to create public opinion in favour of the construction of a temple to Ram.[20] Advani, a soft-spoken, urbane, Sindhi refugee who migrated to India from Pakistan in the 1940s and claims, like most Sindhi Hindus, to be 'spiritually a Sikh', had been a film journalist who reviewed popular Bombay films in his less glorious days. Perhaps appropriately, the chariot in this instance was a decorated, expensive old Chevrolet. The politically alert, however, saw the Yatra as the beginning of the BJP's election campaign. They felt the party had correctly guessed that the general elections were round the corner and it needed a new platform to improve upon its earlier performance. Syed Shahabuddin, Janata Dal MP and no stranger to hard-boiled politics of nationalities, had a perfect understnding of Advani's motives. In the course of an interview he said to us:

The Rath Yatra undertaken by Advani ... is not a religious movement. It is basically a political movement and therefore the reason for the causes must be sought in the political domain....

I shall give you one proof of it. There are many sects in Hinduism. The Ram *upāsaks* are Vaishnavas who worship Ram as a deity. The entire Indian society, as a matter of fact, considers Ram as a *purushottam*. Even Iqbal described him as '*Imam-e-Hind*' and not the Imam of an ordinary mosque or even a *shāhi* mosque but considering India as a place of worship. Therefore, Ram as a great human being, as a moral ideal is accepted by everybody. But

---

[20]Speaking of the symbolism of the chariot, Datta ('VHP's Ram') notes that the chariot invokes the image of Krishna, rather than Ram. He could have added that the chariot is only associated with the Mahabharatic Krishna, not the Krishna of the *Bhāgavat Purāna*. The VHP's imagery in this respect is in continuity with the attempts that began in the nineteenth century to establish the primacy of the Krishna of the Mahabharata—specially the Gita—over the erotic, androgynous, playful Krishna of Bhāgavat.

The VHP iconography of Ram represents the same tensions, the same potency strivings, and the same attempts to disown the androgynous, pastoral, and less technologized maleness that Ram symbolizes. This iconography *has* to reverse the original Ramayana in which Ram fights his climactic battle with the demon Ravana without a chariot, standing on ground and defying his own technolgical backwardness and Ravana's more advanced war machine. In both Valmiki's and Tulsidasa's Ramayana, it is Ravana the demon who uses a chariot, not Ram representing divinity.

as an *avatār* [incarnation] he is accepted only by the Vaishnavas. Now, tell me, is there any prominent Vaishnava in this movement? There is none. There are *aghorpanthis*, there are *tāntriks* who have always fought against Ram; there are Arya Samajis who do not believe in idol worship at all and do not accept *avatārs*, there are Jains. But no Vaishnavas. For the Vaishnavas there is already a site in Ayodhya which for the last 300–400 years they have considered sacred as the birthplace of Ram and that is where the Ram Jan-masthan Mandir stands. Now how can the others say that that place is false and the real site is the inner sanctum of the mosque? It is nothing but an act of political assertion.

By the time Advani was finally arrested in Bihar on 23 October the Yatra had succeeded in creating widespread communal tension to which the activists of the VHP and Bajrang Dal had already con-tributed by taking out Ram Jyoti processions throughout the country (see Tables 6 and 7). And unlike earlier times, this time the violence showed a tendency to spread to rural areas (Table 8).

TABLE 6

INCIDENCE OF COMMUNAL RIOTS BETWEEN
1 SEPTEMBER AND 20 NOVEMBER 1990

State	Places	Killed
Andhra Pradesh	4	27
Assam	1	7
Bihar	8	19
Delhi	-	8
Gujarat	26	99
Karnataka	22	88
Kerala	2	3
Madhya Pradesh	5	21
Maharashtra	3	4
Rajasthan	13	52
Tamil Nadu	1	-
Tripura	1	-
Uttar Pradesh	28	224
West Bengal	2	6
TOTAL	116	558

SOURCE: Collated from newspapers by the People's Union for Democratic Rights for their posters. It has not been possible to separate people killed in communal violence and people killed in police firing during such violence.

At the other end of the spectrum were the *sadbhāvanā* or amity rallies organized by the then Chief Minister of UP, Mulayam Singh Yadav, throughout his troubled state to garner grass roots support for whatever action he had to take. Mulayam Singh's main base was the large Yadav community of the state, politically the most powerful of the 'backward' castes of UP. This was resented by the Hindi press of UP, dominated by the élite castes, which stressed that the riots came in the wake of the BJP's and the VHP's innocuous attempts to take out Ramjyoti processions. Some of these local newspapers were

TABLE 7
DISTRIBUTION OF VIOLENCE RELATED TO THE TEMPLE MOVEMENT

State	Number killed	Affected places	Population under curfew (in millions)
Jammu-Kashmir	-	4	NA
Punjab	-	1	0.04
Haryana	1	7	0.22
Delhi	15	15 police stns.	1.10
Rajasthan	49	10	2.50
Gujarat	258	35	5.70
Uttar Pradesh	170	35 dists.	58.70
Madhya Pradesh	133	17	3.30
Bihar	40	11	2.20
West Bengal	27	6	5.50
Assam	98	12	0.70
Maharashtra	434	32	7.00
Orissa	2	1	0.40
Andhra Pradesh	23	20	3.70
Karnataka	78	13	4.50
Tamilnadu	3	11	NA
Kerala	11	7	2.00

SOURCE: People's Union for Democratic Rights

TABLE 8
SPREAD OF VIOLENCE IN RURAL AREAS

State	Villages	Districts	Dates
Andhra Pradesh	6	1	Oct. 24
Bihar	12	12	Oct. 12–28
Gujarat	9	9	Sep. 18–Oct.22
Karnataka	2	2	Sep. 13–Oct. 9
Madhya Pradesh	18	18	Sep. 28–Oct.22
Maharashtra	2	2	Oct. 10–13
Rajasthan	11	11	Sep. 13–Oct 19
Tamil Nadu	1	1	Oct. 6
Uttar Pradesh	1	1	Sep. 28

SOURCE: C. V. Subba Rao, Seminar on Communal Violence, organized by the PUCL at the Centre for the Study of Developing Societies, February 1993.

to be later found guilty of fomenting communal violence by the Press Council of India.[21]

The campaign against Yadav in the local press took other forms, too. For instance, the BJP had set the date of 30 October for the start of *kārsevā* in Ayodhya. The date coincided with the day of the *pancha kosi parikramā* that year. The party probably calculated that, if there were trouble, the regime could be blamed for it. The press dutifully swallowed the BJP line and blamed Mulayam Singh Yadav for all the violence in the state. His mobilizational efforts earned him the title 'Maulana Yadav' from his opponents and a large section of the local press, unimpressed by his low-brow, street-fighter-like image. As for the more suave Advani, 'he seemed to have', the press said, 'acquired an aura of religiosity for the people who hung on to[sic] every word he spoke.'

While the press wrote about the spontaneity with which the people turned up to greet and hear the BJP president from his chariot, it

[21]*Report of the Subcommittee Appointed by the Press Council of India on 8.11.1990 to Examine the Role of the Press on the One Hand and on the Other the Role of the Authorities in Dealing with the Press Relating to the Coverage of the Ramjanmabhumi-Babri Masjid Issue*, presented at Thiruvananthapuram, Kerala, on 21 January 1991. Also the testimony of Manimala at *Citizens' Tribunal on Ayodhya*, New Delhi, 12 July 1993.

insisted that the local administration had stage-managed the mammoth crowds at Yadav's rallies. When communal riots broke out in the state—among other places in Gazipur, Bijnor, Pratapgarh, Meerut and Colonelganj—the local press blamed Yadav, accusing him of making intemperate statements against the Hindus in his rallies, which had encouraged the Muslims to indulge in violence. Never was the violence or the crisis traced to inter-party competition; the press chose to depict it as a confrontation between the people and the government. Mulayam Singh in his political short-sightedness and arrogance fell almost eagerly into the trap. In one of his several speeches he appealed to the people to perform the *parikramā* in their own villages, since this time it would fall on 30 October. Next day, most newspapers, including major English dailies, carried a report saying that, for the first time in centuries, the *parikramā* would not take place because Mulayam Singh had banned it. The sentiments of religious Hindus were deeply hurt, especially since the government's denial next day was dismissed in a paragraph by the same newspapers. Similarly, in another rally in Kanpur, Mulayam Singh mentioned the well-known fact that, because Muslims had scant faith in the security forces, they tended to arm themselves for self-protection. (The Muslims of UP are said to fear the police, especially the Provincial Armed Constabulary, more than the rioters themselves.[22]) The press claimed that the chief minister was exhorting the Muslims to take up arms against the Hindus. The newspapers' campaign against Mulayam began to have an effect on the readers after a while.

The incident that decisively turned popular Hindu opinion in UP, particularly in Ayodhya-Faizabad, in favour of the VHP and the BJP was the removal of a tin canopy covering the spot where the *shilānyas* ceremony had been performed in November 1989. On the night of 23 October, the canopy was removed under the supervision of the district administration. Mulayam Singh Yadav had visited the site a few days earlier; it is said that the chief minister was alarmed at the transformation of what was just a pit till a year ago into something close to a little temple, with its idols of Ram and other gods and offerings piled up before them. He ordered that the canopy be removed.

[22]The main episode responsible for such fears could be the one at Maliana where the PAC ran its own pogrom against the Muslims. People's Union of Democratic Rights, *Forgotten Massacres* (Delhi: PUDR, 1989); and Indian People's Human Rights Commission, *Report on Meerut* (Delhi: IPHRC, 1989).

Given the prevailing tension, it was a dangerous political error. On 26 October, the Hindi daily *Aaj* splashed the news in bold letters on its front page; the headline in its Ranchi edition said, 'Ram temple broken in Ayodhya'. The Patna edition of the paper reported that the VHP's general secretary, Ashok Singhal, had been injured in the incident and that the idol of Ram had been removed from the pit. Later, the VHP had to issue a statement saying that it was their people, present at the site at the time, who had removed the idol before the canopy was brought down. But few were in any mood to pay heed to the clarification. The damage had been done.

Other Constructions

A journey through Ayodhya–Faizabad around this time revealed much diversity of opinion on the temple issue. A large proportion of the priests, pilgrim guides, holy men and mendicants in Ayodhya seemed to agree with the VHP line that the temple had to be built at any cost and the mosque had to be relocated or destroyed. We were to be proved wrong, but more about that later.

Nrityagopal Das, the abbot of Maniram Chavni and Vice President of the Ramjanmabhumi Mukti Yajna Samiti, was one of the most vocal and active supporters of the cause. A dark, thick-set man with a ready, almost childlike smile, he certainly did not come off as a firebrand religious chauvinist, though it was also obvious that, over the years, he had learnt the jargon and the standard arguments of the VHP rather well. When we spoke to him, he was surrounded by some fawning disciples and political hangers-on. Like his fellow traveller Ramchandra Paramhans, he often seemed to be enacting a role and addressing a large audience even when he was talking only to us. Ironically, he used the famous lines of Mohammed Iqbal's song, '*Sāre Jāhān se achchā Hindustan hamārā*' to emphasize his point that the politicians and their politics were responsible for the controversy in the first place. He added, quoting Iqbal again, '*Mazhab nahin sikhātā āpas mein bair rakhnā; Hindu hain hum vatan hai Hindustan hamārā*' (Religion does not teach us to bear grudges against each other; we are Hindus and our land is Hindustan). It is love of the *kursi*, the "chair", which often, creates tension between people, not their religion,' he explained.

Subsequently, Nrityagopal Das was to tell us on his own that the Ramjanmabhumi controversy had come close to a solution a couple of times. Once, some years ago, the local Shia leadership generously offered to shift the Babri masjid to Sehanawa village where the descendants of Mir Baqi, the builder of the mosque, lived. But, according to Nrityagopal, the politicians on both sides objected to such a solution, saying that the locals did not have the right to barter away things which belonged to the entire community. However, the priest also hastened to add, word for word, the argument of Ramchandra Paramhans that Muslims, when less than 25 per cent of the population of a city or a community, were never a problem; and that, only when their population exceeded this proportion, did they become assertive. He talked of the Muslim refusal to conform to a common civil code, their right to have four wives simultaneously, and their extra-territorial allegiances—all in the language of his colleague in the VHP, Paramhans. But somehow he seemed to lack Paramhans' shrewdness and political sense.

However, there was what seemed at that time to be a minority among the abbots, priest and holy men who thought differently. Chief priest Baldev Prasad Chaturvedi of Kanak Bhavan, one of the biggest temples in Ayodhya, refused to talk about the mandir–masjid controversy. He was, he said, a religious man, and had no interest in anything other than the performance of his daily religious duties. Indian classical music was his other abiding passion; he had trained in it for seven years. The politics of religion, he said, would have interested him only if he was not a man of religion. But since this was not the case, he did not concern himself with it.

According to Chaturvedi, if Hindus and Muslims practised their religion in true faith, there would be no problem at all. It was the non-adherence to religious traditions of the past, their dismissal as 'old fashioned nonsense', which was the root cause of all the trouble. He cited the example of the telecast on Doordarshan of the hit serial Mahabharata:

In the old days only a few great saints recited the Mahabharata and that too after performing special rituals. It was never recited inside a house because it was said that a Mahabharata would take place wherever the epic was recited. If at all it was recited, it was done somewhere outside, in the open. And now it [the epic] is there in each and every house. So why should anyone be surprised at all at these disturbances? If you show Mahabharata on television they are bound to happen, and much worse will come.

Chaturvedi must have seen the happenings of 30 October and 2 November in Ayodhya as the final proof of the truth of his belief.

Even more clear-cut was the position of Swami Laldas who had been appointed chief priest of the Ramjanmabhumi mandir by the court-appointed Receiver of the temple. Laldas stays at a temple formally called Vijay Sundar Vihar Kunj but better known as Kurmi Mandir. Unlike the chief priest of Kanak Bhavan, who was pained by the turn of events and unwilling to talk about the controversy, Laldas is forceful and articulate.

Short, plump and fair, Laldas is only 45 years old, but looks more like a well-preserved 60. He is politically alert and shrewd, but also has a certain social charm and much intellectual stamina. From our various conversations with him, it became gradually obvious that the VHP movement is seen by him, and others like him, as a Shaivite encroachment, if not attack, on the deeply Vaishnava culture of Ayodhya. 'Shaivas consider Ram as a human being and as a king; Vaishnavas consider him the Brahma,' he said to us, as if passing a final judgement.

Laldas was born at a village close to Ayodhya, Shringrishi, in a Kshatriya family. Of course, he went out of his caste when he renounced the world. He had his religious education at Raghunathpur in the state of Jammu and Kashmir and later became a temple priest at Mehsana, Gujarat. A former member of the Communist Party of India (Marxist), Laldas was for a while the secretary of the Party in Ayodhya. As he puts it, he was impressed by the party's commitment to the traditional ideal of *sāmyatā*, equality, not by its hostility to religion, especially to idolatry. Laldas is accused by his detractors of being a maverick. But they also fear him for his aggressive 'in house' criticism which goes down well with those not fully converted to the VHP point of view, both because of his knowledge of the scriptures and his polemical talents. Laldas was in hiding at the time of our meeting, fearing physical attack from both the VHP and the police.

According to Laldas, the BJP supported the movement for political gains. Why did its leaders not demand a Ram mandir on the disputed site, he asks, when they were in power as members of state coalition governments in the 1960s in UP, Bihar, Madhya Pradesh and elsewhere? Why did Lal Krishna Advani and Atal Behari Vajpayee not raise the issue when they were ministers of the central government in 1977–9?? It was only now that they had jumped into the fray, because after winning 86 seats in the last general elections, they were seeing visions of conquering Delhi. 'The BJP does not want the temple to be built. The day that happens, they will be finished politically. Because they will have no issue left to fight elections on.'[23]

Laldas is strengthened in his belief by the record of the RSS. The RSS has never built or helped maintain a temple; it has never even taken an interest in any temple, he affirms. In fact, the RSS, which has supplied the leadership of the entire movement, has been consistently against idol worship. Laldas is deeply suspicious of the new-found enthusiasm for temples in the ranks of the RSS.[24] No important leader of the Sangh family, except the BJP Vice-President Vijaya Raje Scindia, has ever worshipped at the Ramjanmabhumi temple till the time of our interview. As for the VHP, not a single one of its functionaries has even come to the temple with a garland. 'You cannot fill the empty stomachs of people by building temples,' he adds.

He is particularly scathing about the VHP:

Who cares about them in Ayodhya and Faizabad? Not even 10 per cent of the population. When they hold meetings here, they have to bring their workers from outside to attend them. When they wanted to rent a house here to open their office, nobody wanted to give them a place and, so, they were offered houses at double the normal rent. It is largely an organization of the Brahmans and for the Brahmans.

But the VHP propaganda is more dangerous than the organization, he believes. It is like the creeper *bannār,* which is rootless all right but lives on and destroys trees even though, in the process, it dies itself. His opinion of the priests of Ayodhya is no better:

If you want to know what happened to the lakhs of bricks collected from all over the country for the foundation-laying ceremony [of the planned Ram temple], you only have to look at the additions and extensions made in the recent past to the temples of which Nrityagopal Das and Ramchandra Paramhans

---

[23] 'If there is an election today, the BJP would lose,' he was to affirm in February 1992. For the Parliamentary elections held *after* the temple episode in November 1990 had gone aginst the BJP in Rajasthan and Madhya Pradesh where it was a ruling party. The BJP would not have won even the elections in UP, he was to say, but for the 'stupidity' of Mulayam Singh Yadav.

[24] See chapter 3 for a brief discussion of this paradox. Much of the intellectual baggage as well as ideological contradictions of Hindu nationalism come from the religious reform movements of the nineteenth century. Thus, the Arya Samaj, despite its strong tradition of uncompromising anti-idolatry, has also declared its support for a Ram temple at the disputed site.

are the chief priests and you will have your answer. And these are the kind of people who are the local leaders of the movement.

In earlier days, Laldas claims, the heads of monasteries and temples were learned men from good families. But today even a criminal could give Rs 20,000 to the police and with the help of four disciples lay siege to a temple and become a *mahant*. 'It has become like another Chambal valley (the dacoit-infested ravines in central India).' Laldas adds, 'If you ever learn the truth about what goes on in the temples here, you will become an atheist.' These are the very people who, according to him, are recognized by the VHP as religious leaders. Subsequently, in another interview with us, Laldas was to suggest that this attempt to establish links with the criminally inclined had something to do with the criminal or quasi-criminal connections of some of the political parties involved in the dispute. He alleged that a factory of the brother of an important VHP functionary had stored 27 tons of lard; it was reportedly being used to adulterate vegetable oil. The priest was particularly sarcastic about the millions of rupees the VHP had collected and about the salience of Marwari businessmen among its functionaries.

The situation has been worsened by the local police and administration. According to Laldas, the police has always been partisan. As for local administrators, every now and then there have been good officers, but the current lot are entirely with the BJP. The District Magistrate, Ram Sharan Srivastava, was the worst. He was posted in Meerut before being transferred to Faizabad. Both cities witnessed communal violence during his tenure.[25]

The people of Faizabad–Ayodha are sensible and tolerant, Laldas says. If they are communal, he asks, why did they vote a Communist to power from here in the previous general elections? While widespread violence rocked the rest of the state in the wake of L. K. Advani's Rath Yatra, there was relative peace and calm in the area. Left to themselves, Laldas feels, the citizens of Ayodhya would have settled the matter amicably.

Laldas, however, sees no possibility of a solution in the existing atmosphere. It is already too late, unless the VHP withdraws its

[25]In the communal riots that broke out immediately after the demolition of the Babri masjid on 6 December 1992, Kanpur was the worst-affected city in UP. Srivastava was the District Magistrate of Kanpur at the time. When the violence continued for some days, he had to be hurriedly transferred from the city.

movement and—here Laldas shows some political sense, despite lending support to the state government's secular rallies—unless the government of Mulayam Singh Yadav becomes less aggressive. Only then could a solution, acceptable to both the Hindus and Muslims, be worked out.

The Muslim religious leadership of Ayodhya–Faizabad was bitter. 'Now we cannot even say, all right take this masjid and spare us, because they have already staked their claim to 3000 more mosques. Today they want our mosques, tomorrow they will want our homes. There will be no end to it,' said Haji Muhammad Kalim Samshi, the head of the Tatshah mosque in Faizabad. According to him the only thing to do was to accept the court's verdict. But when asked what he would do if the judgment went against the popular sentiments of the Muslims, he remained silent for a few seconds and then mumbled 'I'll go away.' He did not say where.

But despite such strong feelings on the issue, Haji Samshi appeared on television, on the night of 30 October, and said that no damage had been done to the structure of the mosque. He added that he had been to the site and inspected it. It was obvious that apart from being a religious leader, he also had worldly wisdom. At that point in time, the fears of the Muslims of Ayodhya–Faizabad and those all over the country had to be allayed and the aggressive elements in his community had to be prevented from reacting by committing acts of violence which would only have invited the wrath of the majority community.

Despite the bitterness, the local Muslims tried to keep their emotions in check. While talking of a last-ditch effort to save the situation, the fear showed, not the anger. Said a youth leader of Ayodhya, Khalid Ahmed, 'What will happen if Muslims take up arms tomorrow and turn terrorists? The government has not been able to control the Sikh problem in so many years. How will they control us?' A senior Muslim leader of Faizabad, Nasir Sahib, talked of how life had become a living hell ever since 26 February 1986, when the opening of the lock on the Janmasthan was celebrated with fireworks and distribution of sweets in Ayodhya. He said angrily:

For 37 years before that everyone had forgotten about it, and then suddenly all these outsiders came here and made it an issue of life and death. If only we had been left alone to decide for ourselves what we wanted! Instead it is

L. K. Advani and the Shahi Imam, who have never even visited Ayodhya, who are going to decide the fate of its residents.

The leader was open to a suggestion made just that day that the Hindus and Muslims of the twin cities should stage a bigger march than the army's flag march in a show of solidarity and communal harmony. But it was left to Haji Abdul Ghaffar, then in his nineties, who used to read *namāz* in the Babri masjid until it was converted into a temple overnight, to express the depth of the fears of the minority community, which others were too sophisticated to do. 'I have purchased my funeral shroud', said Ghaffar.

The residents of Ayodhya had long regarded the whole town as the Ramjanmabhumi. Neither they, nor the priests of the innumerable temples which dot the town's landscape, could identify with total conviction, one particular site as the birthplace of Ram. As we have already said, there are at least two other spots in Ayodhya, besides the one on which the Babri mosque stood, that have long been considered the site of Ram's birth. One is the Ramchabutra, outside the actual structure of the mosque but within its compound, which has been worshipped as the Ramjanmasthan since the mid-nineteenth century. The other is the Ramjanmasthān mandir which stands close to the masjid and where the worshippers and the priests had long been relatively indifferent to the cause of liberating the Ramjanmabhumi. But the VHP propaganda had made some difference to their way of thinking, as in fact events at the end of October were to show.

The Propaganda Machine

The Hindus and Muslims of India do not constitute, we have said, distinct ethnic groups in any conventional sense. Nor do they constitute, despite differences in their socio-economic and educational profiles, distinct socio-economic formations having distinct political interests. There are 650 million Hindus in India and more than 110 million Muslims. Such large aggregates, in a society as diverse as India, cannot but have internal divisions that are in some cases less and in other cases more significant than religious divisions. Even religious divisions within the two aggregates often bear 'peculiar' relationships with divisions within the other community. Thus, the Pranami sect in Gujarat (the one in which Gandhi was born) is in many ways closer to Islam than it is to many other sects within Hinduism; likewise, most versions of Sindhi Hinduism look terribly

Islamic to many South Indian Hindus and many Muslim communities in Rajasthan, Gujarat, and Bengal look disturbingly Hindu to Muslims in other parts of India.

Such variations mean that all attempts to mobilize Hindus and Muslims as Hindus and Muslims must concentrate on broad ideological issues and subjective configurations of grievances, memories, and cultural differences, specially engineered for mobilizational purposes. The VHP provided such a configuration. Its propaganda in Ayodhya was shrill and vitriolic, especially near the disputed site where it set up a showroom during the movement.

The approach to the disputed structure was through a heavily guarded iron gate. On the other side of the gate was the temple with a sanctum sanctorum that projected into the masjid. In it, there were three low stools on which were placed the idols that miraculously 'appeared' there on the night of 23 December 1949, and pictures of some other gods and goddesses.[26] Besides, there were pictures of four individuals: K. K. Nayar, the District Magistrate of Faizabad at the time the idols made their appearance, Thakur Gurudutt Singh who was the city magistrate at the time, and freedom fighters Bhagat Singh and Chandrashekhar Azad.

Less than thirty yards away from the temple, separated by a fence, was the site of the foundation and adjoining it was an exhibition set up by the VHP, a visit to which was a must for any visitor according to a policeman standing on guard nearby. At the entrance of this showroom was the model of the proposed Ram mandir to be constructed at a cost of five hundred million rupees where the masjid stood. The idol of Ramlalla was placed in this model and all visitors were asked by VHP workers to bend down to have a look at the idol. The psychological impact of the showroom on at least some visitors was profound:

The organized conjunction of the model [of the proposed temple] with the *shilanyas* site suddenly transforms the showroom. It becomes no longer simply a place to exhibit the wares of the VHP.... The showroom makes the spectator complicit in the building of the VHP dream, by making the dream appear

---

[26]By now about six persons have claimed to have stealthily put the icons in their present place on 23 December 1949. See the interview with one claimant, Mahant Ramsohandas Shastri, in Anand Patwardhan, *Ram ka Nam* (Documentary film, 1992). Ramchandra Paramhans is another such claimant.

fully formed. The future becomes inevitable: it transforms into the grand design of fate.[27]

A brief history of the controversial structure was sought to be given through a series of large posters. One showed the miracle by which Vikramaditya found the Ramjanmabhumi, a second detailed the story of the temple, and a third showed its destruction by Babar. On the wall was written: 'It is the religious duty of every Hindu to kill those who kill cows.' There were also two large pictures of K. K. Nayar and Gurudutt Singh. The write-ups at the bottom lavished praise on these great men, honouring them for their great sacrifice.[28]

Outside the exhibition, a few policemen were playing an audio cassette on the public address system. It was a recording of some highly aggressive and somewhat vulgar speeches made by the BJP leader Uma Bharati.

The one who can console our crying motherland, and kill the traitors with bullets, we want light and direction from such a martyr, we want a Patel or a Subhash for our nation....
When ten Bajrangbalis will sit on the chest of every Ali, then only will one know whether this is the birthplace of Ram or the Babri masjid, then only will one know that this country belongs to Lord Ram.[29]

We tried to find out why they were playing this particular cassette. 'Oh, we were just trying it out,' they clarified. The trial lasted more than an hour.

[27]Datta, 'VHP's Ram', p. 2525.
[28]The reason for Nayar's greatness becomes clear from his letter of 27 December 1949 to the then Chief Secretary of UP, Bhagwan Sahay,

... I would if the government decided to remove the idols at any cost request that I be relieved and replaced by an officer who may be able to see in that solution a merit which I cannot discern [quoted by Satyapal Dang, *New Age*, 15 October 1989].

K. K. Nayar was eventually removed from government service after which he served one term as a Jan Sangh M.P.

[29]'*Jo hamāri roti mātribhumi ko sukun de, aur deshdrohiyon ko goliyon se bhun de aise sarfarosh ka hamen prakāsh chāhiye, desh ke liye hamen Patel ya Subhash chahiye....*
Jab ek-ek Ali ki chchāti par das-das Bajrangbali chadhe honge, tab patā chal jayegā ki yeh sthān Ramjanmabhumi hai ya Babri Masjid. Tab patā chal jayegā ki yeh desh Prabhu Ram kā hai.'

The literature being sold in the VHP showroom was not different. Comprising mainly histories of Ayodhya, they centred on one main theme: how the sanctity of the Janmasthān in Ayodhya, attested by its association with miracles that had surfaced in many myths, had been defiled by the Muslims. Two such publications were the book *Ayodhya Guide* and the pamphlet *Angry Hindu! Yes, Why Not?* Both pleaded for aggressive assertion of Hindu power to avenge the wrongs inflicted on them by the Muslims in the past.

Yes, certainly I am angry. And I have every reason to be angry. And it is also right for me to be so. Otherwise I would be no man. Yes for too long I have suffered insults in silence. Uptil [sic] now I have been at the receiving end ... My people have been kidnapped by the enemies. My numbers have dwindled ... my goddess-like motherland has been torn asunder ... My traditional rights have been snatched away from me.

And still you tell me I should not get angry? That I should not stand up and shout 'that's enough'?

My temples have been desecrated, destroyed. Their sacred stones are being trampled under the aggressor's feet. My gods are crying. They are looking to me for their re-establishment in all their original glory. When I speak out my agony, the secularists see it as a threat to our 'secular peace'. You add insult to my injury. You rub salt into my wounded heart and expect me to keep my mouth shut.

I am proud that you called me an 'angry Hindu'. Till now I was an angry zamindar, angry farmer ... or an angry Maratha, angry Bengali ... or angry Jain, angry Arya Samaji ... But now you have given me a new name in which all this is absorbed ...

I now realize I had been too good for this world of 'hard reality'. I believed that others would respect my gods and temples as I respected other's ... I believed generosity begets generosity.... But alas, again and again I was deceived, I was betrayed, I was stabbed in the back. I know now something of the ways of the world. And I have decided to speak to others in the language they understand ... And finally, I have come to know the value of my anger itself.[30]

A poem in the same pamphlet, now known to be written by Atal Behari Vajpayee when he was in high school, sought to define the identity of this new militant Hindu:

Hindu tan-man, Hindu jīvan, rag-rag Hindu merā parichay
Main Shankar kā woh krodhānal, kar saktā jagti kshar-kshar

---

[30]Anonymous, *Angry Hindu! Yes, Why Not?* (New Delhi: Suruchi, 1988), pamphlet.

Main damru ki pralayadhvani hun jismain nāchtā bhishan sanhār
Ranachandi ki atripta pyās, main Durga ka unmatta hās,
Main Yam ki pralayankar pukār, jalte marghat ka dhuandhār
Phir antartam ki jvalā se jagti mein āg lagā dun main,
Yadi dhadak uthe jal-thal-ambar-jad-chetan phir kaisā vismay?
Hindu tan-man Hindu jivan, rag-rag Hindu merā parichay.[31]

(This is the identity of the Hindu body, the Hindu soul and the Hindu life,
I am that rage of Shankar, which can destroy the earth and reduce it to ashes,
I am the devastating sound of his drum to which death dances,
I am the unquenched thirst of the goddess of war, I am the divine laughter
    of Durga,
I am the doomsday call of the god of death, the burning fire from the funeral
    pyre,
If with this fire raging inside me, I burn the earth,
And the water, earth, sky, soil go up in flames on their own, do not be
surprised.)

Towards its end, the poem also spoke of the victimization of the
Hindus in history and their overall martial and moral superiority over
the Muslims.

Mein vir-putra, meri Jānani ke jagti mein jauhar apār;
Akbar ke putron se puccho—kya yād unhe Minā Bazār?
Kya yad unhe Chittor durg mein jalne wali āg prakhar?
Jab hāi! Sahasron mātāen til-til jalkar ho gayin amar.
Vah bujhne wāli āg nahin, rag-rag mein use sanjoye hun,
Yadi kabhi achānak phut pade,
viplav lekar to kya vismay?[32]

(I am the son of the brave, there are many Jauhars hidden in me; ask the
sons of Akbar, whether they remember Minā Bazār?
Do they remember the raging fire in the fort of Chittor?
When thousands of mothers attained martyrdom by burning themselves. This
fire which I have nurtured in every vein of my body is not one which can
ever be put out,
If it suddenly erupts in the form of a revolution, it will hardly be a surprise.)

Both the books and pamphlets were selling briskly.

---

[31]Anonymous, *Krudh Hindu?—Han Main Krudh Hun* (New Delhi:
Suruchi, 1988), 2nd ed., pamphlet.
[32]Ibid.

CHAPTER THREE

V. CREATING A NATIONALITY

The social sources and political motives propelling the Ramjanmabhumi movement were related to the contents of the propaganda unleashed by the movement. Its consumers, in turn, were not distributed randomly over all social segments; they came with a particular social profile.

For more than a hundred years, these sources and motivations have been shaped by the growth of the political culture of Hindu nationalism. The growth parallels similar movements within South Asian Islam, Sikhism, and Buddhism. The emergence of Hinduism itself as the religion of the majority community in urban, modernizing India has its mirror image in the emergence of Islam as the religion of a minority with roughly similar ideological and programmatic content. Both in turn have striking similarities with the emergence of Buddhist Sinhala majoritarianism and Sikh minority consciousness roughly along the same lines.

The Politics of an Idea

Hindu·nationalism does not have a long past in India. Nor for that matter has Hinduism itself in its present sense. The idea of Hindus as a single political community that can be specifically called a nation is relatively new.[1] Its beginnings can be traced to the middle of the

---

[1]As repeated *ad nauseum* these days, the word Hindu is of Arabic/Persian origin and has exactly the same meaning etymologically as the word India, which is of Graeco-Roman origin. None of the Hindu sacred texts even once mentions the word Hindu. Both these foreign words have served, for outsiders unacquainted with the complexities of the country, as a generic name for the different, mainly non-Islamic, but also non-Christian, communities living in the subcontinent. It is doubtful if the word Hindu excluded before the nineteenth century the ancient Christian communities of the present-day Kerala, the Zoroastrians, and the Jewish communities of Maharashtra and

nineteenth century when, in reaction to the onslaught of aggressive modernism of mainly the Utilitarians and the social Darwinists, Christian evangelism, and exposure to European ideologies of nationalism, there began to crystallize a wide variety of 'Hindu' responses in the public sphere of India.

These responses gained strength because the modern and secular ideologies, that came into India primarily through colonialism, began to be backed, since about the 1830s, by the colonial state trying to establish a closer link between colonialism and modernism and using the latter as an endorsement of the Raj's civilizing mission. The resulting feelings of inferiority, insecurity about the future, and moral disorientation provoked responses that were frequently a strange mix of the classical, the folk, and the imported western categories that had produced the cultural and psychological disruption in the first place.

One reaction took the form of a defensive attempt to redefine Hinduism as a 'proper' religion along Semitic lines and to make this redefined Hinduism the pillar of a second, nativized theory of modernization of mind and society in India. In opposition to the liberal-secular model, becoming popular among the more Anglicized sections of the élites, this second strand retained some of the basic concerns of modernization, but gave them a new twist. Concepts such as the nation-state and modern technology continued to be important, but they were now to be pursued through a language that was Hindu in its new, redefined sense. Simultaneously, the ideology of nationalism was nativized in a form that could sanction the attempts to convert the Hindus into a conventional, European-style nation.

This new Hinduism—the political ideology of which was to be later given the name Hindutva and which some of its detractors prefer to call 'toady Hinduism'—had a number of important features. First,

---

Kerala, and even many of the Muslim communities of the subcontinent.

For the West Asian Muslims who coined it in the twelfth century and the pre-British rulers of India who used it, 'Hindu' was an administrative term. The British and, following them, the westernized Indians turned it into a religious category. The definition and parameters of Hinduism are being settled now. There is the other side of the story too; many other communities now widely recognized as non-Hindu are actually becoming so now in India. For example, whatever the official census might say, Sikhism became an identifiably separate 'religion' in the minds of Indians only in the 1980s and, formally, probably after the riots in the city of Delhi in November 1984.

it defensively rejected or devalued the little cultures of India as so many indices of the country's backwardness and as prime candidates for integration within the Hindu/national mainstream. Instead, the new Hindus sought to chalk out a new pan-Indian religion called Hinduism that would be primarily classical, Brahmanic, Vedantic and, therefore, not an embarrassment to the modern or semi-modern Indians in touch with the more 'civilized' parts of the world. It was this high culture, more acceptable to the modern or westernized Indians and to post-Enlightenment Europe, which was sought to be made the basis of the new Hindu nation. The nationhood was also projected into the past and the Hindu cultural uniqueness was reinterpreted as merely the marker of a modern national ideology.

This attempted Brahmanization or, what at that time could be safely called, Aryanization was sustained by the poor access and even contempt that many of the early stalwarts of Hindutva had for the diverse lifestyles that went with Hinduism in South Asia.[2] For these stalwarts mostly came from the uprooted, urban, modernized or semi-modernized sectors of the country and, in fact, their Hindutva was often a reaction to, and compensated for, their distance from the lived traditions of Hinduism. The poor access did not appear a handicap at the time because of the ambience created by the rediscovery of classical Hinduism by sympathetic European scholars,[3] by the spread of Hindu reform movements such as Brahmo Samaj and Arya Samaj, and by the devaluation of the little cultures of Hinduism by aggressive modernism and evangelical Christianity.[4]

[2]Following Majid Rahnema, one could call this the tradition of vernacular Hinduism or vernacular India. Majid Rahnema, 'Reflections on Fundamentalism', *Alternatives*, forthcoming.

Anthropologist Michael Robert has drawn our attention to the parallel split in Sri Lankan Buddhism between vernacular Buddhism serving as a faith of the kind so elegantly depicted in Gananath Obeseykere's *Medusa's Hair: The Cult of the Goddess Petini* (Chicago: University of Chicago Press, 1984) and the ideological Buddhism of the likes of Dhammapal serving as the basis of Sinhala nationalism.

[3]In this neoclassicism and neo-Brahmanism an important role was played by Orientalists such as William Jones and Max Mueller whose enthusiasm for ancient India was sometimes matched by a distinct distaste for the living reality of India and Hinduism.

[4]Particularly revealing in this context are the life and writings of Brahmabandhav Upadhyay (1861–1907), probably the first activist-scholar to systematically develop the ideological content of Hindu nationalism. Already the

The Orientalists and the religious reformers created the impression of there being a 'real' Hinduism which transcended the 'trivialities' of the local traditions. The modernists and the missionaries delegitimized Hinduism as a lived experience and left open, for the increasingly insecure Indian literati, the option of defending only philosophical Hinduism as the real Hinduism.

Second, the redefined version of Hinduism allowed those who saw the new religion more as an ideology than as a faith, to use Hinduism as an instrument of political mobilization *à la* European-style national ideology. This part of the redefinition of Hinduism derived strength from the fact that Indian culture was primarily organized around religion and it seemed natural to some Indians, sold to the new myth of the nation-state, to use Hinduism as a national ideology rather than as a repertoire of religious, cultural and moral categories in politics.[5] In fact, Hindu nationalism had to specifically reject a cultural-moral definition of Hinduism, the political possibilities of which were to be later developed by M. K. Gandhi.

The two strands of consciousness were never to be reconciled, despite the efforts of a number of individuals and parties. Occasional paeans to Gandhi notwithstanding, Hindu nationalism continued to see Gandhism as a mortal enemy. It is not widely known that all three attempts on Gandhi's life in India were made by Hindu nationalists. During his lifetime, his commitment to eternal Hinduism, *sanātana dharma*, was itself seen as one of his stigmata. And fifty years after his death, his Hinduism continues to look to Hindu nationalists openly anti-statist, anti-Brahmanic, disaggregating, emasculating and hostile to modern science and technology. Even more dangerous, his Hinduism brings to politics a cultural-moral

---

culture of the twice-born castes and Aryanism were evident in Upadhyay. It is no accident that Upadhyay's nationalism was tinged with his own marginality, religious and cultural. Upadhyay, brought up as an orthodox Brahman, first embraced Protestant Christianity and then Catholicism, and returned through Christianity to Vedantic Hinduism. An aggressive nationalist, he was the first to theoretically explore the possibilities of using political terrorism as an instrument of anti-imperialism. See the section on Upadhyay in Ashis Nandy, *The Illegitimacy of Nationalism: Rabindranath Tagore and the Politics of Self* (New Delhi: Oxford University Press, 1993). Similar uprootedness characterized the life of Vinayak Damodar Savarkar (1883–1966), also. The nationalism of the early Savarkar, especially as projected in his novel, *1857*, has many similarities with that of Upadhyay's.

[5]Nandy, 'Politics of Secularism'.

critique of Hindutva from the point of view of Hinduism as the living faith of a majority of Indians. The political possibilities of such a critique in competitive, open politics are not lost on the Hindu nationalists. (Suresh Sharma draws attention to the paradox that the ultimate protagonist of Hindu nationalism, Vinayak Damodar Savarkar, had little to say about the content of Hindu religious tradition, whereas Gandhi, whom Savarkar considered a danger to Hinduism, spent his life exploring and redeploying these traditions in politics.[6])

As it happened, many of those who helped to redefine Hinduism as a national ideology were themselves either agnostic or non-believers; some of them were not even practising Hindus.[7] But they were convinced that the Indians had to be pummelled into a single nation through the ideology of Hindutva. In this respect at least, there was no difference whatsoever between Hindu nationalism and statist secularism. Actually, the fanaticism associated with Hindutva at the highest levels of the organizations swearing by Hindutva is political, not religious. At its core lies a secular ideology of the state and a modern rationality. Both have a totally instrumental concept of piety and of the faith of the lesser mortals who supply the personnel and, occasionally, the cannon-fodder for the movement.

Third, this Hinduism sought to masculinize the self-definition of the Hindus and, thus, martialize the community. The more the sense of cultural and personal impotency produced by the colonial political economy, the more pronounced became the attempts to give public shape to these masculinity strivings, to militarize the seemingly un-militarizable.[8] To bring about this change, the Hindu nationalists

[6]Suresh Sharma, 'Hinduism in Colonial Times', unpublished paper presented in the seminar on 'Hinduism: Religion or Civilization?', Max Mueller Bhavan, New Delhi, 2–3 December 1991.

A similar paradoxical situation obtains in the case of Muhammad Ali Jinnah (1875–1948), the best known spokesman for subcontinental Muslims who had little to say about their faith and culture, and Abul Kalam Azad (1888–1958), who lost out as a leader of the subcontinent's Muslims but showed a lifelong concern with Islamic theology and culture.

[7]Once again there is a vague parallel between Savarkar and Jinnah in this respect, apart from the fact that they both embraced a two-nation theory for India. Savarkar's two-nation theory of course predated Jinnah's.

[8]For a more detailed discussion of some of these issues, see Ashis Nandy, *The Intimate Enemy: The Loss and Recovery of Self Under Colonialism* (New Delhi: Oxford University Press, 1983).

systematically began to use the newly discovered discipline, history.[9] They did so not with the Orwellian conviction that one who controlled the past controlled the future, but with the enthusiasm of one who had introjected the colonial estimate of Indians as ahistorical and irrational. Defensive about the traditional Indian emphasis on myths as the major means of constructing the past, they enthusiastically used the colonial histories of communities identified by the British as martial, such as the histories of the Rajputs and the Marathas by scholars like James Tod and Jadunath Sarkar. They then turned these sectional histories into powerful nationalist, often Hindu nationalist, interpretations of the past. In their new editions, these interpretations selected and absolutized elements of history that elicited the passions and the sacredness traditionally associated with myths, without the openness, multiple narrations, and interpretations that went with these myths in an epic culture.

Having done so, Hindu nationalism had to specifically reject the Indian openness to all alternative forms of construction of the past and underplay or ignore the latent Indian hostility to history as conceptualized by Enlightenment Europe. In this respect, the Hindu nationalist commitment to the idea of history was to be matched only by the Leninist-positivist concept of history as internalized by the Indian Left. The Hindu nationalists sought to justify everything by history; they invoked and instrumentally used myths only when history failed them; and they absolutized history in a way that abridged and delegitimized the open hermeneutics of myths, legends and epics in Indian civilization.[10] With the secular liberals and the socialists they also shared a common faith in scientized history; all of them

[9]For an excellent discussion of the process see Vinay Lal, 'On the Perils of History and Historiography: The Case, Puzzling as Usual, of India', ms, 1988.

[10]In other words, they absolutized myths, too. It is not surprising that, in the context of the Ramjanmabhumi stir, when the Hindu nationalists, feeling betrayed by their beloved history, tried to return to myths as a crucial organizing principle of society, they fell flat on the face. See, for instance, K. R. Malkani, Letter to the Editor, *The Times of India*, 15 December 1989. Their discomfiture was matched only by that of their ultra-secular brethren trying to combat the Hindu nationalist exploitation of the Ramjanmabhumi controversy through 'hard' history. S. Gopal, Romila Thapar, and others, *The Political Abuse of History* (New Delhi, pamphlet). See also A. R. Khan, 'In the Name of History', *Indian Express*, 25 February 1990; S. Gopal et al., 'In the Name of History', 'Dr A. R. Khan Replies', Ibid., 1 April 1990.

criticized colonial history, but they did not see history itself as having a colonial connection. We have already mentioned how this historical consciousness has itself become a major contributor to communal tensions in India today.[11]

Fourth, Hindu nationalism not only accepted modern science and technology and their Baconian social philosophy, it also developed a totally uncritical attitude towards any western knowledge system that seemed to contribute to the development and sustenance of state power and which promised to homogenize the Indian population. There is no critique of modern science and technology in Hindutva, except for a vague commitment to some selected indigenous systems that are relatively more Brahmanic and happen to be peripheral to the pursuit of power. So Ayurveda and Siddha can have some legitimacy for the Hindu nationalists, not the traditional folk or tribal systems of healing. Nor has Hindu nationalism shown the slightest sensitivity to the traditional Indian concepts of statecraft or village technology or artisan skills. For there cannot be in Hindutva any acceptance of any traditional technology or skill that diminishes or subverts the power of the state or its centralizing thrust or detracts from its phallic symbolism. Hence, the fanatic commitment both to nuclear weaponry and nuclear power even among those votaries of Hindutva who are ideologically committed to indigenous systems of knowledge in other areas of life.

Consequently, there is a complete rejection of not only the pre-British Islamic concept of state in India—which in any case was seen as totally hostile towards the Hindus, even the traditional Hindu experience of running large states in India is seen as entirely irrelevant. Thanks to the new historical consciousness, acquired through the colonial connection and the systematic delegitimization of the pre-British cultures of politics after the entry of the Utilitarian theories of progress into the Indian scene in the 1830s, any appreciation of the Hindu past could only be an appreciation of the contemporary West superimposed on the Hindu past. Despite all the lip service paid to non-Muslim rulers and warriors such as Chandragupta Maurya, Rana Pratap, Shivaji and Guru Govind Singh, Hindu nationalism has always held in contempt the memories of Hindu polity as it survives in the traditional sectors of the Hindu society. There is not a single

[11]Cf. E. Valentine Daniel, 'History and its Entailments in the Violence of a Nation', in Frederique Apffel Marglin (ed.), *Decolonizing Knowledge: From Development to Dialogue*, forthcoming.

respectable study of the political theories of pre-colonial Hinduism done from within the tradition of Hindu nationalism which is not shot through with western concepts of statism and nationalism. Though the concept of Hindu *rāshtra* was introduced in the middle of the nineteenth century and later systematized by the likes of Savarkar, the concept is culturally hollow; it is nothing more than the post-seventeenth-century European concepts of nationality and nation-state projected back into the Indian past; such a nation-state is expected in contemporary times to be controlled by modernized Hindus and inhabited by their likes. It is this modern content of Hindutva which explains part of the enthusiasm for the idea among urban, middle-class Indians and expatriate Indians in the first world; they see their secular interests as well as private hopes, anxieties, and fears well-reflected in the ideology.

In other words, even the Hindus who would constitute the Hindu *rāshtra* are not expected to be Hindus in the traditional sense. The traditional Hindus are seen as too diverse, feminized, irrational, unversed in the intricacies of the modern world, and too pantheistic, pagan, gullible and anarchic to run a proper state. So, the emphasis is on the new version of Hindus emerging in metropolitan India, with one foot in western education and values, the other in simplified versions of classical thought now available in commoditifiable form in the urban centres of India. This simplified version is expected to be a substitute or compensation for the loss of access to traditional social relations and lifestyles, both in the growing urban jungles of modern India and in the cultural melting pots of the First World. (In a way, the attempt was to take to its logical conclusion Vivekananda's belief that a European society could be built in India on the basis of re-interpreted Vedanta.)

This re-engineered, culturally bipedal Hindu is to be backed by an ideology that is a pasteurized, Brahmanic version of the dominant public ideology of the modern West. This ideology works on the basis of a number of conspicuous polarities—genuine secularism as opposed to pseudo-secularism, genuine history as opposed to false history, true nationalism as opposed to false or effete patriotism, and so on.

No wonder that from the beginning, the ideologues of Hindutva found that a majority of their supporters came from urban India and specially from among the same modern Indians who were unable to

break into the high-status, oligarchic club of the fully westernized
Indians.

The Party

To start with, the ideologues of Hindutva were a small minority in
the public sphere, though their presence in the culture of Indian politics was never insignificant. But their influence grew with the widen-
ing reach of the modern institutions. The major breakthrough came
when the colonial state began to falter due to the growing politiciza-
tion of the Indian middle classes. When the movement against the
partition of Bengal began in 1905, the Hindu nationalists for the first
time made their political clout felt. Though there persisted a powerful
liberal-syncretic strand of political consciousness in the public sphere,
the appeal of Hindu nationalism was visible enough for some, like
Rabindranath Tagore, to register their dissent even during the heady
days of the *Banga Bhanga* movement.[12]

The reason for the visibility is not difficult to guess. The
'syncretism' that had been once so conspicuous in the Indian political
scene had begun to look to many politicized Indians, thanks to the
humiliations being inflicted by the colonial regime, as too compromising and obsequious to the colonial establishment. That syncretism had even failed to produce an adequate critique of the modern
West, these Indian felt.

There was a time when such syncretism had its aggressive, fanatic
proponents in associations such as the Young Bengal group led by
Henry Derozio (1809–31) and Krishna Mohun Banerjea (1813–85).
They were ardent nationalists and modernists, and their syncretism
was actually a not-so-hidden plea for full-scale westernization and
war against Hinduism. In the first decades of the new century, such
syncretism, even when preached by more moderate movements,
began to look like an alliance against the victims of colonialism. The
proliferation of 'terrorist' outfits—many of them inspired by the ideology of Hindu nationalism—could be said to be a direct outcome of
the manifest impotency of the liberals in the Indian freedom movement in the face of the arrogance and arbitrariness of the colonial
regime. What further underwrote the ideology of Hindu nationalism
was the fact that this arrogance and arbitrariness were based on a
Kiplingesque division between the so-called martial and non-martial

[12]Nandy, *The Illegitimacy of Nationalism.*

races of India and on the belief, openly articulated by colonial bureaucrats such as Lord Curzon, that the martial races deserved to rule India. Hindu nationalism in this respect was another case of identification with the aggressors and internalization of the key categories of the colonial discourse.

The battleground of the contestants—Hindu nationalism and modern liberalism—was the middle-class Indian. The influence of both strands of political consciousness was confined to urban India and to those who had some exposure to the process of modernization. Within this sector, by the second decade of this century and especially after the Jalianwalabagh massacre in 1919, there were signs that the Hindu nationalists were gradually winning more and more support, and the liberals were losing out.

This contest, however, was disrupted by the entry of M. K. Gandhi into Indian politics. By the middle of the 1920s, he had consolidated his dominance in the Indian national movement by checkmating both the 'moderates' and the 'extremists'. He had done so by taking his anti-imperialist politics beyond the urban middle classes, into India's sleepy villages. The cultural fall out of the process included the containment of the Hindu nationalists who began to see Gandhi's emergence as a defeat for them. This explains the persistent simmering hostility towards Gandhi, particularly towards his philosophy of politics and perception of India's civilizational future, among the more modernized Indian communities that supplied the clientele of both Hindu nationalism and western liberalism as well as the leadership of the freedom movement till then. Among these displaced communities were the Brahmans of Maharashtra and South India, the *bhadralok* of Bengal, and a sizeable section of the upper-castes in northern India who had come under the influence of the Arya Samaj. Not only were all three attempts on Gandhi's life made by Hindu nationalists, all three involved Maharashtrian Brahmans.

One by-product of this defeat at the hands of Gandhian mass politics—which brilliantly used the strengths of vernacular Hinduism—was the gradual withdrawal of Hindu nationalism from the mainstream of the anti-imperialist struggle. Many stalwarts of Hindu nationalism—starting from Savarkar, who had once made enormous personal sacrifices for the freedom struggle, to Hegdewar, who had started his life as a freedom fighter—veered round to take a more benign view of western colonialism. They wanted to use the British presence in India not only to cure Indians of their unconcern with things like history, nation-state and modern science, but also to free India from the scourge of the Muslims. Anti-imperialism was not abandoned, but it was given a much lower place in the hierarchy of political goals.

This sense of defeat in the Hindu nationalists lasted until the 1960s by when, with the introduction of full-fledged general elections after the partition of the country into India and Pakistan, they had marked out a small constituency that stood by them through thick and thin. The constituency served not so much the old Hindu Mahasabha, with which the likes of Savarkar were associated, but the newly founded Jan Sangh.

The Jan Sangh was established in 1953 by Shyamaprasad Mookerji (1901–53) who, though by conviction and family traditions was sympathetic to Hindu nationalism, had been a respected member of Jawaharlal Nehru's cabinet. His political break with Congress was bound to come, but it took on the colour of a serious policy difference on the issue of Jammu and Kashmir, though the treatment of minorities in East Pakistan was also a contributing factor. In fact, the first session of the Jan Sangh at Kanpur was dominated by two issues: (a) Hindu refugees streaming into India from East Bengal and (b) the India–Pakistan conflict on, and the especial status given to, Kashmir. On both issues the government of India was condemned for taking a soft stand and a demand was made for firm action short of war.

On the refugee problem, Mookerji had the support of most opposition parties, including most sections of the Left. On Kashmir too, Mookerji had the tacit support of a large part of Indian public opinion. Later, when the Kashmir issue became more conspicuously an all-party issue, at least one commentator was to go so far as to say that on Kashmir, after Mookerji, 'the Jan Sangh did not have a more brilliant spokesman of its policies than [V. K. Krishna] Menon....'[13]

The Mass Politics of Hindutva

Before we look at the performance of the BJP in the electoral arena— after all, according to many that was what Ramjanmabhumi was all about—a word on the party's precursors.

The first party to contest elections in India on a Hindu nationalist platform was the Hindu Mahasabha. It grew out of a few Hindu

---

[13]Quoted in Craig Baxter, *Jan Sangh: A Biography of an Indian Political Party* (Philadelphia, University of Pennsylvania Press, 1969), p. 116.

organizations established in the first decade of the century. The Mahasabha was established partly in reaction to the establishment of the Indian Muslim League.

At the beginning, the Mahasabha's programmes were not seen as entirely incompatible with those of the Indian National Congress. Some members of the Congress were members of the Mahasabha, too. Also, despite its style and idiom, the new party maintained a certain openness to political manoeuvrings. It even once formed a coalition ministry with the Indian Muslim League in Punjab. This openness lasted through the early years of independence; in fact, one internal historian of the Mahasabha, deploring the failure of the party to capitalize on the tension between the Hindus and Muslims, blamed its own moderate leaders.[14] This open style was maintained even when Savarkar dominated the Mahasabha between 1937 and 1948.

The political openness was not matched by ideological flexibility, particularly during the Savarkar era, partly because Savarkar, being an intellectual, painstakingly formalized the ideological presuppositions of Hindutva that were only implicit in the earlier leaders of the Mahasabha, and partly because the arrival of pan-Indian electoral politics had created a space for a political definition of the Hindus that could be more exclusivist. Here is what the privately faithless votary of Hindutva said on more than one occasion: 'a Hindu means a person who regards his land of Bharatvarsha from the Indus to the seas, as his Fatherland as well as his holy land.'[15]

In this definition, for the first time, the concept of Hindu is given a predominantly territorial component, a concept of holy land is specifically introduced in a fashion that would create a stratarchy of Indians;[16]

[14]Indra Prakash, *A Review of the Work of the Hindu Mahasabha*, quoted in Baxter, p. 16–17.

[15]We are grateful to Govind Deshpande for pointing out to us that the spatial part of this definition was taken from the *Vishnu Purana*. However, it is doubtful that Savarkar borrowed it directly from that source. More likely, he borrowed it from one of a number of writers and thinkers of nineteenth-century Bengal who had used this definition in roughly the same form.

[16]The tacit assumption was that this concept of the holy land would not be acceptable to the Christians and the Muslims, especially the latter. As it happens, Islam in South Asia, too, has a rich plural tradition even on this score. See chapter 5 of their book. Also, Tahir Mahmud ('Bridging the Hindu–Muslim Gap', *Prout*, 25 January 1992, p. 15) who quotes the prophet's son-in-law, the fourth Caliph Hazrat Ali as saying, 'Of all the places on earth the holiest and most fragrant is India.'

and the imagery of fatherland is borrowed from European nationalism
and introduced into a culture that had specialized in sacralizing the
country as a mother.[17] Trivial though these differentia might be, they
were the ones that distinguished the Hindu nationalism of the likes
of Savarkar from that of his declared precursors such as Bankim-
chandra Chattopadhyaya and Swami Vivekananda, both of whom articulated a more nuanced approach to the politics of culture and were
more willing to celebrate India's diverse cultural traditions.[18]

,   Savarkar's definition was wedded to a few other clear-cut demands
on the Hindus, demands later repeated by virtually every important
Hindu nationalist leader. The Hindus had to profess Hindutva rather
than Hinduism as the first defining characteristic of themselves; they
had to organize themselves as a religious as well as a political community and disown all internal divisions such as caste; they had to
opt for the classical, pan-Indian version of their religious philosophy;
they had to systematically de-paganize their faith, preferably by
giving up all forms of idol worship; and, above all, they had to mod-
ernize and kshatriyaize—read masculinize—themselves.[19]

All these preferred traits were seen as features of the Semitic
creeds and the aim, ultimately, was to engineer the Hindus into a

[17]To thus masculinize Mother India, Savarkar had to even drop the word
bhumi, land, which was grammatically feminine and had been traditionally
used in expressions such as *janmabhumi*, birthplace, and *mātrbhumi*, motherland.

[18]See, for instance, Chaturvedi Badrinath, *Dharma, India and the World
Order: Twenty Essays* (New Delhi: The Centre for Policy Research, 1991),
p. 138: 'Neither does Golwalkar refer to another central perception of
Vivekananda that it was in Islam and Islam alone, that the Vedanta had found
its true practical application, and therefore what was required for the future
of India was a fusion of Islam and Vedanta.'

[19]It is fascinating how the Belgian Jesuit scholar Koenraad Elst, manfully
bearing the burden of the guilt of the colonial record of European Christianity,
has consistently tried to re-read Hindu nationalism as exactly its reverse—as
a defence of paganism. See his *What After Ayodhya: Issues Before Hindu
Society* (Delhi: Voice of India, 1991).

Elst's last book, *Negationism in India: Concealing the Record of Islam*
(Delhi: Voice of India, 1992), even granting the truth of his accusations against
the Eurocentric secularist scholars of India, makes it obvious that at least one
of his aims is perfectly compatible with that of Hindu nationalism. He wants
to establish that the European colonial record in South Asia was far superior
to that of Islam which he finds comparable with that of Nazism. We return
to this issue more than once in this book.

dark-skinned version of the most successful species on earth, the Europeans. One even suspects that the hostility to Muslims came at least partly because they now appeared to have, after the entry of politically truculent monotheism into the Indian scene, similarities with the Europeans in their faith and this similarity was read as a clue to their dominance over India for 700 years and the 'unfair advantage' they enjoyed in Indian public life.[20] Rammohun Roy (1772–1833), the father of modern India, might have put it on behalf of the entire galaxy of Hindu social reformers of the nineteenth century when he said,

I have observed with respect to distant cousins, sprung from the same family, and living in the same district, when one branch of the family had been converted to Mussulmanism, that those of the Muhammadan branch living in a freer manner, were distinguished by greater bodily activity and capacity for exertion, than those of the other branch which had adhered to the Hindoo simple mode of life.[21]

Predictably, Roy traced this difference to Hindu vegetarianism, which he traced to their 'religious prejudices', and their 'want of bodily exertion and industry' brought about by a hot climate and a fertile land.[22]

The BJP

This is the cultural baggage with which the Bharatiya Jan Sangh, the forerunner of the BJP, entered the electoral arena in independent India for the first time in 1952. Its electoral performance was not spectacular till 1977 (see Table 9), but from its beginning, the party carved out a small, reliable, steady, support base among the urban middle classes and sections of the twice-born castes, especially the Banias.

---

[20]Both Islam and Christianity were seen as predatory faiths by the ideologues of Hindu nationalism. See for instance, Badrinath, *Dharma*, pp. 117–18. This entire section of Badrinath's book (pp. 111–39) provides an excellent analysis of Madhav Sadashiv Golwalkar's (1906–73)—and, in the process the RSS's—intellectual mission. The analysis is offered from the point of view of the traditional concerns of Indian society and it reconfirms the colonial roots of Hindu nationalism. It was in Golwalkar's thought that Hindu nationalism found its final fulfilment.

[21]Rammohun Roy, 'Additional Queries Respecting the Condition of India', *The English Works* (Calcutta: Sadharon Brahmo Samaj, 1947), part 3, pp. 63–8; see p. 63.

[22]Ibid.

In 1977, this marginality ended for the Jan Sangh electorally. This was one by-product of the Internal Emergency imposed by Prime Minister Indira Gandhi during 1975–77. The Jan Sangh was one of the first parties to oppose the suspension of civil rights and its cadres suffered imprisonment and other forms of harassment along with the workers of other parties. As a result, the Jan Sangh workers, most of them from the RSS, managed to break down a part of the fear and discomfort they used to arouse in many activists of the other opposition parties and the Left. The RSS itself was banned during the Emergency, nearly 27 years after it had been banned for the first time after the assassination of Gandhi. But, given the political circumstances in the country, the ban this time did not enjoy the legitimacy it had done in 1948.

It was also the time when the Left, with some exceptions, suffered a decline in intellectual influence and political legitimacy. Sixteen other organizations were banned during the Emergency along with the RSS, fourteen of them small Maoist groups of various kinds. But what stuck in public memory was the support given to the Emergency during its early days—and some mealy-mouthed opposition to it afterwards—by important sections of the mainstream communist movement. Also, given the close links many Leftists had with the Congress party through the Nehru-Gandhi family and its entourage, the Emergency years marked the emergence of the Jan Sangh as a serious, authentic opposition for a large section of Indians.

So, when the Janata Party was formed in 1977, it did not hesitate to include within it the Jan Sangh. The founder of the party Jayaprakash Narayan (1902–80) himself insisted on such a united front, perhaps motivated by the belief that this would further smoothen the edges of Hindu nationalism.

When the Janata Party won the general elections and came to power that year, its Jan Sangh component acquired an impressive political presence, with two important cabinet posts and a certain new-found respectability in the public sphere. The process of legitimation acquired further momentum when the Jan Sangh's Atal Behari Vajpayee turned out to be an enlightened foreign minister, sensitive to South Asian issues and especially successful with and respected in Pakistan and other neighbouring countries. L. K. Advani, the other stalwart of the Jan Sangh, also acquitted himself well as minister of information and broadcasting.

TABLE 9

AGGREGATE ELECTORAL PERFORMANCE OF BJS/BJP
FOR LOK SABHA

Year	Total seats	Seats con-tested (%)	Seats won (%)	Votes won (%)
1952	489	19.2	3.2	3.1
1957	494	26.3	3.1	5.9
1962	494	39.7	7.1	6.4
1967	520	48.3	13.5	9.4
1971	518	30.9	13.8	7.4
1977	542	-	17.0	14.0
1980	542	-	-	8.6
1984	542	42.3	0.9	7.4
1989	529	42.7	37.6	11.5
1991	508	87.2	25.3	-

SOURCE: Adapted from Shankar Bose and V. B. Singh, *Elections in India: Data Hand Book on Lok Sabha Elections—1952–85* (New Delhi: Sage Publications, 1986), Table 1.3.; and Election Commission of India, *Report of the Ninth General Elections to the House of People in India 1989 (Statistical)* (New Delhi: Election Commission, 1990).

NOTE: The BJP performance in 1977 and 1980 are estimates because the party contested as part of a larger party/front. Also, for the same reason, the percentage of the party's share of votes is calculated on the basis of the number of seats which it captured as part of the Janata Party. In 1989, too, the BJP had seat adjustments with a major opposition party, the Janata Dal.

The lessons learnt from the experience were not forgotten for a long time by the party. Even when the Janata Party split in 1980, the Jan Sangh was not resurrected. A new party called the Bharatiya Janata Party was launched with Gandhian socialism as its ideological platform. Both the choice of the name of the party and the ideological label indicated that the attempt was to maintain a continuity with the erstwhile Janata Party and the political tradition associated with its founder, Jayaprakash Narayan.

There is a widespread impression in India that the BJP reached the pinnacle of its electoral glory in 1989 and 1991 with 88 and 117 parliamentary seats respectively. Actually, the party did very well in 1977 also, when it won 92 seats with a softened Hindu nationalist stand. What changed the party's stance was its performance in the general elections of 1980 and 1984. In the former it won 16 seats; in the latter two (see Table 9).

The BJP began reverting to its ultra-Hindu posture soon after the 1984 elections. One important reason for that was the Congress party's success in winning over the BJP's mainly upper-caste, urban vote bank as a compensation for the perceived loss of scheduled caste and minority—specially Muslim and Sikh—votes since the Emergency years. Thus, Rajiv Gandhi's landslide victory in the 1984 parliamentary elections was attributed partly to his ability to win over most of the upper-caste support that previously went to the BJP.

After the 1989 General Elections, no party won an absolute majority in Parliament. When the results were declared, the BJP, along with the Left Front led by the two major communist parties of India, decided to support the Janata-Party-led National Front in Parliament. The latter then formed a minority government. It was an obvious attempt by the BJP and the Left to keep the Indian National Congress out of power. Both anticipated that the minority government would not last long and there would soon be a mid-term poll.

This of course also meant that all the major political parties continued to compete to expand their own support bases in preparation for the expected mid-term poll. Things hotted up when Prime Minister V. P. Singh accepted the recommendations of the Mandal Commission, under consideration for several years, and reserved an additional 27 per cent of government jobs for the 'backward' castes. This action immediately identified the Janata Party with the interests of the numerically preponderant backward castes, but also made it a deeply hated formation among the upper castes and the urban middle class, specially the professionals. It also successfully antagonized the media and the intelligentsia, dominated by the upper castes and fearful of losing their easy access to power, ensured by their education and ability to cope with modern institutions.

But, above all, the acceptance of the Mandal Commission recommendations threatened to split the political base of the BJP. The BJP had been working assiduously to expand its upper-caste support by utilizing the ideology of Hindu nationalism. Its targets were primarily the numerically strong and politically mobilized backward castes. Singh's strategy now seemed to strike at the roots of Hindu electoral

consolidation so important to the BJP. The party reacted by organizing its Rath Yatra, from Somnath in Gujarat to Ayodhya in Uttar
Pradesh.

The rest of the story is already known, at least in its outlines. In any
case, we shall describe its specific course in two states in chapter 5
of this book. All that remains to be done here is to give an idea of
the electoral gains the BJP made from its cultural politics (see Tables
10, 11 and 12). They show that the BJP did profit substantially from
its temple agitation and the Rath Yatra. The party's vote base had
already registered a small growth over the previous decade, but that
could be explained away by its decision to put up a larger number
of candidates. Certainly the number of seats won by the party had
little to do with the proportion of votes it won. In 1991, the party
won not merely a sizeable vote but also managed to translate much
of it into seats. Roughly, it doubled its national vote and its gains
cut across state boundaries (see Table 11). Though in some states its
gain in number of seats was small, it made spectacular inroads into
the bastions of other parties. (In Karnataka, for instance, the BJP
seemingly finished the Janata Party, even as an opposition.)

TABLE 10

ELECTORAL PERFORMANCE OF BJS/BJP IN UTTAR PRADESH
(1970 ONWARDS);

Year	Total seats	Seats con-tested (%)	Seats won (%)	Votes won (%)
State Assembly				
1974	424	94.6	15.2	17.1
1980	425	94.1	2.8	10.8
1985	425	81.6	4.6	9.9
1989	421	66.0	20.5	11.7
1991	420	100.0	53.3	- *
Parliament				
1971	85	47.1	10.0	12.3
1984	85	58.8	00.0	6.4
1989	85	36.5	25.8	7.6
1991	82	100.0	60.9	32.7

* Data not yet available.

TABLE 11

SEATS WON AND VOTES POLLED BY THE BJP IN STATE
ELECTIONS IN SELECTED STATES: 1985 AND 1990 (PER CENT)

State	Total seats	1985		1990	
		Seats won	Votes polled	Seats won	Votes polled
MP	320	18.2	32.4	68.4	39.2
Himachal Pradesh	68	10.3	30.6	67.6	42.7
Rajasthan	200	19.5	21.2	43.0	25.2
Gujarat	182	6.0	15.0	13.4	26.4
UP	425	3.8	9.9	13.4	11.6
Haryana	90	16.7	NA	6.7	10.1
Bihar	324	4.9	7.5	12.8	11.0
Maharashtra	288	5.6	7.3	14.6	14.6
Karnataka	224	0.9	3.7	0.0	4.1
Orissa	147	0.7	2.6	1.4	3.9
Andhra Pradesh	294	2.7	1.6	1.2	1.7

SOURCE: Election Commission of India. *Report on the General Elections to
the State Legislative Assemblies 1985–6* for the figures presented in col.
1–3. Figures presented in col. 4–5 are computed from the provisional
results sheets of the Commission.

In India's largest state, UP, its gains were immense and it formed
the new government (Table 10). In the Ayodhya assembly constituency itself, the BJP won a handsome victory, made doubly sweet by
the party's earlier defeat (Table 13).

The victory may or may not have made much of a change in the
sprawling state of UP with its 100 million inhabitants, one of the
poorest in India, but the new dispensation did make a difference to
the politics of Ayodhya. One of the first things the new government
did was to change the Deputy Inspector-General of Police and the
Superintendent of Police of the Faizabad division. The District
Magistrate of Faizabad, Net Ram, was also removed.

The new government also helped the VHP to remove one of the
main thorns in its side, Laldas, the *mahant* of the Ramjanmabhumi
temple. He was replaced by a priest close to the VHP. While admitting

TABLE 12

STATE-WISE DISTRIBUTION OF LOK SABHA SEATS AND VOTES
WON BY THE BJP. IN THE 1989 AND 1991 ELECTIONS (PER CENT)

States	*Total seats*	1989		1991	
		Seats won	*Votes polled*	*Seats won*	*Votes polled*
Andhra	42	0.0	2.0	2.4	8.6
Assam	14	0.0	0.0	14.3	8.6
Bihar	54	16.7	13.0	9.3	17.0
Gujarat	26	38.5	30.4	76.9	51.4
Haryana	10	0.0	8.3	20.0	10.3
Karnataka	28	0.0	2.6	14.3	28.8
Kerala	20	0.0	4.5	0.0	4.7
MP	39	69.2	39.7	30.8	42.0
Maharashtra	48	20.8	23.7	10.4	20.6
Orissa	21	0.0	1.3	0.0	9.7
Rajasthan	25	52.0	29.6	48.0	41.0
UP	85	11.8	7.6	58.5	33.0
West Bengal	42	0.0	1.7	0.0	9.5
Delhi	7	57.1	26.9	71.4	40.1
Himachal Pradesh	4	75.0	45.3	50.0	42.8
All-India	465	18.5	11.4	25.8	19.9

SOURCE: Election Commission of India: *Report of the Ninth General Elections*; Also *India Today*, 15 July 1991, pp. 40–48; and provisional result sheets of the Election Commission.

TABLE 13

PERFORMANCE OF MAIN POLITICAL PARTIES AT THE AYODHYA
ASSEMBLY CONSTITUENCY IN 1991 ELECTIONS (PER CENT)

Year	*Congress-I*	*BJP*	*BSP*	*Janata Dal/Party*	*Indepen-dents/others*
1985	32.9	9.9	-	21.6	35.6
1989	20.3	24.9	13.7	34.8	6.3
1991	10.6	51.3	11.7	19.6	6.8

that there were no specific charges against Swami Laldas, a spokes-man of the VHP vaguely claimed that the *mahant* had been creating various problems for the pilgrims visiting Ayodhya. Laldas also had some altercation with the PAC men at Ayodhya, the VHP alleged, causing serious law and order problems.[23] Supporters of Laldas claimed that the VHP had been looking for an opportunity to get rid of the intrepid priest and the altercation with the PAC men had been stage-managed to frame charges against the priest.[24]

On closer scrutiny, however, some of the gains of the BJP look less impressive. Thus, in Karnataka, according to James Manor, the gains were connected not so much with the temple agitation as with 'continuous problems and decline' of the Janata Dal, the major op-position party, the voters' dissatisfaction with the poor performance of the Congress-I's state government, and the widespread feelings among the two dominant castes, the Lingayats and the Vokkaligas, of being abandoned by both the Congress and the Janata Dal. A very large proportion of the votes cast against the Congress party for its lack-lustre governance, as a result, went to the BJP.[25] Even in UP, it is doubtful if the gains of the BJP were as spectacular as they at first appeared to be. Indeed, they could be considered a gift from Mulayam Singh Yadav. The BJP stalwarts and its new President, Murli Manohar Joshi, more or less admitted this in their interviews on the national media soon after the results of the UP elections were announced. Vajpayee said point blank to one of us that the credit for the BJP's success should go to the other political parties, especially to Mulayam Singh and V. P. Singh.

The BJP's electoral performance, however, is only the manifest poli-tical return of the Ramjanmabhumi movement. Underneath it lie the more important, long-term cultural forces that found systematic ex-pression, perhaps for the first time, in the movement and the politics

[23]Arvind Singh Bisht, 'Priest of Ayodhya Shrine Removed', *The Times of India*, 2 March 1992.

[24]Laldas was shot dead on 20 November 1993 by unknown assailants. According to a press report, he was killed because he got involved in a land dispute. However, the police refused to admit the First Information Report of an eyewitness and, instead, depended on the FIR of his nephew who was not present at the site.

[25]James Manor, The BJP in South India at the 1991 General Elections', unpub. MS, esp. p. 18.

of culture contextualizing it. Let us summarize them before we
on to the next section.

Basically, the Ramjanmabhumi movement represents the recognition by the BJP, and the larger Hindu nationalist formation of which
it is a part, that their day has come. The movement *is* an attempt to
make short-term political gains, but beneath it lies the awareness that
the BJP and its allies are no longer as peripheral in Indian politics
as they once were. For nearly a hundred years the Hindu nationalists
have been a fringe—according to many a lunatic fringe—in the polity. The RSS family now knows that they are no longer so; they have
broken into the mainstream of Indian politics.

This recognition is based on irreversible social changes. Though
the proportion of urban Indians has risen from roughly 20 to 25 per
cent during the last 50 years, in absolute terms, they are now more
than 200 million strong. Likewise, while India may officially be a
less industrialized society, in absolute terms it is as industrialized as
France. Again, only two per cent of Indians know English, but two
per cent of Indians are a lot of human beings; they constitute a
population larger than Australia's and New Zealand's put together,
both of which are entirely English-speaking. These modernized sections have behind them a substantial number of literate and semi-
literate Indians accessible to centralized media, propaganda and
currents of political communications. They have been constantly exposed to what can be called, in the absence of a better expression,
the modern idiom of politics (including the ideologies of nationalism
and nation-state). Especially, the ideology of the Indian state—by
which we mean the constant emphasis on national security,
secularism, development, and scientific rationality—has now a
hegemonic presence among the politically exposed Indians. The
modern means of communication, especially the national media, have
underwritten the presence.

To put it another way, in the culture of Indian politics, modern
India is no longer a mythic reality or statistical artefact. Nor is it
solely an institutional reality built through the dedicated efforts of a
few modernists in key political positions. For the first time, modern
India is a powerful political reality, with a large number of Indians,
uprooted from their local or vernacular cultures and traditional social
ties, living with that reality. These Indians have to make sense of
their environment, their uprooting, deculturation and massification.

The politics of Hindu nationalism allows scope for reconciling these two sets of demands within the terms of discourse of modern India.

As a consequence, the political culture of India is no longer merely a site of contention between the modern and the traditional, with the state clearly on the side of the former. It has become an site of contention between the modern that attacks or bypasses traditions and the modern that employs traditions instrumentally. This has opened up political possibilities for Hindu nationalism that were not open when the traditional idiom of Indian politics was *the* major actor in the culture of Indian politics and when a sizeable section of Indians were not insecure about their Hinduism. As we have said, Hindu nationalism has always been an illegitimate child of modern India, not of Hindu traditions. Such a nationalism is bound to feel more at home when the main struggle is between two forms of modernity and when the instrumental use of traditions—the use of religion as an ideology rather than as a faith—is not taboo for a majority of the political class.

Given this configuration of cultural forces, the *Sangh parivār* has taken full advantage of the keywords of political 'modernism' in India, and taken to its logical conclusion the constant emphasis on nationalism, secularism, national security, history, and scientific temper. It has rightly guessed that, given this idiom, it is possible to mount systematic political attacks on the forms of ethnicity and religious cultures that are identifiably different in their reaction to the mainstream culture of Indian politics and which offer strong resistance to the modern idiom of politics.

The culture of the majority usually comes to enjoy some primacy in the culture of an open polity. The moment nationalism is given a monocultural content and the definition of Indianness ceases to be a statistical artefact to become a reality on the ground, the minority cultures become easy and legitimate targets of criticism, social engineering and, as a leader of the erstwhile Jan Sangh once put it, 'Indianization'. When such targeting takes place, Indianness is no longer defined in terms of what Indians are and the ways in which they live; it is derived from ideal-typical definitions. Such ideal-typical definitions then become the staple of the formations which see the majority itself as flawed in character and as a fit subject for large-scale social engineering. Hence the long and abiding connection between Hindu nationalism and Hindu social reform movements of all hues.

When that is the project designed for the majority, the minorities cannot hope to fare any better. And naturally every marker of difference, howsoever peripheral to the culture of a minority, becomes a marker of the political backwardness and even national betrayal by the minorities. So things like the refusal of some Muslim men to reconsider their customary right to marry four times or the resistance many Muslims offered to the Indian Supreme Court's judgement in the Shah Bano case, sanctioning certain property rights to divorced Muslim women (however much such reactions might have been shaped by the sense of cultural insecurity of the Muslims) become grist to the mill of an absolute, uncompromising, steam-rolling nationalism.[26] Gone are the days when the Dravida Kazhagam and the Dravida Munnetra Kazhagam could openly, in the streets of Madras, burn the flag and the Constitution of India or heap insults on the images of Ram as a symbol of Aryan and upper-caste domination and could still hope to enter into a political dialogue with national leaders and occupy seats of power. Such 'compromises' with national honour and national politics are now seen as unforgivable sins and any government tolerating such anti-national acts is now unlikely to survive in power.

Some scholars, such as historian Bipan Chandra, seem to suggest that what we see in India today is a political contest between the nationalism represented by the Indian freedom movement and a new-found 'pseudo-nationalism' built on the collaborationist past of the *Sangh parivār*.[27] It can be argued that the *parivār* has only taken to a logical conclusion one significant aspect of the nationalism implicit in some strands of the anti-imperialist movement in India. That nationalism, borrowed from the likes of Giuseppe Mazzini (1805–72) and Johann Gottfried von Herder (1744–1803), was an imitative concept to start with. Following the thrust of its European versions, it

---

[26]When this happens, the arguments of the likes of Syed Shahabuddin that the social practices of Muslims that do not harm the Hindus should not be the concern of the latter has no impact in a political culture wedded to a melting-pot model of nationalism. Nor can the arguments of others that polygamy is more prevalent among the Hindus (0.8 per cent) than among the Muslims (0.7 per cent) in India cut any ice.

[27]Bipan Chandra, presentation made in the Seminar on The State and National Identity in India, Pakistan and Germany, organized by the Max Mueller Bhavan, Bangalore, 25–30 January 1992. See also his *Indian National Movement: The Long Term Dynamic* (New Delhi: Vikas, 1988).

always had the potentiality of developing into the particular form of exclusivism that Hindu nationalism has become.

On the other hand, the dominant form of 'nationalism' of the freedom movement—which became dominant only in certain phases, thanks to leaders like Mohandas Karamchand Gandhi—had little to do with the western concept of nationalism. It had its origins in the traditional allegiance to or bonding between the individual and the idea of India as a civilizational and territorial entity, fuzzy at its borders. The civilization, the state and the territory were seen to overlap, but only to an extent. The Gandhian and proto-Gandhian nationalism was clearly predicated on a refusal to define a political cultural mainstream and a periphery, and it even refused to define the West in its entirety as an alien presence in India.

With the significant bridgeheads established by the global mass culture and the European concepts of nationalism and the nation-state in India, this traditional patriotism began to recede in the articulate sections of society.[28] The significant growth of the BJP in Indian politics, whether permanent or temporary, reflects that change.

It would be unfair to the reader, however, if we do not mention that the Indian political culture has usually functioned with a built-in political thermostat. The culture copes with any of its major strands that threaten to establish total dominance by reviving or empowering the strands peripheralized.[29] It is not impossible that the present salience of Hindu nationalism will also be similarly neutralized in the long run by the dynamics of the culture of Indian politics. We shall see that in the case of the Ramjanmabhumi agitation, there *was* a noticeable shift from heroic, high-pitched politics to unheroic, messy, everyday politics and the BJP 'connived' with that everydayness. The very success of the movement contributed to that change. That the change was not permanent is another story.

[28]The political contest between the indigenous forms of patriotism and the imported nationalism has been discussed in Nandy, *The Illegitimacy of Nationalism*.

[29]On this theme see Ashis Nandy, 'The Making and Unmaking of Political Cultures in India', in *At the Edge of Psychology: Essays in Politics and Culture* (Delhi: Oxford University Press, 1980), pp. 47–69.

VI. FAMILY BUSINESS

The BJP is backed by a number of semi-political organizations that have gradually moved centre-stage during the last two decades, the most important of them being the RSS, the VHP, and the Bajrang Dal. Of these, the crucial actor in the Ramjanmabhumi movement is the VHP. There is also a small women's wing of the Bajrang Dal, the Durga Vahini. It is reportedly not doing well. The Akhil Bharatiya Vidyarthi Parishad, the BJP's student wing, has also been somewhat overshadowed by the more flamboyant Bajrang Dal in recent years.[30]

The over-arching organizational frame is provided by the RSS which we shall briefly discuss first.

The Rashtriya Swayamsevak Sangh.

Much work has been done on the history, politics and structure of the RSS and there are a few full-length analyses of the subject.[31] We shall therefore avoid the institutional and historical details of the RSS and instead provide a brief cultural introduction to the organization as a carrier of the principles of Hindutva developed by Savarkar. (Savarkar in his lifetime did not have much to do with the RSS and the RSS has never fully owned him, probably because he was never a part of the organization and could never persuade it to give all-out support to his political party, the Hindu Mahasabha.) Our introduction will be incomplete in another sense; we shall not discuss here the complex and, often, complementary relationship between the RSS and its religious counterpart, the Arya Samaj.[32]

[30]This is why we have not discussed the Durga Vahini and the ABVP in this section.

The BJP also once made an abortive attempt to set up a student wing, Janata Vidyarthi Morcha or JVM, that would be, unlike the ABVP, fully under its control.

[31]The best known account is that of Walter K. Anderson and Sridhar D. Damle, *The Brotherhood in Saffron: The Rashtriya Swayamsevak Sangh and Hindu Revivalism* (New Delhi: Vistaar, 1987). For more partisan but useful accounts see K. R. Malkani, *The RSS Story* (New Delhi: Impex India, 1980); Nana Deshmukh, *RSS: Victim of Slander* (New Delhi: Vision, 1979); and D. R. Goyal, *Rashtriya Swayamsewak Sangh* (New Delhi: Radha Krishna, 1979).

[32]A succint and sensitive discussion of that complementarity is in Daniel Gold, 'Organized Hinduism: From Vedic Truth to Hindu Nation', in Martin E. Marty and R. Scott Appleby (eds), *Fundamentalism Observed* (Chicago: University of Chicago Press, 1991), pp. 531–93.

The RSS was established in 1925 by Keshav Baliram Hegdewar (1889–1940). He was a nationalist and a worker of the Indian National Congress, who lived at Nagpur. Influenced by Savarkar on the one hand, and his friend and senior, Dr Balkrishna Shriram Munje, on the other, Hegdewar gave the organization its distinctive cultural style. All three were Maharashtrian Brahmans and modern professionals who sought to rise above their parochial and local allegiances and their vernacular selves. 'The roots of the RSS,' Anderson and Damle say while talking of its beginnings, were 'embedded in the soil of Maharashtra; its membership and symbols were almost exclusively Maharashtrian.'[33] But between Maharashtra and the RSS mediated the personalities like those of Savarkar, Munje, and Hegdewar, who were, from the beginning, at the margins of the mainstream public culture of Maharashtra and who were to be, from the 1920s, further marginalized by the political rise of the numerically strong non-Brahmanic castes of the region. It would be more appropriate to insist that the roots of the RSS lay primarily in the Brahmanic, westernized, tertiary sector of Maharashtra.

Hegdewar was a successful modern doctor who gave up his practice for the sake of the new organization. He had studied medicine at Calcutta and, during his six years in the city, had become a member of the Anushilan Samiti, a revolutionary group set up soon after the movement against the division of Bengal started around 1905. The Samiti was one of two most distinguished outfits—the other being the Jugantar Samiti—that tried to violently overthrow the Raj. Hegdewar had been sent to Calcutta by Munje who had been a doctor of the British Indian Army and had participated in the Boer War.

Though Hegdewar's name is often associated today with Hindu fundamentalism or fanaticism, like his guru Savarkar, he had scant interest in Hindu religion and culture. His father actually avoided putting him into the traditional vocation of a priest because young Keshav was uninterested in orthodox rituals, much of which he considered 'silly'.[34] The son's main interests were history and politics.

Despite this interest of its founder in politics, from the beginning the RSS was conceived of as a cultural organization that eschewed politics. Throughout the colonial period it remained true to its self-image. This had its in-built advantages. The RSS avoided the wrath

[33] Anderson and Damle, *The Brotherhood*, p. 30.
[34] Ibid.

of the colonial regime; it could create a space within its ideology for categories that were derived through the colonial connection, and it could concentrate on its anti-Muslim stance. Savarkar in any case had already perfected this part of the ideology. He, the one-time intrepid freedom fighter, wanted in his later years to take advantage of the British presence in India to improve the character and culture of the Hindus and to solve the Muslim problem once and for all.

The early writings on the subject by some of the worthies of the RSS show that the motivating forces for the establishment of the organization were two. One, they saw the Hindus as effeminate, spineless and non-martial and, thus, as vulnerable to the more aggressive faiths such as Islam and Christianity. (For that same reason the RSS has always maintained a sneaking respect for the more masculine strands of the two faiths, especially European Christianity.) Two, the founding fathers of the RSS saw the Hindus as unorganized, given to religious superstitions of all kinds and, hence, incapable of resisting the more organized, rational faiths. Anderson and Damle quote Munje, Hegdewar's guru, who said at the time the RSS was founded:

Out of 1.5 lakh (1,50,000) population of Nagpur, Muslims are only 20 thousand. But still we feel insecure. Muslims were never afraid of 1 lakh 30 thousand Hindus. So this question should be regarded hereafter as the question of the Hindus. The Muslims themselves have taught us to behave as Hindus while in the Congress, and as Hindus outside the Congress.[35]

Like most well-known social reform movements in the colonial period, the RSS, during the seventy years of its existence, has tried to become the symbol of martial, organized, rational Hinduism, stripped of its pagan superstitions. Though itself dominated by Brahmans for most of these seventy years, it has been consistently against the caste system, idol worship and most versions of folk Hinduism. In this respect, it is a secular analogue of the Arya Samaj in north India (which has supplied many of the north Indian leaders of Hindu nationalism in recent years).

The RSS has no formal membership, but insiders claim that those who maintain close links with it now number around two million. The number represents an estimated ten-fold increase from the time of independence. These 'members' are linked through a country-wide network of branches, modelled on traditional *akhādās* or gymnasia, and they now represent one of the most organized sectors of Indian

[35]Quoted in ibid., p. 33.

politics. Their discipline and cohesion are matched only by the members of some of the cadre-based Leninist parties of the Left.

Many of the rituals of the RSS are derived from colonial times, including the uniform its members wear when in the gymnasia. The uniform includes khaki shorts and *lāthis* or bamboo sticks, the combination clearly borrowed from the standard gear of the colonial police. The main slogans and heroes of the RSS, too, are predictable, though they have been broadened in recent years to cover the names of leaders such as Mohandas Karamchand Gandhi and Vallabhbhai Patel. Both, but especially the former, were anathema to the RSS even 20 years ago.

This broadening of the ideological platform, combined with faithful adherence to the essential dogmas of Hindu nationalism, was primarily the contribution of Madhav Sadashiv Golwalkar (1906–73) and, to a lesser extent, Deendayal Upadhyaya. Chaturvedi Badrinath has recently written a brief but elegant account of the worldview of the former.[36]

Like the other stalwarts of Hindutva, Golwalkar, too, was not burdened by any noticeable millenialism. He was educated as a scientist and a lawyer. He taught science at Benaras Hindu University from 1930 to 1933. Science remained important to him; he disowned and refused to reprint his first book *We or Our Nationhood Defined*, because it was not scientific.[37] He did not practise law either. He wanted to be a *sanyāsī* and renounce the world, and he received his initiation from Swami Akhandananda of the Ramkrishna Mission, Calcutta. Golwalkar succeeded Hegdewar in 1940 as the *sarsanghchālak* or head of the RSS, but never gave up his saintly style. Savarkar the

[36]Badrinath, *Dharma, India and the World Order,* pp. 119–39.

[37]M. S. Golwalkar, *We or Our Nationhood Defined* (Nagpur: Bharat Publications, 1939). The book's pro-Nazi tone and proto-Nazi ideas also must have been an embarrassment to its author, especially during the war years when the colonial regime was touchy about such ideas and the RSS was keen to be in the good books of the regime.

On Golwalkar's attitude to *We or Our Nationhood Defined*, see Badrinath, *Dharma, India and the World Order*, p. 112. For his analysis of Golwalkar's political ideology, Badrinath depends on writings owned by Golwalkar. His conclusion, that the ideology is *adhārmik*, is therefore likely to be particularly galling to the RSS. Recently an analysis of this disowned book has been attempted in Tapan Basu, Pradip Datta, Sumit Sarkar, Tanika Sarkar and Sambuddha Sen, *Khaki Shorts Saffron Flags* (New Delhi: Orient Longman, 1993).

modernist found that saintliness amusing and made no secret of it. He would have been the last person to notice that Golwalkar's saintliness, too, had no deep roots in tradition. It was processed through his exposure to the cultures of modern professions of science and law on the one hand, and the modernist Hinduism of the Ramkrishna Mission on the other.

Much of what Golwalkar says is standard stuff unlikely to enthuse those acquainted with the colonial interpretations of Indian traditions proffered by psychologically defensive, urban, westernized Indians. However, in one respect he faithfully replicates and builds upon Munje, Hegdewar and Savarkar. Like Munje, Golwalkar believes that the enemies of Hindus are not the Muslims or the English, but the Hindus themselves. For the Muslims and the English are predatory by nature and it is in them to 'overrun, plunder and destroy other weaker countries'.[38] Golwalkar is more concerned that the Hindus do not have a national consciousness and have fought among themselves for the previous one thousand years.[39]

Like most writers deeply impressed with the British colonial enterprise, Golwalkar sees the absence of a developed sense of nationalism and statism as basic flaws of Hindu character. He uses what he sees as three main elements in the modern western concept of the nation and then claims that the Hindus alone meet the criteria of nationhood in the subcontinent. Yet, the Hindus do not seem to know this. Hence, 'the remedy of Indian ills lies in resurgent Hindu Nationalism; for it [is] in the decline of Hindu character that those ills originate.'[40]

Somewhat predictably, the only cultures worse than that of the Hindu are some of the non-Semitic oriental ones, not Islam or Christianity. Gyanendra Pandey has drawn attention to Golwalkar's comment on China (peopled by 'intoxicated monkeys') to show how such evaluations contrast with the RSS theoretician's estimate of the erstwhile rulers of India. According to Golwalkar, 'the Englishmen were a civilized people who generally followed the rule of law. The

---

[38]Quoted in Badrinath, *Dharma, India and the World Order*, p. 118. Of course, the judgment on the West was moderated by a deep conviction about the superiority of the western civilization over the Islamic, which is seen as only predatory, and the Hindu, which is seen as cowardly and effeminate.

[39]Ibid.; see also p. 132.

[40]Ibid., p. 130.

Chinese are a different proposition.'[41] The ideology of the RSS towards the 'lower order' of the Hindus is only a trifle less hostile. Its Aryanism, partly imported from nineteenth century Bengal and partly from pre-war Europe, combines with its Brahmanic worldview to grant the plebian Hindus only a second-class cultural citizenship in the Indian civilization. In the course of time, through social evolutionism and re-education, they are expected to merge themselves into the Brahmanic mainstream as an indicator of their social progress.[42]

The RSS is not uniformly spread all over India, though it now has branches in virtually every state. It provides the main functionaries at the upper echelons of the BJP, VHP, ABVP, Bajrang Dal, and Durga Vahini and acts as their organizational and intellectual hub. All these organizations are open to directions from the RSS headquarters at Nagpur. However, the openness to such directions varies with time and the nature of the organization. For instance, the Jan Sangh was heavily dependent on the RSS for its organizational clout but was founded by a person who had no exposure to the RSS in his formative years. The BJP, after becoming politically powerful, was increasingly becoming more independent of the RSS, but its recent involvement in the Ramjanmabhumi movement has again made it more dependent on the RSS. Likewise, the Shiv Sena at all levels and the Bajrang Dal at the lower levels have always been relatively free from RSS influence and discipline, not always with happy consequences.

Vishwa Hindu Parishad.

Compared to the older Hindu nationalist organizations, the Vishwa Hindu Parishad or VHP is relatively new in Indian public life. Culturally, its uniqueness and strength lie in its ability to draw upon

[41]M. S. Golwalkar, quoted in Gyanendra Pandey, 'Hindus and Others: The Militant Hindu Construction', *Economic and Political Weekly*, 28 December 1991, pp. 2997–3009; see p. 3001.

[42]Pandey ('Hindus and Others', p. 3003) points out that the RSS term for the tribes of India is *vanavāsis*, the forest dwellers, not the more common *ādivāsis*, original dwellers. For cultural life begins in India, according to the RSS ideologues, with the Aryans who, unlike the Muslims, were not invaders.

The standard expression for cultural integration used in the RSS literature is *samaras*, which invokes the idea of an American-style quasi-Brahmanic melting pot.

both the Arya Samaj and the Sanatan Dharma movements. This has given it a geographical spread and resilience, especially in the Hindi-speaking areas of India, that was once only a distant dream of the RSS.[43] But the main heritage is the nineteenth-century attempts to turn Hinduism into an organized creed. The attempts gave most religious activities in the expanding modern sector of the time, even when based on orthodoxy, a reformist tinge.

Deviating from RSS orthodoxy, which permits *only* Mother India or Bharat Mata as a theistic presence, the VHP leadership, mostly

---

[43]For instance, in parts of northern India, the VHP has built upon the heritage of movements committed to the protection of cows and *sanātan dharma* (crudely, eternal codes of conduct) and the promotion of Hindi. All these movements were active in the late nineteenth century along with the Arya Samaj. Though the orthodox and the reformists differed on issues such as image worship, widow remarriage, and the interpretation of caste status, they could unite on issues such as cow protection, reconversion (usually of Christians and Muslims), and the agitation for the adoption of the Hindi language and Devanagari script.

In UP, the most prominent leaders of local *sanātani* or orthodox organizations also promoted Tulsi's *Ramcharitmānas*, increasingly hailed as the 'Hindi Veda' or 'the *sanātani* scripture par excellence'. The *Ramcharitmanas* for these leaders came to symbolize the 'upward mobility' of Ram: ' ... from an earthly prince with godlike qualities of heroism, compassion, and justice, to a full-fledged divinity—or rather, *the* divinity; for in north India today the word Ram is the most commonly used non-sectarian designation for the Supreme Being.' Peter Lutgendorf, *The Life of a Text: Performing the Ramcharitmanas of Tulsidas*, (Berkeley: University of California Press, 1991), pp. 4, 10, 364, 365–9.

The *Ramcharitmānas* also reconciled the traditions of worshipping a formless God with that of a God 'with attributes', a reconciliation that was to pay indirect dividends to the RSS family when the Ayodhya temple became a public issue.

The reader may get the impression from these details about movements that the Sanatānīs were fighting for the cause of the vernacular and local. Actually, from the beginning, the cow protection movement made a clear distinction between cows consumed by the British in India and those consumed by some sections of the Indian Muslims. The movement was directed only against the latter. Likewise, the movement for Hindi was also a movement for the abolition of the local and vernacular. The Hindi that the 'orthodox' fought for was built on the ruins of at least three well-established languages with rich cultural traditions and literary heritages. These languages were politically reduced to the status of dialects to produce an artificial new language that would serve the purposes of an emerging nationality.

Hindi-speaking north Indians, admit the greater power of theistic Hinduism as compared to that of the Neo-Vedantic Arya Samaj. This theism, though, is given a monotheistic slant, as an antidote to Hinduism's 'embarrassingly' non-revelatory, pagan character. Thus, in some northern Indian states the temples at the VHP offices have icons of Ram-Sita-Laxman-Hanuman, along with the regulation plaster-of-Paris Bharat Mata spreadeagled across a map of India. True to the Hindu-nationalist tradition though, the Bharat Mata dwarfs the icons and the temple is called Bharat Mata Mandir. And the new greeting, 'Jai Shri Ram', has to accompany the standard RSS farewell, 'Bharat Mata ki Jai' (Victory to Mother India).

The VHP was formally registered in 1966 with Swami Chinmayananda and S. S. Apte as its working President and General Secretary. Jaichamraj Wodeyar, the erstwhile Maharaja of Mysore and at the time Governor of Madras, was its first chairman.

The decision to constitute the VHP was, however, taken in 1964, at a conference convened in Bombay at the instance of the then head of the RSS, Golwalkar.[44] The meeting, in his words, was aimed at 'inspiring all those faiths and beliefs that have sprouted from the *ashwath* (banyan) tree, to unite on a single platform and safeguard their common interests.'[45] Hence, apart from such prominent religious Hindu leaders as the five Shankaracharyas and Sant Tukaraoji Maharaj, the meeting was also attended by, among others, the Dalai Lama, Jainmuni Sushil Kumar and the Sikh leader, Master Tara Singh.[46]

[44]The decision to found the VHP during the mid-sixties was no accident. M. K. Gandhi's assassination by a Hindu nationalist in 1948, the political success of Nehru's secular policies, and the post-independence consensus on the style of 'nation-building', all combined to push the aspirations of the RSS leadership for a Hindu state into the background for well over a decade. The failure of their political wing, the Jan Sangh, in the general elections of 1952, 1957 and 1962 marginalized the RSS family even further (see Table 8). But, in 1962, Nehru's image was severely damaged by the Indian debacle in the Indo-China border war. It marked the beginning of the end of the Nehruvian era. In 1963 the idea of founding the VHP was floated.

[45]Narayan Rao Tarte, 'Vishva Hindu Parishad ki Kalpanā', Hindu Vishva, Vishva Hindu Parishad Rajat Jayanti Vishesh ānka, August 1990, 25(12), pp. 13–16; see p. 13.

[46]The word 'Hindu' was defined at this convention to mean 'one who respects, has faith in, and adheres to the principles of all those moral and

The VHP was conceptualized by Golwalkar as an organization that would be 'totally non-political, so that people of all castes, faiths and parties could associate with it'. This was also probably an attempt by the RSS to further distance itself from politics, especially from the Jan Sangh that had failed to sell the RSS ideology to the electorate. The RSS might have felt that such distancing would widen its base.

One other objective could have been to attract the leaders from the various national parties who, despite their diverse political ideologies, were one on the issue of Hindu unity (such as the second chief minister of UP, Sampoornanand, who was sympathetic to the VHP when it was being constituted). Thus, when the first convention of the VHP was held, there was no mention of any senior Jan Sangh leader, or for that matter of any prominent RSS leader except Golwalkar, attending.[47]

After the VHP was formally formed, a Marg Darshak Mandal was set up to direct its activities. These activities were broadly listed as:

---

spiritual lifestyles which have their origin in India.' Jaswant Rao Gupta, '*Vishwa Hindu Parishad: Gathan aur Kramik Vikāsh*', ibid., pp. 17–20; see p. 17. This automatically made outsiders of Muslims and Christians whom Hindu nationalist literature calls 'invaders', and Parsis and Jews, who are called 'refugees'. On the other hand, the definition proposed that Shaiva, Lingayat, Buddhist, Jain, Sikh, Dadupanthi, Nanakpanthi, Ravidasi, Kabirpanthi, Arya Samaji, Brahmo and other cognate faiths were all part of the larger Hindu faith, the tolerance of which allowed such diverse beliefs to exist and thrive under it.

The same line of thinking informs the newly constituted minority cell of the BJP. It is made up entirely of Muslims. None from other 'faiths' finds a place in it, simply because most of them are not considered non-Hindu.

[47]Even today, the VHP hopes to attract Hindu politicians from different parties, not only from the BJP. In an interview with one of us, the VHP's President, Vishnu Hari Dalmia, while commenting on the success of the BJP in the 1991 elections, repeatedly differentiated the VHP members who had been elected to Parliament on the BJP ticket from the rest of the party candidates. He stated categorically that if the BJP failed to keep its promises on issues that concerned the VHP, it would not hesitate to part ways with the BJP. Because, unlike the BJP, the VHP's aim was not to capture political power, but to establish a Hindu *rāshtra*.

This statement bears comparison with the frequently repeated assertion of the leaders of the BJP like Advani that India is already a Hindu *rāshtra,* the implication being that nothing further need to be done in this regard.

strengthening, organizing and energizing Hindu society; conservation
and promotion of Hindu moral and spiritual values; liberating Hindu
society from outdated social customs and practices and general backwardness, a result of centuries of foreign rule; and protection of Hinduism by maintaining strong ties with Hindus living outside India.[48]

As anyone with even tangential acquaintance with the RSS literature
would immediately sense, these goals are a direct response to some of
the main anxieties of the nineteenth-century Hindu religious reformers
and the early twentieth-century Hindu nationalists. This linkage acquires
another meaning when one consults some of the manuals which the
VHP produces for the training and guidance of its grass roots workers.
The operational definitions of the larger goals at that plane become close
to the stereotypical anti-minorityism for which the organization is
known.[49]

To meet these goals, the VHP has divided the country into 5 zones,
10 regions, 25 provinces, 210 divisions, 706 districts, and 7,180 *prak-
hands*. It itself has also expanded considerably, with 18 departments
currently functioning at the national level. Each of them looks after
one programme of the Parishad, ranging from cow protection to the
use of Sanskrit. (Sanskrit in Devanagari script is identified as the
premier language; other Indian languages are seen as its offshoots.
Urdu, is naturally excluded from the list.)[50] The VHP also has a unit
in every state, with branches at district, subdivisional and block
levels. Special emphasis has been placed on making inroads into
tribal areas and into areas with a large concentration of 'backward'
castes and dalits, 'so that they can be educated regarding the Hindu
way of living and the Hindu gods and godesses and ultimately be
absorbed in the mainstream of Hindu Society.'[51]

Predictably, this emphasis on Sanskritic Hinduism and the attempts
to abolish the little cultures of India go hand in hand with attempts
to reach out to the westernized middle-class Hindus as the 'natural

[48]Tarte, *'Vishwa Hindu Parishad ki Kalpanā'*, p. 14.

[49]See for example the privately printed *Pradesh Padādhikārī Shikshan Varg*
(Ahmedabad: VHP, no date), a Gujarati training manual used by the VHP in
Gujarat.

[50]This is depicted visually in a VHP pamphlet from Rajasthan (Jaipur:
VHP office, undated) which shows languages such as Vedik (sic), Gurumukhi,
Gujarati, Malayalam, Bengali and Assamese as deriving radiance from
Sanskrit/Devanagari.

[51]Shrivastava, *Hindu Visva*.

clientele' of the VHP. The Parishad has tried to bring expatriate Indians into its fold in a big way. It has divided the world, excluding India and its neighbours, into four regions—USA, Europe, Africa and Middle East, and South Asia—to facilitate easier access to expatriates. It began functioning in the USA in 1970 and currently it has branches in forty states. The VHP has compiled a list of all the ethnic Indian students studying in American universities and born in that country, and is now trying to establish contacts with them. It runs summer camps and has also instituted an 'adopt a child scheme' through which it has so far collected one million dollars for the education of poor children back home. This scheme has also been introduced in Hong Kong.

In Britain, where it started functioning in 1972, the VHP has fourteen branches, and is also supported by some local Hindu organizations. The VHP has five branches in West Germany, one in Spain and, although it does not as yet have a set-up in the Netherlands, efforts to establish one received a boost in 1988, after a successful European Hindu Sammelan was held there. It was attended by, among others, the mayor of The Hague, the Dutch home minister, the envoys of India and Nepal, and the chief justice of the International Court of Justice. (The VHP attaches importance to Netherlands because droves of Surinamese of Indian origin have migrated to that country.)

Except for Zambia, where the VHP has a branch, the organization does not have a formal presence in Africa. It has, however, developed contacts with many Hindu organizations throughout the continent and works through them. For instance, it organized an African Hindu Sammelan in 1988 at Nairobi under the aegis of a 'Hindu Council of Kenya'. In some other countries like Mauritius, Burma, Guyana, Malaysia, Tanzania, Indonesia and Fiji, the VHP is trying to establish itself by forging links with local Hindu organizations.

As the activities of the VHP have continued to grow, it has constituted several bodies and trusts to look after them. One of them is the Dharma Sansad. It is a synod of saints and seers of 'all faiths prevalent in Hindu society' as well as of VHP-chosen representatives of the religious heads of the various tribes.[52] Some of the more

---

[52]One of the achievements of the VHP in recent years has been its ability to bring together on one platform some of the religious leaders who were previously at loggerheads with each other. But still, a dissenting note was struck by Swami Swarupanand, the Shankaracharya of Dwarkapeeth, who was against the movement launched by the VHP.

important functions of the Dharma Sansad are: to provide a religious
order capable of sustaining the integrity of Hindu society in the present age; to develop shrines and places of pilgrimage into powerful
cultural centres; to help those who voluntarily opt for conversion to
Hinduism; and, for those who might otherwise miss the touch of the
parivār's usual paranoia, to provide effective measures for countering
the evil designs of non-conformists.[53]

These goals, too, are obvious extrapolations from the core concerns of Hindu nationalism, especially if one scrutinizes the way they
are sought to be operationalized for purposes of training and organization.[54]

The Dharma Sansad has held three conventions since its inception
to provide 'guidelines' to Hindu society. In the first convention held
in Delhi in 1984, the religious leaders deliberated on the problems
of re-acquiring Hindu property in Bangladesh and on the liberation
of the Ramjanmabhumi and Kashi Vishwanath temples. In addition,
a twelve-point code of conduct was drawn up to safeguard Hindu
culture and values. At the second, held at Udipi in 1985, the main
concerns were riots in the name of religion and the take-over of
monasteries and temples by the government. The third convention,
held in Prayag in 1989, tried to work out ways of ending the 'in-
justices being heaped on Hindus'.

The VHP has also set up two trusts, the Bharat Kalyan Pratishthan,
to provide education and medical aid to the poor and needy, and the

[53]Omkar Bhushan Goswami, 'Dharma Samsad', *Hindu Visva*, pp. 21–3;
see p. 21.

The VHP has revived the Arya Samaj's *shuddhi* or purification movement
with the concept of *parāvartan*. *Parāvartan* is said to be different from mere
conversion, but is actually only an attempt to introduce the standardized concept of proselytization in Hinduism. The VHP claims that in Rajasthan, for
instance, a total of 48,310 persons or 8311 families have been converted out
of a national figure of 120,000. The VHP in Rajasthan acknowledges, however, that they have achieved little success in reconverting the Meos, the
largest Muslim community in the state.

Such reconversion is supposed to counter the phenomenal growth of minorities in India—the increase in the number of Indian Muslims from 30 million
in 1947 to 141.2 million now and their reported attempts to convert 200
million of the lower strata of the society to Islam; and the proselytizing goals
of the 20 million Christians who threaten to convert the 100 million of tribals
and backward castes.

[54]See the Gujarati training manual of the VHP.

Vishwa Hindu Parishad Foundation, to work for the upliftment of the rural poor and the backward castes.

Patently, neither when it came into being nor for years afterwards did the VHP have very specific objectives, other than the vague and general one of bringing about Hindu unity through the better organization and the Hinduization of the Hindus. This objective was obviously in continuity with the nineteenth-century Hindu nationalist conviction that the Hindus had suffered the indignity of Muslim and British rule, despite having a superior civilization, because they had been divided and had strayed from true Hinduism. We have already told this part of the story.

This single-issue concern persisted till the beginning of the 1980s. Only around 1983 did the VHP begin to come into its own and start acquiring a more differentiated set of concerns.[55] That year it organized the Ekātmatā Yajna in which the waters of different sacred rivers were intermingled. For instance, pots carrying the water of the Erawati river in Burma, were taken in a chariot to Gangasagar and released there. Similarly, water from the Pashupatinath temple in Nepal was released into the sea at Rameshwaram and so on. This demonstration of the unity of waters was followed by the Shri Ram Janaki Rath Yatrā. The Yatrā commenced its journey from Sitamadhi in Bihar in September 1984, but was cut short in the wake of Mrs Gandhi's assassination.

In April 1984, the VHP announced for the first time its intention of liberating the Ramjanmabhumi. In 1986, the lock on one of the gates of the disputed structure was ordered to be opened by the court and, as a result, the VHP's movement gained in momentum. Taking full advantage of the unexpected turn of events in which it had played no role, the VHP by the end of 1987 had formed Shri Ram Janmabhumi Mukti Samitis throughout the country. Realizing how invaluable the financial support of the expatriate Indians could be to their movement, the VHP in 1988 alone organized as many as six major

[55]The time when the VHP became active is significant. After Operation Bluestar, Indira Gandhi's popularity was at an all time low and, had it not been for her assassination, it is doubtful whether the Congress would have won the General Elections that were due in 1985. The VHP leadership sensed that the people were in a mood for change, and it launched its programmes by the end of 1983. Mrs Gandhi's assassination was a setback for them for a while, but not for long.

conferences of Hindus spread over the world—in Nairobi, Kathman-du, Singapore, Kuala Lumpur, Bangkok and the Hague—followed by one in England in 1989.

After deciding to perform the foundation laying ceremony of the Ram temple at the Prayag Kumbh in February 1989, a joint programme was launched by the RSS family to make a door-to-door collection of sanctified bricks for the Ram temple.[56] The response was massive. It was obvious that a political ritual had been invented and marketed successfully as each brick—wrapped in red cloth, tied with a sacred red-yellow thread and marked with a swastika—became an object of worship. The worship of the bricks took place on 10 November the same year. The first brick was laid by a Dalit from Bihar, Kameshwar Chopal.[57]

Following the foundation-laying ceremony, the VHP spent considerable time and energy mobilizing public passions and support for the issue. This culminated, almost a year later in October 1990, in the storming of the Babri masjid and the tragedy of 2 November. The communal riots that broke out throughout the country following the events in Ayodhya did not deter the VHP from organizing an Asthi Kalash (urn of ashes) Yatra of those *kārsevaks* who had died in the police firing. More riots followed in the wake of this *yatra*.

Encouraged by its success in Ayodhya and the subsequent fall of the V.P. Singh government at the centre, the VHP became more vocal about its immediate intentions. Not only did it want to construct the Ram temple at any cost, but also to liberate the Kashi Vishvanath temple complex at Varanasi and the Krishnajanmabhumi in Mathura. They also tasted victory when more than twenty of their members were elected to the Lok Sabha on BJP tickets from UP and Madhya Pradesh in the 1991 elections and several more got elected to the UP Legislative Assembly.

---

[56]Workers of Astha, an NGO that works in the tribal areas of Sirohi and Udaipur in Rajasthan, say that despite their poverty, tribals contributed Rs 5 or Rs 10 each. Cf. the report on Gujarat below.

[57]The VHP leadership for the first several years of its existence was mainly drawn from the trading castes. Even now, its topmost echelon is dominated by Banias. Slowly, however, Rajputs and Brahmans have also become important in the organization. Except for Vinay Katiyar, who heads the Bajrang Dal and belongs to a backward caste, no other VHP leader has emerged from among the backward castes or classes.

A word on the composition of this group of legislators. A number of them are religious leaders and priests, such as Mahant Avaidyanath from Gorakhpur, who is also the President of the Ramjanmabhumi Mukti Samiti, Sakshiji Maharaj from Mathura, Swami Chinmayananda from Badayun and Swami Yogeshwarananda from Bhind, Madhya Pradesh. They have entered Parliament they say, with the sole purpose of pressuring the government of the day to meet their demands. A few of these MPs, such as Shrish Chand Dikshit from Benaras, are former high-ranking government officials. Dikshit was at one time Deputy Inspector General of Police, UP, and the reader may remember that it was he who led the *kārsevak*s in the assault on the Babri masjid on 30 October. Bhartendu Prakash Singhal, a former police official and chairman of the Film Censor Board during V. P. Singh's tenure as Prime Minister, was also in the fray at Moradabad. He, however, lost to a Janata Dal candidate. Yet another high-profile VHP parliamentarian is the former Chief Justice of the Allahabad High Court, Justice Devaki Nandan Agrawal.

Currently, the VHP seems preoccupied with the Ramjanmabhumi agitation and has threatened to go ahead with the construction of the temple irrespective of the stand that the BJP takes.

Bajrang Dal

Bajrang Dal was formed in July 1984 as the youth wing of the VHP and, according to its chief, Vinay Katiyar, Member of Parliament from Faizabad, its main purpose is 'to implement the policies of the VHP'. The name of the Dal invokes the imagery of the army of monkey warriors in the Ramayana, led by their king Hanuman, also known as Bajrang. As the functionaries of the Dal never fail to remind one, Hanuman was the most devoted and obedient of all disciples of Lord Ram and fought on the side of the Lord against the demon-king Ravan, to ensure the triumph of good over evil.

Probably because it is primarily seen as an instrument of another organization, the Dal is neither registered as a society nor does it have any constitution or code of conduct. There does not appear to be even a formal record of the names of its members and it is difficult to estimate its size. No data are available on the officials and representatives of the Dal. Though this gives the impression that the Dal does not have a structure and is plagued by organizational chaos, it is not a light-weight political outfit. In the temple agitation, it has certainly pushed the ABVP, the student wing of the BJP, out of reckoning. At least one commentator had said,

The uniqueness of this force lies in its ill-defined and amorphous character and extremely loose organizational structure. In this respect, it was, and remains, an oddity in the *Sangh parivār*. The *parivār* takes pride in its strict discipline....[58]

The same commentator goes on to hint that this looseness may not have been a matter of choice: 'Acutely aware that it is almost impossible to discipline this riff-raff, the VHP has left the Bajrang Dal largely to its own.'[59]

Katiyar himself is a traditionally low-caste Kurmi, an uncommon presence among the upper-caste dominated *Sangh parivar*. He belongs to a small town in west UP. His family originally owed allegiance to the Indian National Congress during the Raj and participated, Katiyar claims, in the freedom struggle. Others dispute the claim.

Katiyar lists the tasks the Bajrang Dal has taken upon itself since its inception. They include protecting cows, fighting the 'abduction of Hindu mothers and sisters', preventing innocent Hindus from 'being lured by petrodollars' to convert to Islam, spreading education, stopping infiltrators (mainly Pakistanis) from entering India, and identifying and weeding out 'foreigners' from the country (mainly Bangladeshis). If the Bajrang Dal's concern with these issues appear vague and undirected, it is because of its almost full-time involvement till now with the VHP's programme for the liberation of the Ramjanmabhumi. The Dal was, after all, founded for that purpose.

The VHP had all the essentials to launch a massive agitation of the kind it wanted—a well-planned strategy and financial and political backing. The only thing that was missing was somebody to take the issue to the streets. The VHP required, to put it plainly, substantial muscle power under its control to meet the needs of agitational politics. In time, the youth power of the Dal came to fulfil this need of the VHP. Though a few of the functionaries of the Dal had been RSS volunteers, the organization as a whole had little patience with the kind of discipline, personal integrity, ideological cohesiveness and austerity which the RSS was known for. The goal of the VHP was

[58]'Angry Members of the Family', *The Pioneer*, 6 December 1992.
[59]Ibid.

obviously to have easy access to a reservoir of street-smart muscle power.

The youth exercizing this power are drawn mainly from the ranks of the poor, upper-caste population of the smaller cities and the semi-urban areas. They are partly educated and socialized to the burgeoning modern sector of India and are often jobless. The VHP helps them to cope with their anxieties by handing them a cause to fight for and by persuading them that on their young shoulders lies the responsibility of restoring to the Hindus their lost honour and pride. As if out to prove their worth to society and to themselves, the Bajrang Dal youth have expressed their restlessness and frustrations through some of the more violent incidents that have taken place as part of the Ramjanmabhumi agitation. The Dal has become better known after these as the militant outfit of the VHP.

In defence of the Dal, Katiyar draws an analogy with the incident in the Ramayana where Hanuman burns down Lanka. According to him, Hanuman had no other choice after the demons tied a burning rag to his tail to reduce him to ashes. Similarly today, a new set of demons have put a torch to the hearts of the youth. So why should anyone complain if they now spit fire. They are only following in Hanuman's footsteps. Katiyar claims that his 'boys are fully disciplined and fully aggressive.' According to him, they indulge only in 'disciplined aggression'.

Similarities between the Bajrang Dal and its far older counterpart in Maharashtra, the Shiv Sena, become clear at this point, both in the social background of their members and in their participation in a well-developed cult of violence. The Shiv Sena, though, is a full-fledged political party now; the Dal merely an affiliate of one.

The Bajrang Dal first came into the limelight in December 1985, when it called for a general strike in UP to demand the removal of the lock on one of the gates of the Babri masjid. In the following years it was in the forefront when the VHP organized a number of programmes in connection with the Ramjanmabhumi Mukti Andolan. In October 1988, the Dal forcibly closed down for a day all educational institutions in UP to protest against the Ayodhya march organized by the Babri Masjid Action Committee and the latter's plan to read *namāz* at the mosque.

Later in the month, the Bajrang Dal announced that its volunteers were going to recite the *Hanumān Chalisā*, a religious text associated with the epic Ramayana in some parts of north India, at the Jama Masjid in Delhi. It also added that Dal members in Rajasthan, Madhya Pradesh and Maharashtra were going to sing Hindu religious songs at the mosques in their respective areas.

The countdown to the events of 1990 began for the Bajrang Dal in July 1989. This was when the Dal held a Bajrang Shakti Diksha Samaroh (a training programme given the form of an initiation ceremony) at Ayodhya 'to strengthen them [the boys] for the fight that lay ahead'. More than 6,000 volunteers, it is claimed, went through the initiation rites.

Before the BJP government was installed in UP, any action of the Bajrang Dal volunteers—ranging from raising anti-Muslim or anti-government slogans to active participation in communal riots, to damaging the Babri masjid—was dismissed by their peers in the VHP as 'natural over-enthusiasm'. But now, the Dal is being increasingly regarded as an embarassment. Senior BJP and VHP leaders privately confess that the Dal's volunteers are beginning to get 'totally out of control'.

This tension between the political leadership of the temple movement and their fighting arm became obvious during November 1991 in Ayodhya, where the *kārsevaks*, of whom a large number were Bajrang Dal volunteers, had assembled to observe the first anniversary of the storming of the Babri masjid and to honour those who died in the violence associated with the event (see chapter 5). Despite warnings and entreaties issued by the top brass of the VHP not to mount any attack on the Babri masjid on 1 November, some of the *kārsevaks* once again succeeded in causing further damage to the structure. On the other hand, the general feeling among the Bajrang Dal volunteers, who had come from places as far as Surat in Gujarat, was that of being let down. Many of them had slowly come to believe that they had been used. As one of them summed it up, 'the priorities of our leaders have changed; politics has won over the temple.'

This was true at that point of time. But it was clear that the VHP was not going to distance itself from the Bajrang Dal or disclaim responsibility for it. For the VHP knew that, if it was to achieve its goals, it needed the muscle power of the Dal.

Because we have avoided in this book the details of the actual nature of the quarrel about the Babri mosque and the legal position of the two sides as irrelevant to our story, we must re-emphasize that the groups that we have described here, though deriving inspiration from the tradition of Hindu nationalism, have not really been constrained by the tradition in any serious fashion in the matter of the Ramjanmabhumi movement. None of the exemplars the *parivār* claims to respect—from Shivaji to Swami Vivekananda and Bal Gangadhar Tilak to V. D. Savarkar and Deendayal Upadhyay—ever demanded the destruction or removal of the Babri mosque. Nor did the RSS ever show any interest in the construction of any temple, least of all a Ram temple. The attitude of Hindu nationalism to Ram was defined by the major nineteenth-century Hindu reform movements which were primarily anti-idolatrous. The choice of Ram as a symbol in the 1990s was determined by political strategy and cost calculation, not by religious fervour or theology or by any attempt to return to the fundamentals of faith. It was a perfectly instrumental, hard-headed, secular choice made possible in an environment where the dispassionate, cynical use of the faith of others has acquired certain political legitimacy.

The little-known story of Mohandas Karamchand Gandhi's sole visit to an RSS office is worth recapitulating here. Seeing on the wall pictures of the martial Hindu leaders of the past, Gandhi, a life-long devotee of Ram, had reportedly asked why a picture of Ram was not there. The elders of the RSS present there explained for his benefit that Ram was too effeminate a figure to serve their purpose.[60]

---

[60]The metamorphosis that Ram himself had to undergo, to serve the purposes of the RSS has been studied by Anuradha Kapur, 'Deity to Crusader: Changing Iconography of Ram', in Gyanendra Pandey (ed.), *Hindus and Others: Question of Identity in India Today* (New Delhi: Viking, 1993), pp. 74–109.

CHAPTER FOUR

VII. HINDUTVA AS A SAVARNA PURĀNA

Ayodhya, everything said, is not an isolated pilgrim city. What happened there in 1990–91 had links with intercommunal relationships in other regions of India. These regions have often brought into the Ayodhya conflict their distinctive pasts. Ayodhya in turn has contributed to these regional conflicts both a pan-Indian issue and a potent new political symbol. On this plane the local, the national and even the international have merged at the sacred city.[1]

It is impossible to cover here the entire political process that Ayodhya has come to represent. What follows are thumbnail sketches of the politics of hate and fear that has informed the Ramjanmabhumi controversy in two states, Gujarat (from where, the reader may remember, Advani's chariot began its fateful journey towards the city of Ayodhya in 1990) and Rajasthan (which has never previously figured in studies of riot-prone states). To keep our account brief, in the case of Gujarat we focus upon the larger political process and mobilization that produced the violence in the wake of the Ramjanmabhumi movement; in the case of Rajasthan we emphasize the actual process of violence associated with the movement.

Gujarat: Political Mobilization of the Middle Classes

The reactions to the Ayodhya episode in Gujarat are framed by the changing political sociology of self-validation. For more than two decades, like characters in search of an author, the expanding and modernizing middle class of Gujarat has been looking for a new

---

[1]Not only have there been reverberations of the Ayodhya episode in Pakistan and Bangladesh, in both countries similar attempts are on to redefine traditional lifestyles and communities as conventional nationalities and minorities and similar roles are being played by the cultures of the nation-state and the westernized middle classes.

purāna, a sacred if non-canonical myth or epic, to validate its past and protect its future. By the end of the eighteenth century, the Brahmans, Rajputs and Banias of the region got their pedigrees authenticated through one of the eighteen *purānas*, with the help of interpolations carefully arranged by obliging *shāstris* or small-time Brahmanic theologians. Now the new Hindu middle class of Gujarat is searching for a new *purāna* to explain and legitimize its domination.

The search has been part of the attempts to cope with rapid urbanization and industrialization coupled with the breakdown of the caste society among the *dvija* or twice-born castes and the absence of traditional validation for the enhanced status of landowning middle castes like the Patidars, who were considered low-caste until the late nineteenth century.

By the 1970s, the twice-born castes, after being stripped of land by the land reforms initiated in the 1950s, began to move into Gujarat's fast-growing cities and towns on a massive scale. Those among them who had migrated to the cities before Independence were satisfied if they were able to establish their own caste associations. These associations started schools, hostels or scholarship schemes for students from their own caste in big cities and district headquarters. But within three decades of Independence, the demands of urban living compelled many to look for new, broader identities that would transcend caste. For such dvijas a more generic Savarna or high-caste identity seemed both viable and rewarding. For landowning castes like the Patidars, too, who acquired economic power through the 'green' and 'white' revolutions and political power through the Congress Party, only a Savarna identity could provide the social recognition they so badly sought.[2]

As long as the undivided Congress Party in Gujarat remained the main vehicle for social mobility and political self-expression for the upper castes and the Patidars, they felt secure. This sense of security also allowed them to co-opt the emerging Dalit and Adivasi leaders into the power-structure of the Congress. The Congress split of 1969 changed these caste equations. The Congress now tried to mobilize the disgruntled elements in the lower castes and classes through populist slogans such as *garībī hatāo* (remove poverty). This new

[2]This was, of course, less true for the high-status Leva Patidars of central Gujarat than for the newly rich, low-status Kadva Patidars of north Gujarat and Saurashtra.

formula attracted not only those from among the have-nots and the
minorities who had till then not broken away from the politics of
patronage of the party but also some sections of the emerging, cash-
crop-cultivating Patidar farmers of north Gujarat and Saurashtra.

The youth-led Navnirman Movement of 1974 and the debacle of
the Congress Party in the general elections of 1977 brought new sections of the people into the party and smoothened the exit of others
from it. When the re-christened Congress-I prepared, under the
leadership of Indira Gandhi, to fight the 1980 general elections, it
was forced to look for a new electoral formula in Gujarat. It came
out with one known as KHAM—an electoral combine of Kshatriyas,
Harijans, Adivasis and Muslims. Between 1976 and 1980, the Congress-I leadership in Gujarat virtually eliminated the Brahmans,
Banias and Patidars from core positions in the party.

KHAM succeeded in wresting political power from the upper castes. For the first time in the history of Gujarat there was not a single
Patidar minister of cabinet rank. A Dalit was sent to the Union cabinet
as Minister of State for Home. And, for the first time, not only did
a tribal find a seat in the Gujarat cabinet but also held the important
portfolio of irrigation, with which the rich Patidar cash-crop farmers
were directly concerned. Even more important, the Dalit, tribal and
Kshatriya leadership was no longer subservient to upper-caste establishments. In fact, the chief minister of the state himself was a low-
status Kshatriya.[3] Above all, the low castes, the tribes, and the
minorities held more than 100 of the 180 seats in the legislature, the
Congress strength being 140. For the first time the upper castes in
the state, particularly the Patidars, sensed a political and economic
threat to their domination.

The electoral performance of KHAM in 1980 created the impression
of a massive transfer of power from the upper castes to the backward
castes. However, the latter never really tasted the fruits of power.

[3]The Kshatriyas in Gujarat are not a traditional or homogeneous caste.
They are a political caste in which the Rajputs and other backward castes
like the Kolis, Barias, and Patanvadias are projected as one single caste. The
caste was created soon after Independence to counter the domination of
Patidars in electoral politics by some Rajput leaders. In the political sociology
of Gujarat, Kshatriyas constitute the largest caste bloc, covering a quarter of
the population. Of them, the Rajputs account for about 5 per cent and the
low-status Kshatriyas about 20 per cent.

The educated middle class—mainly Brahmans, Banias and Patidars—reacted sharply by starting an agitation against the reservation system in 1981. The myth of Gandhi's Gujarat—peaceful, tolerant and non-violent—exploded in the first quarter of 1981. For the first time in independent India, a modern industrial metropolis stood witness to extreme forms of caste violence. The clashes between the Savarnas and the Dalits in the industrial periphery of Ahmedabad gradually became a caste war that spread to the towns of 18 out of the 19 districts of Gujarat and to many villages dominated by the Patidars in north and central Gujarat.

The first anti-reservation agitation was aimed at the Dalits who were beneficiaries of the reservation system which gave them access to medical and engineering colleges. Although the second anti-reservation agitation in 1984 was against the hike in job quotas for the backward-but-not-'untouchable' castes (the Mandal communities) in government and in educational institutions, the victims were all Dalits. During these two agitations, the Brahman-Bania-Patidar combine acquired a Savarna unity. In both the agitations, the *Sangh parivār* directly or indirectly supported the Savarnas.

However, after the 1981 agitation the national leadership of the BJP became conscious of the growing anti-BJP feeling among Dalits and, by the mid-1980, they had systematically started co-opting Dalit and Adivasi communities. By 1986–87, they had some success with the urban Dalits using the VHP's Hindutva-based programmes.[4] The party's anti-reservation stance was also corrected and, after 1985, the ABVP started talking in favour of a reservation system for the Dalits and the Adivasis. The following year, the VHP, in one of its Hindu Yuva Sammelans, asked the youth to dedicate themselves to the abolition of untouchability. They were also asked to work for the all-round development of their 'economically and socially backward Hindu brothers'. All this paid dividends. In the 1986 communal riots in Ahmedabad, which broke out during the Rath Yatra of Lord Jagan-

---

[4]There are many reasons for the Sangh *parivār*'s success in recruiting and mobilizing the Dalits, which is a source of much discomfort and defensive denial amongst Dalit leaders. One of the most important of these reasons could be the apparent capacity of the *parivār* to provide an easy channel of upward mobility to the Dalits *within* Hindu society. It seems that a sizeable section of the Dalits, despite popular stereotypes, have been looking for such an alternative model of Sanskritization. In this model, a violent or heroic defence of Hinduism allows one to transcend one's lowly caste status, at least temporarily.

nath, the impression was widespread that the Dalits and Muslims were killing each other.

By the mid-1980s the message of the VHP, that the idea of Savarna had to be supplanted by that of Hindutva as the binding cement for Hindus, had spread. Earlier the ultimate symbolic target of hate was the Dalit; now it was the Muslim. At last the Gujarati middle-class— spread out over large cities like Ahmedabad, Baroda and Surat and more than forty other large towns, and consisting mainly of Savarna, but also Dalit and Adivasi government servants, teachers and petty contractors—had begun to find security within the ideology of Hindutva. Cut off from older cultural and social ties, the class had learnt to use the ideology as a ready cure for rootlessness and as a substitute for traditions. Hindutva had become for this class a new *purāna* to validate their pre-eminence.

From Hulladia Hanuman to Shri Ram Temple

Let us now turn to the way the tempo of communal violence has risen in Gujarat in recent times. Over the past two decades the whole of Gujarat, Ahmedabad in particular, has witnessed a series of communal conflicts between Hindus and Muslims. The most violent of these took place in 1969, when five weeks of clashes left more than two thousand dead. A few medieval *dargāh*s or mausoleums and mosques were also destroyed or damaged; overnight some of them were transformed into Hanuman temples with faceless stone icons. The most prominent among these new temples is the Hanuman temple at Raipur Gate in Ahmedabad city, the icon of which is called Hulladia (riot-related) Hanuman.

In 1990, too, a few *dargāh*s were destroyed or damaged during the communal violence which rocked Ahmedabad following Advani's Rath Yatra. The most prominent of them was a medieval *dargāh* that was razed to the ground in the elegant Navarangpura area of Ahmedabad on 30 October 1990. While earlier the desecration of places of worship was entirely the work of lumpen proletariat mobs and unemployed youth, in 1990 it was often the handiwork of educated, middle-class youth belonging to the upper castes. At least it was clearly so in the case of the Navarangpura *dargāh*. These youth later, with the consent and active support of their elders, managed to build a new cement temple of Ram at the very site where till recently the *dargāh* had stood. Neither has the state government moved against those who were actively involved in the episode nor have the Gujarati media projected the issue.

The change in the sentiment of the Hindus is evident in the shift from the Hulladia temple to the Shri Ram temple. In 1969, the Hanuman temple built on the ruins of the *dargāh* was stigmatized by the very use of the adjective *hulladia*; in 1990, the Shri Ram temple fails to remind anyone of the fact that a *dargāh* had once stood in its place. It was almost as if nothing had changed.[5]

At present, the communal configuration in Gujarat is triangular, with the Muslims occupying one corner, the Savarnas and the Avarnas (Dalit castes and tribes) the other two, respectively. In 1981, when the first anti-reservation movement was launched by the Savarnas in Ahmedabad, the whole of Gujarat witnessed a polarization along caste lines. In Ahmedabad the Dalits were physically attacked and their houses burnt down; in many villages they were socially boycotted.

Throughout the three-month-long caste riot, Muslims either remained aloof or, whenever possible, tried to protect the Dalits. The slogan 'Dalit–Muslim *Bhai Bhai*' also echoed in a number of Dalit–Muslim neighbourhoods of Ahmedabad. Some Muslim and Dalit leaders even got together and organized a state-level conference that stressed the need for 'minority unity to withstand the communal cyclone of Gujarat'. However, after the conference, no further attempt to mobilize the minorities was actually made and the whole thing eventually petered out.

Between 1981 and 1985 when the second anti-reservation agitation was launched, the unity of the Dalits themselves was damaged by caste divisions within their ranks.[6] Also there was little understanding

[5]This collective complicity of the middle class, supported by the state's political and cultural establishments, bears comparison—far-fetched though such a comparison may at first look—with a similar event in the eleventh century that gives clues to the traditional cultural norms of the region. During the reign of Siddharaj Solanki of the Chaulakya dynasty, one of the earliest mosques built in India was damaged by some members of the majority community at Cambay following one of the earliest Hindu–Muslim riots. The caretaker of the mosque went to Patan and complained to King Siddharaj. Not only was the mosque rebuilt by royal order, but the local officers as well as the minister who tried to hide the facts of the destruction were punished.

[6]The Dalits of Gujarat are traditionally divided into at least seven castes, located in a hierarchial order. Each caste is again divided into *paragna* or marriage circles. Though the allegiance to these circles is now giving way to feelings of caste solidarity in urban Gujarat, the divisions persist.

among the Avarnas about the second anti-reservation agitation in 1985. The agitation was against quotas for the OBCs (the other backward castes, as they are called in Indian officialese). Hence the OBCs were more active in the counter-agitation. But the target of the Savarnas remained the Dalits, although in north Gujarat violent clashes between the Patidars and the Thakardas took place in at least 33 villages, and in the city of Surat in south Gujarat a few clashes were reported between tribal and Savarna college students.

The disintegration or the absence of solidarity among the Avarnas was matched by the counter-integration achieved by the upper castes during 1981–85 on the issue of reservation. A new 'we-ness' emerged among at least the Brahmans, Banias and Patidars. Today for the first time in Gujarat, these three castes are being identified as one single unit. The word Savarna has become more common in day-to-day conversation in the castes which between themselves dominate the political, economic and cultural spheres of Gujarat and constitute a majority of the urban, educated, middle class in the state.

Significantly, the ABVP, the student wing of the BJP, was the first organization to raise the banner of protest against reservation in postgraduate medical studies introduced by the Gujarat government in 1981. The ABVP not only initiated the agitation but also took it to the middle-class localities of Ahmedabad. By the middle of 1982 however, the BJP leadership had changed its strategy and dropped its anti-reservation stance. Instead, the BJP workers in Gujarat started developmental and relief work in tribal areas and by 1983 they had begun to win over the Dalits. During the Ekatmata Yatras of 1983, the local BJP–VHP leadership systematically involved Dalit leaders. Again, when communal riots broke out in Ahmedabad during 1986, at the time of the annual Rath Yatra of the local Jagannath temple, the Dalits were repeatedly invited by the BJP and the VHP to join the holy war to protect Hinduism. The detailed narratives of the local police and media on the violent clashes that took place in industrial Ahmedabad conveyed the impression that the Dalits and Muslims were out for each other's blood. In the wake of the 1986 communal riots, a series of stabbing incidents took place; the police reports made sure that they all appeared to involve only Muslims and Dalits.

The growing distance after 1986 between Dalits and Muslims, and between Hindus and Muslims in general, should be also viewed against the five successful mobilizational efforts made by the VHP

in Gujarat between 1983 and 1990 to actualize its national programmes. The following are thumbnail sketches of the five efforts.

The Politics of Yatras

The VHP planned three major 'pilgrimages' between 16 November
and 16 December 1983, for the whole of India: the Gangajal or Ekatmata Yatra from Haridwar in the foothills of the Himalayas to
Rameshwaram in Tamil Nadu; the Ekatmata Yatra from Pashupatinath
in Nepal to Kanyakumari; and the Ekatmata Yatra from Gangasagar
in West Bengal to Somnath in Gujarat.[7] Twenty-three subsidiary pilgrimages were planned for Gujarat. They were to originate from different places and merge with one of the main ones from Gangasagar
to Somnath. Their aim was to rise above caste, sect and denominational differences and invoke the spirit of unity amongst the Hindus.[8]
Signatories to the appeal to join the Yatras included the ABVP, the
RSS, the Arya Samaj, the Rotary Club, the Lions Club and also,
more notably, the Jain Sampradāya, Vaishnava Parivār, Sikh
Sampradāya, Bauddha Sampradāya and Bhartiya Dalit Varga Sangh.
In other words, an attempt was made to associate virtually all the
non-Hindu communities with the Yatras and to isolate the Muslims.

The Yatras used not merely the symbol of sacred Ganges water
but also that of sacrificial rituals and pilgrimages. The routes of the
Yatras were so charted that they touched the maximum number of
shrines and centres of pilgrimage. Advantage was also taken of the
fact that these temples were identified for centuries with different
sects belonging to three main streams of Hindu tradition—Shaivism,
Shaktism and Vaishnavism. They also often bore the signatures of
Jainism, Buddhism and Sikhism. In this respect, the Gangajal Yatra
contained all the main features of subsequent programmes of the
same kind. For instance, the route and the form of Advani's Rath
Yatra, the links with the symbols of religious traditions that have
originated in the subcontinent, and the attempt to construct a Hindu
nationality that would span the major and minor sects and the different castes—they were all there.

Only after 1984 did the VHP begin to use Ram in its mass mobilization programmes. The first organized effort was the Ram-Janaki

[7]VHP pamphlet, published by the Mehsana branch of the VHP (Mehsana:
no date).
[8]Ibid.

Dharma Yatra in 1987. It took place throughout Gujarat including the tribal areas.[9] The stated aim was to transcend caste and sect differences in the worship of Lord Ramchandra and to affirm the unity of the Hindus.

The meaning of that unity became clear during the Yatra itself. Virpur is a small town at the junction of Kheda, Sabarkantha and Panchmahal districts of Gujarat. On the day the Ram-Janaki Dharma Yatra was to pass through it, the town witnessed violent clashes between the local Hindus and Muslims and, for the first time in Gujarat, the tribals of nearby villages rushed in to attack Muslim localities and burn down Muslim shops and houses.[10]

The second effort was the Ramshila Pujan—worship of sanctified bricks meant for the projected Ram temple at Ayodhya. The VHP organized the Pujan in 1989. After Gandhi's Dandi March, which took place as a part of the independence movement, the Pujan turned out to be by far the most impressive mobilizational effort in Gujarat. It was successful beyond the VHP's wildest dreams, as even villages with no more than fifty to a hundred houses participated in the worship. Apart from sacred bricks made from the soil of their own land, they offered vast sums of money. Dalit slums of Ahmedabad and less accessible tribal villages in far-flung areas took enthusiastic part in the programme.

According to the state government, in the wake of the Ramshila Pujan, 180 towns and villages witnessed Hindu–Muslim clashes. Even after the processions with sanctified bricks were banned by Chief Minister Amarsingh Chaudhari of the Congress-I, there was communal tension at 95 more places.

Next in the series were the Ram Jyoti and Vijaya Dashami Vijay Yatras. Even before Advani's Rath Yatra was announced, the VHP had announced its own plans to launch these pilgrimages before 30 October 1990, the day *kārsevā* was to commence at Ayodhya.

---

[9]Pamphlet published by the Virpur town unit of the VHP, 10 April 1987.

[10]Two days later, a study team of Ahmedabad Ektā, a voluntary group fighting communal violence, visited the town for an on-the-spot study of the situation. When the team complained to the district collector about the tribal attacks on the Muslims, the collector's response was: 'one should not be surprised if the tribals come out to protect their Ram.' A more likely explanation, offered by a sociologist, is the old hostility of the tribals towards Muslim money-lenders that got generalized to the entire Muslim community, thanks to the charged atmosphere created by the *yātrā*s.

This time communal violence had broken out even before these events were announced, during the Ganesh immersion celebrations. The continuous efforts by the VHP to mobilize the Hindus had spurred the religious fervour of some sections of Hindus to find expression in more and more grandiose ways. Every passing year saw bigger and bigger icons being worshipped at a larger number of places during the annual Ganesh festival. Simultaneously, reports of communal violence, coming from the Muslim-dominated areas through which the Ganesh processions passed, grew in number. The explanations were always the same: either stones had been thrown from a mosque on a procession, or offensive anti-Muslim slogans had been successful in provoking what they were trying to provoke. Often the two explanations went together. On 4 September 1990, the day of the immersion, 15 persons were killed in communal clashes in Baroda, Anand, Surat, Bardoli and Ankaleswar.

On 16 September 1990, Pravin Togadia, General Secretary of the VHP in Gujarat, announced that 101 Ram Jyoti Yatras and 15,000 Vijaya Dashami Vijay Yatras would cover the entire state. He also announced that 1,00,000 volunteers from Gujarat would participate in the *kārsevā* in Ayodhya, including 50,000 trident-carrying Bajrang Dal volunteers and 1,000 tribals with bows and arrows. He added that 18,000 religious conferences would also be held in all the 18,000 villages of Gujarat. Apparently, even before the public announcement of Advani's Rath Yatra, the VHP had started preparing for it on a large scale.

Every mobilization since 29 September 1990 left behind a record of communal clashes. The Vijaya Dashami Yatras brought in their wake clashes in Palanpur and Vijapur towns of north Gujarat; the Ram Jyoti Yatras led to clashes in Baroda, Balashinar and Lunawada in central and east Gujarat and in Bharuch in south Gujarat. In the predominantly tribal areas of Bharuch and Surat districts, in at least 33 villages there were attacks on isolated Muslim houses by tribals.[11]

Advani's Rath Yatra, already briefly described in chapter 2, was the last of the big mobilizational efforts. On 13 September 1990, Narendra Modi, the General Secretary of the BJP in Gujarat, announced the programme of Advani's Rath Yatra from Somnath to

[11]Gujarat is one of the more urbanized states in India, with about 50 large urban settlements. As a result, the villages in the state are more accessible and more exposed to the culture of urban India and more frequently affected by communal tension as compared to villages in most other states in India.

Ayodhya at a press conference. He gave a stern warning to the Central
and UP governments that the BJP was even prepared for a repetition
of the Jalianwala Bag massacre at Ayodhya. When a journalist asked
him about the possibility of communal riots breaking out during the
Yatra, Modi replied that this would not happen, but added that communal tension was woven into the life of Gujarat.

When Advani commenced his pilgrimage on a chariot from Somnath on 25 September 1990, the Muslims in Gujarat were feeling
very insecure. For instance, in Veraval, the city adjoining Somnath,
they sent off the children, women and the aged to nearby 'safe' villages having sizeable Muslim populations. The Yatra, however,
passed off peacefully in the state, mainly because the entire state
machinery was on the alert.

The Yatra was a great political success. Nearly half of Chimanbhai
Patel's cabinet were from the BJP. They used their official position
to promote it in their own way. They piloted it in their own areas
and used the government's wireless service to relay information on
Advani's movement, so that he could be given a proper welcome
everywhere. The VHP was one up on the BJP; it put up big
signboards in each city and town *en route*, declaring them to be cities
of a Hindu state.

The communal situation in Gujarat worsened after the arrest of
Advani at Samastipur, Bihar, on 23 October. That afternoon, curfew
was declared in two of the most sensitive areas of Ahmedabad,
Dariyapur and Kalupur in the walled city. Riots also broke out in a
number of cities in Saurashtra, north and east Gujarat and continued
till 30 October, by which time almost the entire state was affected.
Sporadic rioting continued till 6 November at Ahmedabad.

We shall briefly describe the riots in Ahmedabad here but, before
we do so, a word on the changing human geography of the city.

The Ahmedabad Riots

Actually there are three Ahmedabads. The first is the five-century-old
walled city founded by Sultan Ahmed Shah. It features a number of
medieval mosques, representing Indo-Islamic architectural styles, and
innumerable *pols*—groups of densely packed houses in narrow wind-
ing lanes that together have a main entrance by way of a huge wooden
gate that can be shut. Most of the *pols* are occupied traditionally by a

homogeneous community or caste—Savarna Hindu, Dalit or Muslim—and each has a separate subculture.

The second Ahmedabad developed during the latter half of the nineteenth century around old villages on the periphery of the city, after the rise of its famous textile industry. In these medieval villages turned industrial townships, slums and *chalis* mushroomed around the textile mills and other factories having huge compounds and high walls.[12] While this Ahmedabad retains much of the traditional caste-based lifestyle of the old villages, the slums and *chalis* also carry the imprint of the social composition and segregated diversity of the textile mill workers. Those who migrated into the second city during the last century and in the early decades of this century settled in *chalis* and those who migrated after Independence were forced to live in slums. Almost one-third of the textile workers before 1980 were Dalit and another one-third Muslim. This Ahmedabad has also seen large-scale immigration from Hindi-speaking North India and from areas around the river Godavari in South India during the last three decades.

The third Ahmedabad is new; it is separated from the first two by the river Sabarmati. An élite area, populated by the upper and middle classes with a minuscule and scattered Muslim population and a few Dalit housing colonies and slums, this part of the city hosts most of the modern institutions of higher learning, including the university. During the last decade, the character of this Ahmedabad has changed. After each riot, the middle and upper classes in the walled city have felt more insecure, and the traders with their shops and the professionals with their practices in the other two Ahmedabads have moved to the new Ahmedabad. The process quickened after 1985, with the rise of multi-storeyed offices and residential buildings and Singapore-type shopping arcades. These made the élite areas of the new Ahmedabad even more exclusive. Whereas the membership of housing societies established before or immediately after Independence in the new Ahmedabad were caste-or community-based and recreated the lifestyle of the walled city in a modern guise, housing societies established during the last two decades have exclusive Savarna memberships that transcend caste differences among the Savarnas and reflect their new we-ness.

---

[12]A *chali* or *chawl* is a multi-storeyed, concrete slum; a 'proper' slum usually has an assortment of hutments which in some ways duplicate a village.

The 1980s saw two major changes in the life of Ahmedabad. First, the century-old textile industry started crumbling and, by 1982, around 50,000 textile workers became jobless. About two-thirds of them were Dalits and Muslims. The proportion would have been higher but for the gradual elimination of Muslims and women workers from the textile mills during the previous three decades. Many of the jobless joined the unorganized sector and the children of families that had lost their income due to joblessness or the elimination of women workers, were attracted to the expanding underworld of the city, with its close links with the police and the politicians.[13]

After the two caste riots and the numerous communal riots, this underworld in turn began to reflect, from about the middle of the 1980s, the triangular polarization among the Dalits, the Muslims and the Savarnas. The gang rivalries within it also became more violent. The polarization reached its political climax in 1987 when Abdul Latif, an underworld don, got himself elected from five Muslim-majority constituencies at the same time, presumably to enter both the Ahmedabad Municipal Corporation, where the BJP otherwise got a thumping majority, and the Guinness Book of World Records. The emergence of such local heroes further underwrote the decline of the traditional community leadership. According to Rameshchandra Parmar (political activist, a pioneer of the Dalit movement in Gujarat and a schoolteacher for more than 30 years), the older culture of the merchant guilds and trading castes—the tradition of the *mahājan* or the *shreshthī*—and the more recent Gandhian tradition, had previously served, despite their many limitations, as powerful cultural forces that imposed some social control and moral restraint on the working classes and younger generations of Ahmedabadis. By the 1980s, other forces had begun to replace them.

The second change was the impact of the Urban Land Ceiling Act of 1976 (ULCA) on landholding patterns in Ahmedabad. According to a 1976 survey of slums undertaken by the Ahmedabad Municipal Corporation, at least 78 per cent of the city's slum houses were on private land. After the introduction of the ULCA, private land could not be used for slum creation; only municipal or government land remained available for such use. This encouraged the growth of a new

---

[13]Prohibition being in force in Gujarat, a relatively more urban and industrialized state, suppliers and producers of illicit liquor formed an important section of this underworld.

class of quasi-criminal entrepreneurs capable of illegally occupying open land through their powerful political connections. These slum-lords took money from poor immigrants to first settle them on such land and then, after a while, eager to profit from soaring land prices, turned against the settlers and tried to oust them through 'communal' riots. The cleared land was then again 'sold' to the highest bidders. Today it is not unusual to meet at Ahmedabad a slumlord-turned-builder who at the same time is a municipal councillor or office-bearer of a national political party.

While Ahmedabad was witnessing a shift from its organized textile industry to unorganized industries (such as powerlooms), of the kind which are usually in search of a location, in the walled city there began a scramble for old houses nearer to one's own community. After the communal riots of 1985 and 1986, the distress sale of houses increased so enormously that the government had to issue an ordinance denying, with retrospective effect, registration of such sales. But communal exodus continued and, while the well-to-do migrated to the third Ahmedabad, the lower-middle-class and backward-caste families moved into their community *pols* in old Ahmedabad. By the end of the 1980s, living had become communally homogeneous in all the three Ahmedabads. But homogeneity did not lead to the sustenance or restoration of a stable community life, for many of the inhabitants were now newcomers and there was always a trickle of migration to the new Ahmedabad.

It is against this background that the events of 23 October to 6 November 1990 should be seen.

On 22 October, the General Secretary of the BJP in Gujarat, Narendra Modi, declared a red-alert, anticipating Advani's arrest. It was to be observed during 24–26 October. He also gave a call to observe 23–30 October as a 'week of determination' and declared that meetings would be organized in 1,500 towns and villages of Gujarat. There was tension in the air.

As an immediate reaction to Advani's arrest, the local BJP and VHP workers called a general strike on the morning of 23 October in the Khadia and Raipur areas of the walled city. They were soon out on the streets, to throw stones or erect barricades with the help of uprooted electricity poles. By the afternoon, in Kalupur and Dariapur, two predominantly Muslim areas, large-scale group clashes began. In the walled city, rioters riding two-wheelers began to move

around stabbing people randomly; they killed four and seriously injured another ten. Among those killed was a ten-year-old girl. (This
was the first time that a child had been attacked thus in Ahmedabad.
In 1985 for the first time a woman was stabbed in the city. Earlier,
attacks on women and children were taboo in Gujarat riots; they are
now common.) Banks closed by noon and so did the General Post
Office in another couple of hours. There was an exodus of people
from the walled city who rushed home to the other side of the river
Sabarmati, and wild rumours and exaggerated casualty figures freely
circulated in the city.

For more than four decades riots had always begun in the walled
city but all the three Ahmedabads had rarely been affected simultaneously. This time the violence spread rapidly outside the old city
walls. Two banks, two post offices and an office of the Life Insurance
Corporation of India were set on fire and a jeep belonging to a
government corporation was burnt—all in Hindu middle-class areas
in the new Ahmedabad. Industrial Ahmedabad was also affected by
the evening, though less so. Within one day, the situation was so
tense and the communal divide so intense that rampaging crowds
attacked each other at many places, like two small armies fighting a
battle to the finish.

A general strike was called on 24 October and most of the markets
remained closed. City buses were withdrawn from the roads in the
morning itself. Yet, in Bapunagar and Gomtipur in industrial Ahmedabad, confrontations took place between Dalit and Muslim
crowds. The reason was obvious. To make a complete success of the
strike, the workers of the BJP and the VHP tried to close down Muslim shops; this led to pitched battles and, before noon, curfew was
clamped in these areas. By the afternoon, some more areas of industrial and walled Ahmedabad were brought under curfew (for map
of areas under curfew, see endpapers). But the main battleground had
already shifted to the Naranpura area of the third Ahmedabad. The
targets there were the properties of the Central Government.
Telephone cables worth 30 million rupees were destroyed and even
railway tracks were damaged.

By the next day Ahmedabad had calmed down and there was only
sporadic violence, though half of the industrial and walled city was
still under curfew. The city continued to be tense, though not as much
as its politics. All kinds of speculation and rumours floated around
because Chief Minister Chimanlal Patel had asked the ten BJP ministers

in his cabinet to resign. By the following day, the seven-month-old coalition government came to an end. So did the relative calm of the previous day, as if the exit of the BJP from power was a trigger.[14] Random stabbings by youths on scooters resumed, especially in the walled city. In industrial Ahmedabad, a woman was stabbed and passions rose again.

The next two days, 27 and 28 October, were quieter; only stray incidents of violence took place. On 29 October curfew was lifted from the entire city, though violence continued elsewhere in Gujarat.

The Gujarat units of the BJP and the VHP called another general strike on 30 October. It was a great success in Ahmedabad. That morning *Ramdhun* was sung at most of the important temples of the city. The BJP mayor of the city, Gopalbhai Solanki, set up the first road blocks at Asarwa at around 9.00 AM On the main Ashram Road, close to the statue of Gandhi, the deputy mayor, another BJP stalwart, set up another blockade, while the Gandhi Bridge on the river Sabarmati, was blocked by the President of the BJP's women's wing and other party activists. Soon all the bridges on the river Sabarmati were closed. All buses run by the city municipal corporation were withdrawn from the roads. People on bicycles and two-wheelers were stopped and forced to say '*Jai Shri Ram*'. Those who refused or even fumbled were either beaten up or allowed to go after their tyres were deflated.

Within minutes of the first arrest by the police, violence erupted. Roads were barricaded with the help of heavy iron road-dividers, uprooted electricity poles, dismantled bus stands, and broken signboards of ransacked shops. By the afternoon, life had come to a halt in the city, though not for the more dedicated rioters. A number

[14]The breakdown of civil order in Ahmedabad was certainly worsened by the political situation. The chief minister had to sack the BJP ministers in his cabinet when his seven-month-old coalition ministry was reduced to a minority in the Legislative Assembly after the BJP withdrew support to it. He claimed on 26 October that he would prove his majority on the floor of the Assembly on 1 November. So while the state capital burned, the chief minister was busy trying to save his ministry. He managed to do so, by establishing his majority in the Assembly with Congress support, but at an enormous cost. In the absence of clear political authority and regular political monitoring, the law and order machinery in the city of Ahmedabad gave way on 30 October. In contrast, some 120 miles away, at Rajkot, a road blockade by the town's powerful RSS family flopped because the police commissioner acted firmly.

of houses and shops were set on fire, including some near police stations. Fire engines trying to fight arson were also attacked. At some places, mobs clashed too. By the evening, the army was called out and it staged flag marches on both sides of the Sabarmati.

But even as the army was marching, mobs were burning shops and looting houses in many places. In the narrow lanes and by-lanes of the walled city, stabbing and heavy stoning were going on, and burning rags wrapped on bicycle tyres were being thrown from the terraces of old multi-storeyed houses on the mobs below. As in the earlier riots, these burning rags were supplied by women of both communities. On the outskirts of new Ahmedabad, frenzied crowds of Savarnas and Muslims in mixed neighbourhoods attacked each other with swords, sticks and iron rods; and in crowded industrial Ahmedabad, where Dalits and Muslims lived in adjacent localities, both sides used crude acid bombs, petrol bombs and even private guns.

The situation in the new Ahmedabad was particularly bad. Opposite the Gujarat Vidyapith, the university established by Gandhi, the handicrafts emporium of the Government of West Bengal and a large retail outlet for *khadi* were torched.[15] Some small roadside wooden cabins belonging to Muslim petty shopkeepers were also destroyed and then used as road barricades. Near the Vidyapith, a medieval *dargāh* in an upper-middle class locality was razed to the ground and by the evening the place was declared a Ram mandir. We have already commented on this episode.

Further west on Ashram Road, near the National Institute of Design, a number of Muslim upper-middle class localities were attacked by a large mob that set fire to parked vehicles. Muslim shops in some of the debonair shopping complexes were also burnt down or ransacked. Sometimes, the ransacked goods were burnt on the main road though, usually, they were simply taken away. In the same area, a young Muslim chemist was killed by a mob that attacked the Seven Heaven Apartments where he lived. He fired from his revolver in self-defence and the angry mob rushed to his apartment, broke open the door and dragged him downstairs to burn him alive in front of his brother and mother, both of whom were seriously injured when they tried to intervene.

A few miles further west in Juhapura, late in the afternoon, mobs armed with swords, daggers and iron rods, attacked three Hindu, middle-class

---

[15]The emporium probably became a target because the West Bengal government had belligerently opposed the Ramjanmabhumi movement.

co-operative housing societies—Shailesh Park, Venugopal Society and Zalak Apartments. They burnt at least 21 houses to cinders and damaged 9 others. In retaliation, within one-and-a-half hours the Usmane Haroon Housing Society was attacked and 17 houses were either looted or set on fire. Attacks and counter-attacks continued till late evening. The last target was yet another housing co-operative, Sham Society, where nine houses were plundered or damaged. Three persons died in the clashes and 73 were injured. To control the violence, the police opened fire and killed another 6 persons.

Juhapura-Vejalpur had never had a communal clash. In Juhapura, a predominantly Muslim suburb of some 20,000 people, twelve Hindu temples had existed for years. Even during the earlier riots they had not been touched. Several huts belonging to Dalits and other 'Backward' communities and a large Hindu housing society, situated just across the highway at Juhapura, had also remained intact. This time, it was said, some real estate developers were interested in an expensive piece of disputed vacant land in the area. The outbreak of violence in other parts of the city gave the builders the opportunity they were waiting for and sealed the fate of the community.

Even the élite residential area around the campus of the Indian Space Research Organization did not escape the rioters. Gangs of youngsters moving about there on two-wheelers set on fire a number of isolated Muslim upper-class houses that had been marked earlier and then disappeared on their vehicles. The victims included a number of professionals—a doctor, a college professor, a social worker and a Muslim architect married to a Hindu who lived just opposite the Satellite Police Station. In some cases, Hindu neighbours did resist the mobs; in others they did their best but failed. For instance, when a gang of rioters on two-wheelers entered the grounds of the Indian Institute of Management looking for the house of a Muslim plumber, his neighbours saved him by swearing that he was not a Muslim. Again, when a mob broke open the locked house of a Muslim teacher and made a bonfire of all his belongings, his Hindu neighbours tried to stop them, but failed. Later, they collected whatever was left of the household goods and gave them to the teacher when he returned home. The victim himself was stoic:

At the beginning, I turned down the request of my Hindu neighbours to move to a safer place. But on 27 October, I realized the seriousness of the situation and moved to a Muslim locality. When the boys came to my locked house on 30 October, one of my Hindu neighbours telephoned me and then, every ten minutes, I was given a blow by blow account of what was happening. How the boys broke open my iron grill, then my front door and collected our clothes, furniture etc. outside our house and made a bonfire of them. They were also planning to burn our locked kitchen. But when they saw from the window the cooking gas cylinder [they] probably thought that the explosion would damage the first-floor apartment of a Hindu ... .'

Of his new residence he said, 'I have spent my childhood and youth in a Muslim locality of the walled city. To again live in that environment is not much of a problem. But my two school-going daughters will certainly suffocate in that conservative locality; that is my only worry.'[16]

Never before had such systematic attacks been mounted on upper-class Muslim houses. Though there had been widespread arson during the communal riots of 1985–86, the rioters were careful not to attack Muslim shops covered by any kind of insurance since eventually the government paid the damages. And most upper-class Muslim houses were insured. No such consideration was shown in 1990.[17]

[16]This fear of re-ghettoization also haunted a Muslim researcher working in a well known research institute of Ahmedabad. He said:

Coming from a Muslim lower-middle-class family of a village near Allahabad, when I got my doctorate in social science, I thought that now onward I would enter mainstream society and my children would grow up in a cosmopolitan environment. But after witnessing the current riot in this city and realizing what is happening to educated Muslim families, I feel, we are being pushed back to our ghettos.

The problem was even more acute for Jamindar, a Bohra social reformer and social worker whose house was burnt:

You know that because of the *fatwa* of the Bohra chief priest, we were forced to leave our ancestral house in Voharvad. There was a total social boycott by my Bohra relatives earlier. Since the last few years I have been living in a mixed locality. Now where should I go from here?

[17]Actually, the property of the Central Government was a major target of the rioters. Mobs had set on fire reels of telephone cable worth about Rs 30 million near the new telephone exchange at Naranpura on 24 October, during the first Gujarat bandh. This time a violent mob attacked the Jammu-Tawi Express near Chandlodia railway station and set one of its carriages on fire. Municipal property was also attacked. According to the Municipal Commissioner of Ahmedabad, P. Basu, a mob set on fire the furniture of the Bal Bhavans at Usmanpura and Khokhara and the octroi collection centres at Shara Mandhir and Ghatlodia. The more serious attacks were on the municipal fire brigade. A water tanker and an ambulance belonging to the brigade were burnt.

On 31 October, more than two-thirds of the city was under curfew and the army continued its flag marches. Elsewhere in the State, 14 towns were brought under indefinite curfew. By then 5,000 people had been arrested, of whom 1,000 were held under the harsh Terrorist and Disruptive Activities Act (TADA). In Ahmedabad alone 1,300 were arrested, 94 of them under TADA. Thanks to such measures, the situation improved on 1 November, but the following day, just when a semblance of calm was returning to the city, two women were stabbed to death at Gomtipur when curfew was relaxed. This was the third time that the tradition of sparing women and children, that had survived through a series of riots in the city, was flouted to rekindle violence.

By this time trade and industry were getting nervous about the long-drawn-out routine of violence. Apart from the loss of their business, there was also the fact that most of them stayed in the new Ahmedabad and they had not bargained for a long stretch of insecurity in their part of the city. The office-bearers of the Gujarat Chamber of Commerce and Industry met the police commissioner in a group and suggested the creation of a separate cell to give correct information about the situation in the city in order to contain provocative rumours. The suggestion was accepted and two telephone numbers were allotted for the purpose, and an effort was also made to fight rumours through the newspapers.

As if to reaffirm the class affiliation of the rioters and their distance from the local residents, on 4 November, five young men in a car were caught; they were carrying stolen goods worth Rs 80,000 as well as equipment for breaking open shops.

The riots went on till 6 November. By then, 63 persons had been killed in Gujarat. Even after the Government declared normalcy in the state, hundreds of families who had fled their homes and taken refuge in relief camps refused to go back. In Ahmedabad, the local administration seemed to be in a hurry to disband these camps, but a steady stream of new arrivals and persisting tension even after 6 November, did not allow them to do so.[18]

---

[18]Describing two of the largest relief camps, located at Shahalam Roza, a five-hundred-year-old *dargah*, and in an open ground at Charodia in Bapunagar, the Ahmedabad edition of *The Times of India* (7 October 1992) wrote: 'the government authorities claim that the new refugees are allured by the cash dole and other benefits available at the camps, not all the new arrivals agree.

As for the distribution of violence, in the industrial areas of Ahmedabad clashes took place in all the localities where Muslim houses bordered Dalit houses. In the upper-middle-class areas, well-to-do Muslim families were the targets—as if the social success and the very entry of the Muslims into these areas was being grudged. So even the homes of families resulting from Hindu–Muslim marriages were not spared. Most such victims left their homes and went into hiding in safer places. Though some of them might have come back, ghettoization, in some cases re-ghettoization, of middle-class and even upper-middle-class Muslims has become now a distinct possibility in Ahmedabad.

If the Muslim upper-middle class was a prime target this time, the complicity of large sections of the Hindu upper-middleclass was also clearer this time. That complicity also introduced into the culture of riots in Gujarat a new form of youth participation. In the last two days of October, it was fairly common to come across teen-aged boys and girls from well-to-do families, often only ten or twelve years old, moving around in small cars (usually Marutis) and looting Muslim shops located on the main roads. These teenagers were often egged on by their parents and, in some cases, scolded for not doing a good job of the looting.[19] The symptoms might have been new, the

---

'... Iqbal Mohammed and a part of his family had left the house even before the trouble broke out. The others stayed back to take care of the house and their belongings. But the following day after some incidents of violence, the police forced them to abandon their homes. The police allegedly told them that they were likely to be attacked and should seek shelter elsewhere, Iqbal Mohammed said "the police even beat up some of us who were reluctant to leave our homes." ... A man from the camp had gone to his house this morning to see if things had improved. But he came back terrified because he had been threatened with dire consequences if he, his family and other neighbours returned to their houses....

'Mustaqbhai, a resident of Bhilnivas in the Behrampura area also alleged that he and others were forcibly asked to evacuate their houses by the police after some violence in the neighbourhood. Some have suffered lathi blows inflicted by the police, while others have suffered burn injuries when burning rags were thrown at them. Ramzanbhai, another resident of the same area, alleged that his house was also attacked by the police and some medals belonging to his father, who was in the army, were stolen by the police.'...

'A similar situation prevails at the camp at Charodia'.

[19]One informant, staying in an élite area, described how her prosperous next-door neighbour, a respectable housewife, rebuked her teenaged daughter for hurriedly plundering from the showcase of a Muslim shop only shoes and sandals meant for the left foot.

affliction was not. To many, the city of Ahmedabad now showed all the signs of large-scale anomie, a breakdown of community life and the erosion of traditional social norms.

In the 1985 riots, 210 persons were killed in Gujarat; in 1990 the toll was 220, the highest for the decade. If one went by numbers, the difference was insignificant. However, if one goes by public sentiments, the divide between the Hindus and the Muslims had deepened during the five intervening years. In Ahmedabad in 1985, only one high wall came up between a Patidar and a Muslim neighbourhood in the old city. By the end of 1990, the residents of almost all Dalit *chawls* in the industrial areas had erected high walls around them, interrupted by iron gates. At places where Hindus and Muslims lived side by side, the dominant sentiment now was one of fear and mistrust. When talking to their friends from other parts of the city, they usually referred to their own· place of stay as a frontier.

The divide between communities was obvious even to outsiders. Those in the affected neighbourhoods had drastic solutions to offer to whoever was willing to listen. The Hindu driver of our autorickshaw, realizing that we were returning from a relief camp meant for Muslims, asked point blank, 'Don't you think Nehru committed a blunder? He should have sent the Muslims to Pakistan!' A retired government official was only slightly more suave. He said that he knew it was impossible to drive the Muslims out of India, but many problems could be solved if their voting rights were taken away. Others sought more violent solutions. And when some volunteers of Ahmedabad Ekta went to purchase bread for riot victims, a Muslim bakery owner near the railway station said straight out, 'Sir, why do you give us bread? Give us gunpowder'.

These sentiments went with a growing demand for guns for self-protection. In industrial areas like Gomtipur and in outlying areas like Juhapura-Vejalpur, the demand did not slacken even after the riots subsided. When we visited some households in Vejalpur, most residents spoke of the need to acquire firearms. Still deeply distrustful of the police, members of both the communities felt that only direct access to arms would give them security. A Dalit textile worker staying in a Gomtipur slum, close to a large Muslim settlement, thought that we were from the VHP and said: 'Sir, only milk and medicine will not do, give us guns and teach us how to use them.' Just across the road, a Muslim college student lamented:

Now my friends are so desperate that they are asking for guns. No one in my community trusts the local police after the recent experiences. All my friends think that now they have to protect themselves on the basis of their own strength and create a line of defence.

The demand for arms paralleled an almost paranoic concern with security; people seemed to think in strategic terms. In Juhapura-Vasna, an area new to communal violence, a business executive 'explained' for our benefit the 'gameplan' of the Congress–Muslim leadership. Pointing at the highway, he said:

Look, the earlier Congress mayor of our city, Rafiuddin Shaikh, allowed the Muslim slum to grow near Chandala lake as well as Juhapura so that they could blockade us. After the BJP came to power, the new Hindu mayor has not allowed the Muslims to get concentrated on the approach roads to Gandhinagar. Now it will be difficult for the Muslims to blockade us.

TABLE 14
SUMMARY OF MAJOR RIOTS IN GUJARAT FROM 1980

Year	Location	Comment
1981	Ahmedabad city, Ahmedabad, Gandhinagar, Kheda and Mehsana districts	First anti-reservation agitation. Main contestants Savarnas and Avarnas; main feature violence and social boycott directed against Dalits.
1982–83	Baroda city	Clashes between Hindus and Muslims on Ganesh Chaturthi festival.
1985	Ahmedabad and Baroda cities Ahmedabad, Baroda, Mehsana, Sabarkantha and Kheda districts	Second anti-reservation agitation —it was anti-Dalit in the beginning, then got transformed into a communal riot directed mainly against the Muslims —counter-agitations by the tribals and other 'backwards'.
1986	Ahmedabad city	Rath Yatra: between Hindus and Muslims —Dalit areas affected —Growing distance between Dalits and Muslims.
1987	Kheda (Cambay, Thasra, Dhundara, Virpur, Nadiad, Dakor) and Sabarkantha (Prantij, Himatnagar, Modasa) districts	Clashes between Hindus and Muslims over the Ram-Janki Shobha Yatra —Tribals attacked Muslims in Virpur.

| 1989 | Banaskantha, Panchmahal, Mehsana, Kheda and Bharuch | Clashes between Hindus and Muslims around Ramshila Pujan Shobha Yatra. |
| 1990 | The whole of Gujarat (except Jamnagar, Dang, Sabarkanta, Junagadh, districts) | Clashes between Hindus and Muslims over the Rath Yatra. |

VIII. VIOLENCE AND SURVIVAL

The communal violence that broke out at Jaipur in 1990, in the wake of Advani's Rath Yatra, bewildered its citizens. Some were surprised that the violence took place at all, for it was wholly unprecedented. 'The riots did not happen, they were made to happen,' was the refrain of many. Others like Khandelwal, a Hindu broker in the gemstone trade, were incredulous because they felt that the Hindus and Muslims of Jaipur 'just could not carry on without each other'. When we interviewed him, Khandelwal was helping Yusuf and Vasif Ali, two of five brothers who ran their own business. The three were classifying gleaming garnets and aquamarines according to their lustre into packets to be delivered to showrooms of Hindu traders. Zahoor Mohammad, a resident of Jaipur's Pahadganj area, insisted that the city's Hindus and Muslims lived lives that were completely interlocked—'*aise jude hue hain jaise āpas me ali se sali mili hui hai.*' Nonetheless, hundreds participated in the loot, arson, killings and in the rapes that were often not reported because of the stigma that attached to the victims. What ruptured the social fabric woven over the centuries?

The Social Fabric of Jaipur

The riots were not a 'spontaneous' or inevitable clash between two communities given to primordial religious sentiments. On the other hand, to regard them as the work of only criminals would also be an over-simplification. The conflict had been planned by people other than the underworld and enjoyed ample political backing. And when it came, it did exteriorize the latent or implicit violence within several sections of society. In this section, we show how the diverse accounts of violence coming from the ruling party, the written media, the state, and the police gradually converge to produce a single narrative framing social consciousness and action. This narrative constructs the Muslim as a foreigner, invader, fanatic and traitor, and it acquires legitimacy from an ideology in which the Hindu community and faith are seen as requiring protection from the enemy within. This emerging narrative has ensured widespread *post facto* sanction for the riot from the city's middle class. As one refrain of Jaipur's educated middle class goes: 'It was right; the Muslims needed to learn a lesson. In every riot they attack unarmed Hindus. Look at the way the Muslims are multiplying and the number of the Hindus is getting reduced.'

Jaipur has obviously changed since 1947. When much of north India was gripped by the great Partition riots Rajputana, present Rajasthan, remained mostly unaffected. With the exception of Alwar and Bharatpur, where massacres, large-scale evictions from villages, and forced conversions of the Muslim Meos took place, the princely states, by and large, maintained communal peace. In Jaipur, Jodhpur and Udaipur, the rulers themselves intervened to prevent violence. That relative insulation of Rajasthan from the pan-Indian politics of ethnic violence has now ended. The state is already on the list of communally sensitive states, one of the ten which will soon have a special riot squad. Riots in Rajasthan previously meant anti-Jain riots in the late eighteenth century and Jat–Rajput riots in the early twentieth century; they have now come to mean Hindu–Muslim clashes.[20]

Before we proceed with our story, a word about our major concern in this section. As we have said, most studies of communal and ethnic violence take for granted the existence of two antagonistic groups engaged in violence and counter-violence. In the context of South Asia, such antagonisms are often presumed to be a part of the natural state of the communities. Yet, it is pretty obvious that such antagonisms, and the ideologies and social theories that justify them, are contested at each stage. Report after report on riots in South Asia reveal the elaborate planning and mobilizational effort that go into them. And it must have become obvious to the reader from our account of the growth of Hindu nationalism that at every stage the movement has faced not only passive non-cooperation but spirited

[20]Ashim Kumar Roy, *History of the Jaipur City* (Delhi: Manohar, 1978), p. 186.

resistance from a large majority of Hindus. In this respect, the Jaipur riot was no exception.

It is our belief that no description of the spread of an ideology of hate and violence can be complete without an awareness of this resistance which it faces at the ground level. The resistance finds expression in the ways in which people behave or intervene in events during a crisis, sometimes to protect others at enormous risk to their own life and well-being. Our account of this resistance implicitly uses an expanded version of Robert J. Lifton's concept of the survivor, to cover not only the victim who experiences violence and survives but also the survivor who has experienced protection and care from members of the 'other' community.[21] Such a concept allows one to look at communal violence not as a clash between two exclusive groups but as a complex encounter between man-made suffering and human empathy and care. Such encounters, perhaps more frequent where communities are more intact, keep open the possibility of social healing, of the kind that has allowed some of the older civilizations to survive and triumph over their experiences of violence, exploitation and uprooting.

Jaipur, a city situated in the plains bound by the Aravalli range of hills, was founded by Raja Jai Singh in 1727 and was the capital of a prosperous princely state of the same name. An important aspect of this prosperity were the Muslim and Hindu craftsmen brought in by its rulers from various parts of the country. Jaipur came to be known for its marble and stone carving, brass work, block printing, carpets, gold and silver thread work, tie and dye, handmade paper, and other crafts. But the premier industry was that of jewellery. Jaipur became famous in the late nineteenth century as one of the world's largest centres for cutting emeralds. Gemstone cutting and polishing gradually became Jaipur's core industry, involving the participation of some of the major communities in the city.

Jaipur today is founded on an interweaving of castes and communities that is not fully reflected in its demographic data. Jaipur district has, the 1991 census says, a population of 4.72 million, of which 78 per cent are Hindu.[22] Though the densely populated walled

---

[21]Robert Jay Lifton, *Death in Life: Survivors of Hiroshima* (New York: Random House, 1968). Also Amrit Srinivas, 'The Survivor in the Study of Violence' in Veena Das (ed.), *Mirrors of Violence: Communities, Riots, Survivors* (New Delhi: Oxford University Press, 1990), pp. 305–20.

city of Jaipur has a large concentration of both Hindu and Muslim upper castes, Jains and Muslim artisans, the Muslims are a little more than 18 per cent in a population of 1.45 million in urban Jaipur and the Scheduled Castes and Tribes about 10.5 and 2.3 per cent respectively.[23] But it is the traditional economy of Jaipur that reflects the city's plural culture most accurately—the grain trade, the vegetable market, the textile hand-block printing, and the gemstone industry. If Muslim craftspersons require Hindu patrons and marketing, Hindu festivals and rituals are inconceivable without Muslim craftspersons. The Manihar women make the mandatory lac bangles for Hindu married women, and strands of the *kalāvā* (Hindu sacred thread required for *yajna*) can be found hanging from the balconies in the Nilgaron ka Mohalla behind Ramganj. Sankrānt, a major festival in Jaipur, when kites literally crowd the city's sky, is inconceivable without Muslim kite-makers, exactly as Diwali is unthinkable without Muslim firework manufacturers.

The category 'Muslim', however, includes a world of cultural and occupational variations and social stratification. The conventional *ashraf* of Sheikhs, Saiyads, Pathans, Khojas, and Bohras are better off. The poorer Muslims consist of Mochis (leather-workers), Kasais (butchers), Lohars (blacksmiths), Darzis (tailors), Nilgars (dyers), Manihars (bangle makers), Pannigars (silver paper makers), Pinnaras (quilt makers), Chipas (block printers), kite- and firecracker makers. Besides these traditional crafts, Muslims are also mechanics, rickshaw pullers, and unskilled labourers. As in Ahmedabad, by and large, the Muslims are concentrated in the old walled city. Frequently occupational groups live in *mohallā*s or localities, named after their occupation. The Kayamkhanis, Pathans, Bhishtis, Mochis, Pinnāras, Kasais (called Querishis), Julāhas, Pannighars constitute well-knit *birādari*s with systems of internal decision-making and adjudication.

Jaipur is getting further urbanized. Increased migration has ensured a growth of over 37 per cent in the last decade. While the medieval

[22]Ashish Bose, *Demographic Diversity of India: 1991 Census* (Delhi: B. R. Publishing, 1991), pp. 315–20. In Rajasthan, Hindus are 89.3 per cent and Muslims 7.28 per cent. Boileau's *Narrative* of 1835 mentions 17 per cent Muslims, that grew to 25 per cent in 1901. Apparently, there were not many artisans then except for the *chipas* (printers).

[23]Government of Rajasthan, *District Census Handbook, Jaipur 1981* (Jaipur: Government of Rajasthan, 1981).

walled city has grown, there has also been a movement from it to the new residential colonies that have proliferated in recent years, many of them built by the Housing Board or the Jaipur Development Authority (JDA). Their new-found prosperity in the gemstone industry has encouraged many Muslims to purchase plots or homes in these colonies. (As in Ahmedabad, these were major sites of rioting in 1990, even though communal riots are usually associated with congested areas in walled cities.)

With this urbanization has come Hindu nationalism. In the last two decades it has brought about a pronounced shift in the attitude of many Hindus in Jaipur though, as we shall see, it has not succeeded in eliminating the voices of many others.

The rise of the BJP in the state has paralleled these shifts. As in some other states, the party is no longer dependent in Rajasthan, as its precursor the Jan Sangh was, on the support of urban shopkeepers and traders. The first break came in the 1977 elections, when the Jan Sangh cashed in on the anti-Congress sentiments as part of the Janata Party which, after a resounding victory, formed the first non-Congress government in the state. They had come a long way from the 3 per cent of the popular vote they had won in 1952, for they were now the major constituent of the Janata Party.[24] Rajasthan's BJP government has had one of the longest runs among the non-Congress regimes in India. In the elections of 1990 the BJP again swept the polls in alliance with the Janata Dal and formed the government.

As a consequence of changes in the BJP's national policy, the attitude of the leadership of Hindu nationalism in the state has also changed, though it is still led by a known moderate within the BJP, Bhairon Singh Shekhawat. A decade or so ago, Jan Sangh leader, Satish Chandra Aggarwal, stepped in to prevent a conflict over the killing of some cows by a Muslim Kasai. 'The entire Muslim community cannot be expected to pay for what one Muslim has done,' he reportedly said at a public meeting. On another occasion, tempers were similarly cooled when a Muslim driver ran over some children. Today, even minor issues, such as a dispute between a shopkeeper and a customer, or a boy teasing a girl, tend to polarize a *mohalla*, Satyabhan Singh, Station House Officer (SHO) of the Ramganj police station, complains.

---

[24]In 1977 the Janata Party won 65.2 per cent of the votes. It fell to 31.7 per cent in the elections of 1980.

The huge success of the Ramshila Pujan in Rajasthan had much to do with this increase in communal tension. Rajasthan was one of the states which contributed the largest number of *shilā*s, 20,000, for the Ram temple. It also collected the largest purse, VHP's Jai Bahadur Shekhawat proudly claims. Unlike in Gujarat, much of the money came from the Banias, Brahmans and Rajputs, the dominant castes of Rajasthan and the VHP's main support base.

The Shri Ramshila Pujan Rath Yatra and the Shri Ram Mahayajna Rath Prasthan went along nine sub-routes in Rajasthan. As in Gujarat, the names of the *yātrā*s were carefully chosen, to define the VHP's inclusivity. The Ekalavya Rath that went through Banswada, Dungarpur and Udaipur appealed to the tribal, mainly Bhil, sentiments; the Vir Durgadas and Hadarani Raths, that travelled to Jodhpur–Nagaur and Kota–Bundi–Tonk respectively, invoked local Rajput heroes.

All nine *rath*s converged at Jaipur following shilapujan ceremonies at 26,000 places. Shilapujan and Mahayajna Samitis had been formed in each *prakhand* and each important village to organize the rituals and processions that passed through each lane and *mohallā*.[25] Pradeep Vyas, a Congress party worker, described his experience around Sanganer in the following words:

In each village a specially selected brick was placed in the Ram temple following worship. It was kept there for eight days. The order then came that all bricks be sent to the tehsil headquarters (Sanganer). In the village a *boli* (auction) was held. The wife of the person who made the highest *boli* (bid) was given the honour of carrying the brick on her head and leading the procession through the village. From each home people participated in the procession. They went through the village singing songs. The brick was then placed

[25]The VHP has divided India into 5 zones, 10 regions, 25 provinces, 210 divisions, 706 districts, and 7180 subdivisions. For the *pujan*, Rajasthan was organized into 3 zones (*sambhāg*s), 10 divisions (*vibhāg*s), 298 subdivisions (*prakhand*s), 2,980 *khand*s, and 14,900 *upkhand*s of 2,000 population each. Shilapujan was organized at 26,601 places from where 22,416 *shilā*s were sent to Ayodhya. In all over 10.2 million men and 7.1 million women took part. The VHP also held Shri Ram Mahayajnas at 318 places, large religious conferences at 653 places, and exhibitions at 104 places; 414 processions too were taken out. People from all over the state bought coupons worth 15.6 million rupees to assist the temple construction. Over 300 Muslims participated in the Shilapujan and offerings. '*Rajasthan main Shrirām Shilapujan*', *Shrirām Shilā Smārikā, Rajasthan*, p. 20. It was indeed a majestic organizational feat.

in a jeep and taken to the tehsil. All the bricks from all the villages were then loaded on to trucks.[26]

According to some eyewitnesses, the level of mobilization achieved through such programmes exceeded that achieved by the freedom movement.

Riots in Rajasthan

The first communal riot took place at Jaipur in November 1989.[27] It was preceded by a conflict on 6 October at Shastri Nagar, a new residential area dominated by Sindhis. Forced to migrate from Pakistan at the time of the Partition in 1947, the Sindhis are usually strong supporters of the BJP. The salience of Advani, a Sindhi, in the BJP has also given them a new stake in the party; it is not often that the numerically small Sindhi community throws up a national leader. The conflict began, the BJP spokesmen say, when a Muslim overturned the cart carrying sacred bricks for Ayodhya at the head of a procession.[28] Others claim that the cart was overturned by a local Sindhi leader of the BJP who wanted a communal altercation. The events then followed the standard pattern. The local BJP now insisted on taking the procession through Muslim areas and shouting 'provocative' slogans. Violence broke out in Jalupura and Kalyanji ka Rasta in the walled city. It was followed by the imposition of curfew for nine days. One person was killed.

The riot at Kota was said to have a similar beginning. On the day of the Anant Chaturdashi festival, the VHP says, the Muslims 'attacked' a Ganesh procession.[29] An article in a VHP journal, titled

[26]Vyas, while talking to one of us on 12 March 1992, added that the Rath Yatra touched the feelings of everyone, irrespective of party affiliation. Only later did some realize, Vyas said, that they had been duped.

[27]The Sampradayikta Virodhi Samiti, a voluntary organization fighting communal violence, calls this Jaipur's first communal riot. However, there had been communal conflicts in other cities of Rajasthan in the 1980s: at Beawar in 1986; at Sojat and Pali in 1987; at Makrana and Tonk in 1988; and at Bigodh, Kota, Fatehpur and Udaipur in 1989.

[28]The BJP testimony, filed by Ghanshyam Tiwari before the Tibrewal Commission on 13 December 1991 (Exhibit B-77), says the cart was overturned by the Congress-I which then led the procession with a new cart that deliberately passed through Muslim majority areas.

[29]As a VHP pamphlet put it, this was not unnatural, for 'the Muslims, true to their nature, began the riots all over the country.' *Shriram Shilā Smārikā, Rajasthan*, p. 3.

FIGURE 2
AREAS OF JAIPUR CITY AFFECTED BY VIOLENCE

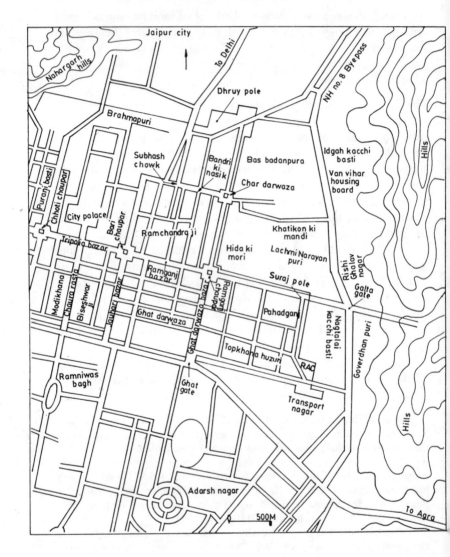

'Why do only Muslims begin Riots?', explains the riots of Varanasi, Sultanpur, Faizabad, Aligarh (UP), Munger (Bihar), Indore (MP) in terms of Muslim attempts to obstruct shilapujan processions.

Muslim sources in Kota say that the VHP, RSS, Bajrang Dal, Shiv Sena and several *akhādās* carrying a large number of weapons were part of the 10,000 strong procession. Those in the procession were shouting slogans such as *'Hindustan mein rahnā hai to Hindu bankar rahnā hogā'* (If you want to live in India, you will have to live like Hindus), and *'Bābar ki santānon ko Hindustan mein nahin rehne denge'* (We will not let Babar's progeny live in India).[30] Two persons were killed in the rioting according to official figures, and huge losses were sustained by the Dawoodi Bohra Muslim business community.

It was, however, the riot at Jaipur on 27 November 1989 that involved large numbers from both the communities. It came after the campaign for Parliamentary elections had already polarized Jaipur, with the BJP seeking Hindu votes to build the Ram temple at Ayodhya and the Congress being backed by the Muslims. The presence of the ultra-Hindu Shiva Sena had also heightened tension. Handsome contributions to the polarization were made by Chittaranjan Sharma, President of the Sena, through his speeches and pamphlets.[31] The riot itself was set off by the BJP's victory procession after the elections. The victors at Jaipur and Dausa, Girdhari Lal Bhargava and Nathu Singh, led the procession. A section of the procession under the leadership of Bhanwar Lal Sharma, President of the state BJP, after assuring the police that it would not do so, entered the 'communally sensitive' Ramganj area—with predictable results.

The First Information Report (FIR) filed with the police says that, although Sharma had between 1,000 and 2,000 followers only, they did not fail to repeat their favourite slogans: 'Every child is Ram's, the rest are bastards' and 'The Muslims have only two places, Pakistan or the cemetery'.[32] A mosque, too, was damaged at the Chandi ki Taksal. As the news spread in Ramganj, the latter part of the

[30]Asghar Ali Engineer, 'Kota: Another Graveyard of Secularism?' (Bombay: Institute of Islamic Studies, 1989), Occasional paper, No 12(5).

[31]Testimony of Dr Bhupendra of the Indian Police Service, Tibrewal Commission, 30 April 1992.

[32]FIR 410/1989 of Rajendra Tyagi, Sub-Inspector (SI), Ramganj police station.

procession was stoned.[33] A Hindu mob then looted and burnt the guns in Shikar store and a Muslim mob set fire and threw gas cylinders at the crowd. The Muslims burnt Hindu shops in Ghat gate and Ramganj; the Hindus reciprocated at Jauhari, Tripolia and Chand Pole markets.

Although the rioting and arson primarily affected the walled city, there were also attacks on individual houses in the outer city. At 5.30 PM, roughly two hours after the rioting broke out, curfew was imposed. Eventually the army was called in at 11 PM. The rioting left 5 persons dead and 200 seriously wounded. About 70 Hindu shops were looted or burnt; the Muslims lost 41 shops, 44 brick houses and 104 hutments.[34]

Next year a rash of violence broke out in Rajasthan following Advani's Rath Yatra. On 4 October there had already been rioting in Udaipur, and the political temperature in the state was still rising. The anti-Mandal agitation had spawned numerous organizations of students and traders. They were now remobilized under a different guise. The supporters of the ABVP among the youth were now part of an anti-Muslim formation whose influence had begun to sweep the middle classes, especially the young and the educated, as Advani's chariot proceeded on its 4,000-km journey from Somnath to Ayodhya.

As in Gujarat, plans for a grand reception to Advani went with other kinds of mobilizational efforts. The Ram Jyoti Shobha Yatras, for instance, were the reverse of the worship of the bricks; the *jyoti* or sacred light brought back from Ayodhya was used to light lamps in local temples, beginning with the highly venerated Govind Deo temple. A series of processions then went to the 56 subdivisions of the state. In each case, the Ram *jyoti* was kept in a prominent village and people were exhorted to light the lamps in their homes with the

---

[33]A human rights group points out that the first stone-throwing incident occurred approximately three hours after the slogans had begun to be raised. People's Union for Civil Liberties, 'The Jaipur Riots', *Lokayan Bulletin*, 1989, 7, pp. 43–4. According to the report the riots could have been averted had the district administration acted on intelligence reports, quoted even by the press, that anticipated communal tension in four cities in Rajasthan, and had the victory procession been banned in Jaipur as had been done in Udaipur, Sikar, Jalore and Bharatpur.

[34]PUCL, 'The Jaipur riots,' pp. 41–6.

sacred fire. While the welcome given to the Rath Yatra was organized by the BJP and to the *jyoti* by the VHP, the RSS busied itself with preparations for the *kārsevā* at Ayodhya. The Rajasthan Karseva Samiti declared that 1,00,000 youths would be sent for the *kārsevā*.[35] An Akhil Bharatiya Sarva Dharma Sammelan was organized on 6–7 October 1990 at Jaipur. It brought together BJP leaders of Delhi and Udaipur and several religious leaders. Subsequently, meetings of the 'Hindu society' were organized across the state.

From Gujarat Advani's chariot entered Banswara where chief minister Shekhawat and his cabinet went to receive it on 10 October. Shekhawat had been a strong critic of the Rath Yatra in private, like the party's well-known national leader, Atal Behari Vajpayee, an erstwhile foreign minister of India. Both were afraid that the Yatra would isolate the BJP politically and destroy its image as a responsible all-India party built assiduously over the previous fifteen years. But like Vajpayee, Shekhawat had to conform to the party line in public.

In two days the *rath* covered half a dozen districts of Rajasthan. The atmosphere, according to several Jaipur residents, had begun to deteriorate.[36]

As we know, Advani's arrest a few days later led to violence in many parts of the country, particularly in Gujarat, UP and Rajasthan. In Rajasthan clashes took place at Kota, Churu, Udaipur, Jaipur, Jodhpur and Beawar. At several places the army had to be called out. In Jaipur, on the day Advani was arrested, a meeting was held in the evening at the Choti Chaupar, and when the crowd dispersed, it shouted offensive slogans.

The next morning around 9 AM, as though in response to a signal, the burning of tyres began simultaneously at several main thoroughfares in many parts of the city: on Amber road and Subhash chowk in the north, Tonk road towards the south, the bridge of the Ajmer road, and behind the Governor's residence in the west, in Purani

[35]Later, returning *kārsevaks* were to be put in areas near Muslim *mohallā*s. See letter of Ghulam Mustafa, MLA, to the Chief Minister, 5 November 1990.

[36]It improved according to Ghanshyam Tiwari, as the *rath* came closer to Jaipur. See BJP affidavit, exhibit B-77, Tibrewal Commission. But there was certainly a determination among BJP cadres not to let violence take place when the *rath* was on the road.

Basti and on Agra road.[37] Also, large groups of people began gathering in the main streets of the walled city to enforce the BJP's call for a general strike. They moved about obstructing traffic, shouting slogans, and threatening the shopkeepers who had not downed their shutters.[38] By 9.30 AM, the crowds had grown larger. According to the BJP version, the rioting by the Hindus was sparked off by a rumour that Hindu children had been held captive in a mosque at Ramganj. This rumour was said to have sprung from an actual episode involving a struggle between some Muslim kidnappers, their screaming child victims, and a courageous *kārsevak* who had stepped in to save the children. People poured into the streets and moved towards Ramganj.[39]

Why were tyres burnt all over Jaipur? One answer is: the thick black smoke rising from burning tyres in different places could easily be seen from people's rooftops; it could be both dramatic and awesome. As for the captive children, the SHO of the Ramganj area said in his deposition to the Tibrewal Commission, set up to inquire into the riots, that he had checked the mosque and found no child there.[40] The kidnapping story, it appears, was planted.

The simultaneous burning of houses and shops in different parts of Jaipur also seems to have been planned. The 'style' of setting fire was similar: holes were made in the walls of houses and burning rags doused in kerosene thrown in. Some women reported seeing these rags being supplied by jeeps to various localities.[41] Besides, there was widespread use of audio cassettes, even after curfew was imposed on the city later in the day. As in 1989, the cassettes of Uma Bharati were used; in addition, this time some cassettes simulated scenes of riots: recorded voices shouted '*Allah ho Akbar*,' '*māro*

[37]Testimony of Jagmal Singh, Additional Superintendent of Police (north), Tibrewal Commission, 26 April 1992. See also the affidavits of Jagmal Singh and Hetram Vishnoi, SHO, Ramganj Police Station, exhibits FW28 and A18, Tibrewal Commission.

[38]Testimony of Hetram Vishnoi, 19 May 1992.

[39]Later, to establish that the kidnapping actually took place, the 'rescuer', Ashwini Kumar, was produced. But he was unable to explain during cross-examination why, despite his training in law, he had failed to register an FIR or report the matter to the police till more than a year had lapsed.

[40]This was also confirmed by the Additional Superintendent of Police (ASP) Jagmal Singh's testimony to the Tibrewal Commission, April 1992.

[41]The *Navbharat Times* (8 October 1990) reported that the simultaneity of incidents also created a special problem for the police.

māro' and *'Jai Siya Ram'*, followed by the voices of screaming women and children.[42]

In other words, as is usual with riots in India these days, the Jaipur riot was methodically planned and professionally executed. In this planning and execution, apart from some BJP leaders, important participants were from Jaipur's 92 *akhādā*s or wrestling clubs, especially the 14 or 15 branches of Balwant *akhādā*. Members of Balwant *akhādā* ransacked and burnt shops at Purani basti and Brahmapuri. More unusual, considering the by-now standardized technology of riots in the subcontinent, were the artificially produced clouds of smoke, the cleverly floated rumours, the use of audio-cassettes, in addition to the intense emotions aroused by the Rath Yatra.[43]

Let us get back to our story. At Ramganj bazar, the crowd by all accounts was initially a procession intent upon closing the few shops that had opened despite the call for a general strike.[44] It was shouting, according to police officials, *'mandir vahin banāyenge ...'* and *'Bacchā bacchā Ram kā, bāki sab harām kā'*—two slogans that had become hot favourites of the Hindu nationalists over the previous year. Stoning began either from Muslim houses reacting to the slogans or from the enforcers of the strike, keen to close Ramganj's Khan Hotel which refused to join the strike. By 10.30 AM, police reports say, a crowd of Muslims were also out on the streets. There was mutual stoning, abuse, attacks on shops, and arson. Both sides were well armed with bottles, iron rods, sticks and stones. At first, the police and administration mostly stood by. The Muslims say that the pro-strike crowd disappeared after the police arrived; it then became

[42]Affidavit of Abdul Bashir, C1 exhibit of Tibrewal Commission. Also, Binu Gupta's interview with Gopal Lal, Kumharon ki Nadi, Jaipur, 10 May 1992. Gopal Lal, a potter, claimed that cassettes were used by both Hindus and Muslims.

[43]Interview with K. B. Garg, Member, Coordination Committee for Relief, Rehabilitation, and Communal Harmony, Jaipur, March 1992.

[44]The owner of the Islamic Book Center recounted, 'We said "Why should we close? We shall not participate in the general strike. The organizers of the strike are against the mosque [at Ayodhya] and the Qur'an".' The owner of the book shop is one of the few members of the Jamaat-i-Islami in Jaipur.

However, in politics, even if it is the politics of religion, things are rarely that simple. According to Jagmal Singh, then Additional Superintendent of Police (North) in the Ramganj Chaupar area, Congress party members instigated the shopkeepers to keep their shops open, Tibrewal Commission, 25 April 1992.

a clash between the police and the Muslims.[45] Several Muslims claim that the SP himself shot Ishaq, a butcher, at point blank range at about this time. The police call Ishaq a rioter; the Muslims say he was an ordinary butcher, shot even as he was closing his shop.[46] A barber who was among the rioters at Ramganj and Hida ki Mori recounts, 'The police were with us and told us to go ahead: "Beat them up; we are with you." They [the police] gave us support; the Muslims could not do anything.'

Curfew was imposed only at 11.15 AM, after over two hours of violence (despite the prior warnings that the police and the administration had and despite a ready contingency plan prepared by the local SP on 20 October). But violence continued during the curfew. A police jeep was burnt almost next to a police station, though a force of 75 men was present right there. At Ramganj, to begin with, seven shops were burnt, six belonging to Muslims and one to a Hindu. The death of a police constable, Braj Mohan, started rumours that a Hindu policeman had been killed by Muslims even though he was the victim of a police bullet. Among the Muslims the rumour spread that Shahzad, a Muslim policeman, had been killed by Hindu rioters.

At about the time the general strike went out of control at Ghat gate, Hindus collected at Ghosiyon ka Rasta shouting, '*Tel lagāo Dabur kā, nām mitāo Babar kā*' (Use the oil of Dabur, erase the name of Babar), '*Hindustan mein rahnā hai to choti rakh ke rahnā hogā*' (If you have to stay in India, you shall have to sport a sacred tuft of hair), and '*Jo māngegā Bābri uskā bacchā ākhri*' (The child of anyone who asks for the Babri mosque will be the last of the lineage). The Muslims collected at the Machlivalon ka Rasta on the opposite side shouting '*Allah ho Akbar*' and '*Jo hamse takrāyegā, sīdhe kabr mein jāyegā*' (Those who clash with us will go straight to the grave). Despite police intervention, both sides returned with arms and began stoning and arson. Firing had to be resorted to.

Roughly at the same time violence also broke out at Bandri ka Nasik, Tripolia, Chaura Rasta and at the Jauhari, Kishan Pole and Chand Pole markets. Mostly young persons were said to be involved

---

[45]Hetram Vishnoi's FIRs, 449/1990 and 457/1990, 24 October 1990, Ramgunj Police Station.

[46]Affidavits of Naimuddin, Abdul Sattar and Gafur Khan, Tibrewal Commission.

on both sides, and there was much use of slogans. Once again, there were signs of prior preparation.[47]

In retrospect both sides see this riot as more lethal (*jāni*) than that in 1989 when the damage was mainly material. This time, besides the killings, there were a large number of incidents of knifing and acid throwing. The targets of attack were often religious places such as mosques and *dargahs*.[48] As in Gujarat, at several places they were converted into temples and renamed. For instance, Pir's *mazhar* at Kagdiwara was renamed Pir Pachar Hanuman and Gaffareshwar Mahadev was built on Gaffar's land. The official tally of the dead was 50. The loss of property was estimated at 1,000 million. The situation could be brought under control only after the army was called out.

The Police Narrative and Rishi Ghalav Nagar

The police narrative that emerges from the hearings of the judicial inquiry into the riots, now under way two years after the event, has a few clear components. First, the riot was sudden ('*ākasmik*') rather than planned or systematic.[49] So the police and the administration could not have anticipated or prepared for it. Second, not only were the losses of the Hindus and the Muslims equal, the two communities were present in roughly equal strength in all the areas where rioting broke out. For instance, the deposition of Satyendra Singh, a police officer, says that the crowd at Suraj Pole bazar consisted of Hindus and it faced the Muslims who flooded the streets of Ramganj bazar.[50] The police were caught between the two at the crossing.

Third, the action of the Hindus was retaliatory and defensive; all the FIRs except one implicate Muslims. Sub-Inspector Hari Narayan's testimony is a case in point. It blames the Muslims for the burning

[47]On the Muslim side, neighbourhood organizations played an important role; less important were political groups such as the Jamaat-i-Islami or the Muslim League. Interview with Hetram Vishnoi, SHO, Ramganj Police Station, 20 May 1992.

[48]The affidavits of Manoj Sharma and Pawan Kumar describe a large mob of between 2,000 and 3,000 Hindus moving towards New Gate and Phool Shah Baba ki Mazhar. Exhibit B-12, Tibrewal Commission, 13 October 1991.

[49]Statements of police officials at the Tibrewal Commission hearings during April 1992.

[50]Deposition of Satyendra Singh, Tibrewal Commission, 22 April 1992.

of the ASP's jeep[51]; and for beginning the sloganeering.[52] Only under cross-examination did Narayan admit that the crowd that initially burnt waste on the streets supported the general strike. He also acknowledged that they raised the slogan 'Use the oil of Dabur, erase the name of Babar.' Narayan, however, refused to confirm that the procession was led by BJP's Mohan Lal Yadav; he only said that the procession later fell into the hands of musclemen, as the BJP leadership 'lost control' over the processionists. Most police accounts also claim that the use of force by the police was 'sufficient' and 'effective'.

There is striking similarity between the constructions of the sequence of events by the police and the BJP. The BJP claims that the first day's violence was caused by the rumour that some Hindu children were being held captive in a mosque, the second day's by the news of the killing of seven persons at Koliyon ka Mohalla, headlined by the *Navbharat Times* on the morning of 25 October. Since the Mohalla had a predominantly Koli population, it was assumed that Hindus had been killed. The carnage of Muslims at Rishi Ghalav Nagar was explained away as a reaction to the killing of the Kolis. In the police version, the events of Rishi Ghalav Nagar are located in the evening; both Natwarlal and Hari Narayan explain Rishi Ghalav Nagar as a response to the happenings at Koliyon ka Mohalla.[53]

Others dispute this thesis. Many people in the Pahadganj area, who can see Rishi Ghalav Nagar in the distance from their rooftops, told us that they saw smoke rising and people moving about in groups between 9.00 AM and 11.00 AM. Civil liberties groups and the residents

---

[51]FIR 450/1990, 24 October 1990 of Hari Narayan, Ramganj Police Station, names Mazhar, Khurshid and Gomak. According to Narayan, a wild crowd at Ramganj was throwing stones and shouting slogans. After a lathi charge, there was stone throwing from the roofs. From Bisaytiyon ka Mohalla hundreds came armed with iron rods, bottles and lathis shouting *'Allah ho Akbar'* and *'Mār do mār do'*. They came to the main road and moved towards the main crossing, breaking shutters, throwing stones and setting shops on fire.

[52]Testimony of Hari Narayan, Tibrewal Commission hearings, 24 April 1992. Hari Narayan's one-sided account needs to be read along with Nanha Singh's FIR. The latter says that an excited crowd of 400 to 500 Hindus came from Ramganj to Suraj Pole shouting anti-Muslim slogans. See FIR 451/1990, 25 October 1990, of Nanha Singh, SI, Ramganj Police Station.

[53]Testimony of Jagmal Singh, Tibrewal Commission, April 1992.

of Rishi Ghalav Nagar, too, maintain that the events in their colony began early in the morning and were simultaneous if not prior to the incidents at Ramganj. One eyewitness was precise enough to say that the events began between 10 and 11 AM. The first body was found at the crossing of the Galta temple in Rishi Ghalav Nagar around noon.

Police testimony at the Tibrewal Commission hearings tries to cover up police inaction and the tacit police support to the Hindu rioters. As we found out, in one case, a policeman told a Muslim that day, 'Say "Jai Siya Ram" or we shall beat you'. Ashok Panchal, a self-confessed rioter, even named a policeman who told them, 'Go and grab guns from the police. In the course of the grabbing, we shall begin firing on the Muslims.' Panchal adds, 'We looted Muslim shops while the police fired on the Muslims. The SP shot a Kasai from the back as he was locking the shutter of his shop.'

Also, the reports which several victims wanted to lodge with the police were either disregarded, censored or edited by the police. In Rishi Ghalav Nagar, only one FIR was accepted. And Shabuddin, who filed it, does not recognize more than half the names of the accused in the statement he himself gave to the police.[54] The police, he insists, have added names that were in their diary. In another instance, a Muslim, who had a case involving a jeep pending against him at the police station, was forced to give a statement that the police came to the neighbourhood at 11 PM, when the residents openly say that they came much later in the night.

Rishi Ghalav Nagar is a JDA planned colony that came up in the 1980s. Originally the plots in it were given to the dwellers of various slums. Many, however, resold them to others who built houses. The plot owners then moved into hutments in a new slum in the same area. The Muslims who came into Rishi Ghalav Nagar range from the lowly to the fairly well-to-do. Several were in the gemstone business earning between 200 and 250 rupees per day. Among some Hindus in Rishi Ghalav Nagar there was a sense of being encroached upon, both geographically and economically. Their sense of space was also partly defined by Jaipur's sacred geography, especially by their proximity to the local Galta temple. But the growth of an aggressive Hindu self-definition was almost certainly a product of the Ramjanmabhumi movement, for at the local level the Hindus and the Muslims had been participating in a large number of co-operative activities,

[54]FIR 480/1990, 24 October 1990, of Shabuddin, Ramganj police station.

such as protests against poor water supply and absence of drainage facilities, the construction of a park, a tank and even a temple. Deep and enduring friendships had also developed between some Hindu and Muslim neighbours. In fact, the FIRs filed at the Ramganj police station from the area suggest many more conflicts within communities than between them. In 1989, when there was rioting elsewhere in Jaipur, both Hindus and Muslims of Rishi Ghalav Nagar had participated in a day-and-night vigil to maintain peace.

The demand for a local mosque by the Muslim leaders and the purchase by them of two plots for the purpose, however, re-invoked the controversy over the Babri masjid. To the Hindus the demand showed aggressive affirmation of Muslim identity and social cohesion, not religious sentiments or piety. The local Masjid Committee was strongly opposed by a group of Hindus led by Shyam Sunder Gupta and Mohanlal Sharma. The polarization was aggravated by local conflicts such as a brawl involving a drunken Muslim and some Dalits.[55] Simultaneously the new leadership of upper-caste and better-off Hindus established links with a wider network in the neighbouring areas. A skirmish was reportedly planned at a *goth* or feast hosted for several neighbourhood leaders at the temple of Kolevale Hanuman. A branch of the RSS became active in the area and was in the forefront of both the shilapujan and *kārsevā*, in both of which the local Hindus participated enthusiastically.[56]

On the eve of the general strike, Rishi Ghalav Nagar's Hindu homes were distinguished by decorative red lights and fluorescent stickers. Ganesh statues in niches over the front door (compulsory for the Hindus in this colony) also served the same purpose. The Muslims thus got automatically marked. In the walled city, communities and castes live together in clusters; modern living caters to the individual and the family but not to the security of the community. At Rishi Ghalav Nagar the 500 Muslim homes were scattered among the 2,000 Hindu homes. Not only that, but the geometrical patterns of crossings and lanes alternating with rows of houses could be particularly helpful to mobs. A mob standing at a crossing could effectively prevent escape and access to the outer world.

---

[55]FIR 354/1990, 19 August 1990, Ramganj police station.

[56]Rishi Ghalav Nagar had its own Shri Ram Karseva Samiti; grand preparations were made for welcoming it, and a huge religious conference was organized. *Navbharat Times*, 8 October 1990, p. 7.

On 24 October, at the major crossings on the National Highway, groups of people had collected by 11 AM, shouting '*Jai Shri Ram*'. According to an insider, RSS activists led the mobs drawn from the nearby areas of Govardhanpuri, Lachminarayanpuri and Ganeshpuri. They had the active support of persons from Rishi Ghalav Nagar, particularly of gangs whose leaders belonged to the Nav Yuvak Mandal. Another informant, Wazid Ali, confirmed the beginning of disturbances in the colony at around 11 AM. From the roof of his two-storeyed house he saw fire and smoke and 200 persons coming to the colony armed with lances, spears, swords and sticks. Persons from the locality were behind the outsiders, who had been positioned in front.

The mosque was smashed and Hindu icons placed in it. Muslim leaders of the Masjid Committee, who sought shelter in Gupta's house, were attacked.[57] One Shahid was surrounded and killed. His mother, who went to collect the clothes of her dead son from the hospital morgue, found those of her second son there as well. Yusuf had learnt of his brother's death and had come on a scooter along with a friend to take home his sister-in-law and her child. A mob stopped his scooter at a bridge and asked his name. As Yusuf's friend (who was with him on the scooter but managed to run away) tells the story, Yusuf mentioned a Hindu name but was asked to strip. When it was found that he was circumcised, acid was poured on him.

Salma, also called Munni, is a widow with three daughters and three sons. She was doing embroidery on a salwar-kameez when interviewed. Her gem-cutting machine had been destroyed by the rioters, apparently as part of a now-not-uncommon attack on the sources of livelihood of the Muslims.

They came at around noon while I was washing. They were shouting '*Musallā katallā, hum tumko jindā nahin chodenge*' (Circumcised Muslims, we shall not leave you alive). We locked ourselves in one room. I was so scared; I nearly fainted. My three young daughters and no man to protect us. They

[57]Gupta, an RSS leader and chief of the Shanti Samiti from Rishi Ghalav Nagar, was later arrested. His wife claimed that the Muslims had come shouting slogans and throwing stones and, later, dragged him and his daughter away. Gupta's affidavit states that the Muslims dragged him to the mosque; his screams brought his wife and friends to his rescue. Exhibit B31, Tibrewal Commission. Gupta's school-going son, however, gave away that Gupta's wife and sons had been been sent off a day earlier to his grandmother's place in anticipation of violence.

broke our lattice, windows, television set, electricity meter, and sewage pipe; they took the three *tolas* of gold and all the vessels I had collected for my two daughters' weddings. They broke my gem-cutting machine. I used to do turquoise cutting and get 50–60 rupees a day. All our family worked on it. Now for this golden thread embroidery I get only 25 for one set. We live in the dark as I have no money for the meter. I cannot send my seven-year-old daughter to school, because I cannot pay the 22 rupees that they are demanding as a deposit. My sons are learning gemstone work at Babu ka Tiba, Hida ki Mori and Ankur cinema. The *ustād* [master craftsman] gives them very little.

The attack on the Muslims—looting, arson and killings—started again around 9 PM and continued till 2 AM. The police knew of the killings by noon, but made no attempt to stop further violence. They had taken a round and had tea at Gupta's place at about 4 PM and that was that. All appeals to the Ramganj Police Station were ignored. The attackers, to judge by the list of those indicted, came from a variety of castes but were mostly young. A few of them were unemployed or had criminal records, but most were by no means poor. A prominent leader of the exclusively Hindu colony of Govardhanpuri describes how the attack on Rishi Ghalav Nagar was planned at the office of the BJP's 'anti-riot squad' called the Shanti Sena (Peace Brigade). The main gate of the office, known as Alakh Math, opened on to Rishi Ghalav Nagar. Previously it had been a temple of the Nath sampradaya. But Ramcharan Vyakul, a relation of the Bajrang Dal leader Acharya Dharmendra, had forcibly occupied it two months before the riot. When some questioned his illegal occupation of the temple and the destruction of the existing icons and sacred places— eleven of Rudra Mahadev or Siva, one of Devi and three *samādhis*— they were beaten up by the police. When the subject was raised in the Rajasthan Assembly, the temple was overnight declared a Shanti Sena office.

One by-product of the riots is the consolidation of the dominance of the Brahmans and the Banias in Rishi Ghalav Nagar, for many Muslims have sold their homes and moved out. Ironically, despite the mutual enmity of the Hindu and Muslim leaders on the issue of the mosque, some of them have got together after the riot to sell the plot meant for the mosque and re-register it, presumably to pocket the proceeds. Among the few exceptions to the general atmosphere of violence, suspicion, greed and conspiracy in Rishi Ghalav Nagar was a house where Hindu neighbours locked in some Muslims for safety and a row of houses inhabited by poor Dalits and Muslims where the Dalits either helped the Muslims or were themselves so terrified that they left their own homes. Elsewhere in Rishi Ghalav Nagar open involvement or a conspiracy of silence was more common. This is how part of a conversation between a Hindu couple, Rameshwar and Chatardevi, and one of us went:

Question: What happened at Rishi Ghalav Nagar?

Husband: We don't know. We were sleeping.

Question: But during the day did you hear anyone.?

Wife: I heard them say, 'kill kill'.

Husband: We don't know who they were, Hindu or Muslim. No we didn't hear anything.

Question: What were they shouting?

Wife: They were shouting slogans.

Husband: What do you know. Keep quiet.

Question: Did you see anything burning.

Husband: No nothing.

Wife: Yes, I saw, in the back lane. They were setting fire.

Husband: She is mad (*pāgal hai*).

Question: What time was this?

Wife: They came around 1 PM. Then they came again at 4.30.

Question: Didn't the police come?

Wife: The police? Only late at night.

The Newspapers and Mohallā Koliyon

The vernacular press contributed generously to the growth of communal hatred in Rajasthan by stoking ill-defined fears of the Muslims. Some wrote of the 'declining' ratio of Hindus to Muslims in the country and restated the stereotype that the Muslims, in contrast to the Hindus, did not practice family planning.[59] More lethal were, however, other kinds of lapses.

[58]For instance, see the editorial page article published just before the riots, titled 'Decreasing Population of Hindus in India', in the *Navbharat Times*, 4 October 1990.

For two days corpses were being hauled in from Rishi Ghalav Nagar but the media and politicians seemed possessed by the events in the Koli Mohalla.[59] Milap Kothari wrote in the *Rajasthan Patrika* of the 'funerals of the living' in the Koli Mohalla[60]; the same newspaper, when it came to the Muslim-dominated Pahadganj, wrote of the two-hours of firing (presumably by the Muslims) which killed one jawan of the Rajasthan Armed Constabulary. Was the news of Koli 'deaths' deliberately leaked by the police? One clue is the parallel between the newspaper reports and the FIR of Jagmal Singh, Additional SP (North), which mentions stoning and firing by the Muslims as a result of which constable Sada Sukh died. According to Singh, 'some person with the intention to kill the policeman fired and killed him.' That person later turned out to be not a Muslim but another RAC constable whose bullet had killed Sada Sukh.[61]

Similarly the seven persons killed in Topkhana Huzuri were instantly assumed to be Hindus. Mohalla Koliyan is in Topkhana Huzuri, one of the later *chowkris*. This is the heart of the gemstone area; the *jawahrat mandi* or traditional gem market is held here in which rough and finished gemstones exchange hands. The population is 90 per cent Muslim, many of them affluent Julahas. Mohalla Koliyan is an island of Kolis, a Dalit group, within Topkana Huzuri. When a newspaper carrying the headline 'Seven killed including two children in Koli Mohalla' was distributed in the area on 25 October, it was assumed that the Muslims were the culprits.[62] The Chief Minister immediately announced a compensation of Rs 100,000 for each person killed. Only much later did it become known that not a single Koli had been killed in the mohalla itself. By then the locality had become the locus of media attention, police protection, and relief.

Two Kolis were indeed killed, but that was in the Nathji ki Bagichi and in the carpet factory adjoining Mohalla Koliyon. A Hindu police constable, too, had been killed during an attack by the Rajasthan Armed Constabulary (RAC) on Muslim homes at Pahadganj. Pahadganj residents give a stark account of the RAC rampage in the

[59]For an example of this contrast, see *Rajasthan Patrika*, 25 October 1990.

[60]*Rajasthan Patrika*, 26 October 1990.

[61]On the other hand, the seven-year-old girl in the house where the incident took place was so terror-stricken by Sada Sukh's behaviour with the women and children that she broke down while describing him to us.

[62]See front pages of both *Navbharat Times*, 25 October 1990 and *Rajasthan Patrika*, 25 October 1990.

area. On the other hand, in an adjacent lane, three of the seven Hindus allegedly killed belonged to a single Muslim family, that of Qazi Daud Khan who had been burnt alive in their jeep. Several persons interviewed alleged the involvement of two Nepali brothers, Manoj and Dinesh Thapa, whose father worked for the RAC and maintained links with the RAC camp.

Previously there were between 2,000 and 3,000 houses in the Koli Mohalla; they are now deserted. The Kolis say that the Muslims first assured them of their security, then suddenly turned on them and burnt their homes after returning from *namāz*. But some questions remain. First, photographs and other evidence suggest that the Kolis had been evacuated by the RAC on the morning of the 24th itself. The evacuation began at 11 AM and continued till 2.00 PM, whereas Koli homes were set on fire just before 4 PM. Second, the police for some reason did not record the testimony of the mother and sister who according to them were eyewitnesses to the killing of the Koli in the Bagichi.[63] There is also the strange case of Nauliya, a Koli, who burnt his own house to get compensation. He was persuaded to do so, some sources say, by an RAC tenant.

Did the Kolis then burn their own houses with the assistance of RAC personnel after their families were in safe custody in the nearby RAC camp? Several informants held that the burning of the Koli homes did not do much damage and left the structures of the houses intact. Almost immediately after the riot these homes were sold to the local Muslims for prices up to Rs 4,00,000. The Kolis were given

[63] On the whole, the police have tended to disparage women's testimony on the 1990 riots. Radheshyam Pujari and Nandram were killed in the presence of their mother and sister respectively. But Nandram's sister Shanti's version was ignored. Interestingly, she had sought protection with a Muslim family for 4 to 5 days. Instead of the testimony of these two women, we have the affidavit of Kesar Lal, Nandram's brother, who claims to have seen it all till the police arrived. Exhibits B-1 and B-2, Tibrewal Commission. Oddly enough, the police FIR did not note his presence. Was Kesar Lal really an eyewitness?

At Pahadganj, too, the police did not record the testimony of the Muslim woman in whose house the RAC constable had been shot dead. Again, at Rishi Ghalav Nagar, a woman's account of how her husband was killed, and the identity of those who stripped her naked and left her with a dozen or so corpses in the dry rivulet behind Rishi Ghalav Nagar, could have been critical. The police say she was not approached because she was *manda buddhi* (dim-witted).

alternative residential sites at Jamdoli, in close proximity to Keshav Vidyapith, an élite RSS school.

Sources of Violence and Resistance

The Jaipur riot was shaped by public responses to three issues that have during the previous five years deeply affected the political culture of Rajasthan: the Deorala sati, the Mandal Commission recommendations, and the Ayodhya temple controversy. Each led to the mobilization of new sections for political purposes and spawned organizations such as Sangharsh Samitis and Dharma Raksha Senas. They introduced a new idiom and a certain frenzy in Rajasthan politics.

The pro-sati movement tried to tighten Rajput solidarity cutting across clans and lineages, and sought to form a broad coalition with the Hindu and Jain mercantile castes and with chunks of Rajasthan's culturally insecure and defensive middle class, particularly students, retired government servants, and army personnel.[64] The anti-Mandal and Ram mandir agitations appealed to increasingly larger constituencies.

The emergence of these constituencies has coincided with the gradual merger of different narratives on Hindu–Muslim relations originating from the ruling party, the written media and the police. This has given a new meaning to the role of the state in communal

[64]The Jaipur riots were contextualized by the larger political process in Rajasthan and the attempts of some social groups to rectify their perceived marginalization. For the preceding thousand years or so the region was marked by Rajput rather than Brahmanical dominance in the princely states. See on this, Iqbal Narain and P.C. Mathur, 'The Thousand Year Raj: Regional Isolation and Rajput Hinduism in Rajasthan before and after 1947', in Francine R. Frankel and M. S. A. Rao (eds), *Dominance and State Power in Modern India: Decline of a Social Order* (Delhi: Oxford University Press, 1990), Vol. 2, pp. 1–58; and Suzanne H. Rudolph and Lloyd I. Rudolph, *Essays on Rajputana* (New Delhi: Concept, 1984).

During the freedom movement Rajput hegemony was challenged by Congress-affiliated praja mandals and parishads under largely Brahmanic leadership. Although in the three decades following independence Congress stayed in power, in 1952, 1957 and 1967, the ex-rulers and large landlords made major dents in the Congress support-base. The Congress came back dramatically on a populist platform, cornering most lower-caste and minority votes in the elections of 1971 and 1984. The marginalization of the Rajputs seemed complete, until the Deorala sati gave them an opportunity to remobilize.

politics. And not only has a distinct police narrative on the riots taken shape, but it has begun to provide a defence of the police and Hindu nationalism in urban violence. As in Gujarat, the state-police-local media narrative in Rajasthan, too, has begun to cohere with the narrative of the more articulate among the lower castes. The theme of the Muslim-as-a-traitor is pervasive in a large number of FIRs filed by the Kolis. 'First the Muslims reassured us and then attacked us after their return from the *namāz,*' is the bottom line.[65] The theme recurs in the Banjara basti, Suraj Pole bazar and Mina Mohalla affidavits. It could simply be an attempt to please the BJP regime of the state and profit from it. It could be an attempt to justify the hostility in the lower castes towards the upwardly-mobile Muslims; Koli accounts did frequently refer to the multi-storeyed houses that the Muslim gemstone dealers had been able to make at Topkhana Huzuri. However, as in Gujarat, in Rajasthan, too, the growing distance between the underprivileged castes and the Muslims is partly a product of the serious efforts made by the RSS family to accommodate the former within the Hindu fold on a new basis, as in fact the fighting arm of Hinduism, and to give them a new feeling of social worth as Hindus.

The converging narratives of the RSS family, the police and the local press also draw upon the changes introduced by the recent riots into Jaipur's urban geography. The last two years have seen much cross-migration in the city. There are now only a few Muslim families in Rishi Ghalav Nagar. Some have needed great persuasion to stay, others are waiting for a decent price before selling their houses. In the Bhishti Mohalla, a Muslim area, six Hindu families have moved out and only one remains. In Mohalla Koliyan not a single Koli can be found; the houses have all been sold to Muslim occupants. This despite a complete ban on the registration of such distress sales by the district administration. Jaipur is fast becoming a city of *mohallā*s organized on religious rather than occupational lines, akin to the black or white neighbourhoods of the North American cities. Many call the areas beyond Rishi Ghalav Nagar 'Pakistan', as they include Bas Badanpura, Idgah and Van Vihar. Around it lie the Hindu areas:

---

[65]See Chunni Lal's and the large number of near-identical Koli affidavits that uniformly harp on the theme of weak Hindus surrounded by Muslims. Likewise, Ganesh Narain Mina's affidavit complains of how after namāz the Muslims attacked at the Balaji ki Kothi rasta. Exhibits B15, B16, B17, B18, Tibrewal Commission, 10 December 1991.

Govindpuri, Lachminarayanpuri, Mandi Khatikan and, now, Rishi
Ghalav Nagar. Similarly, some of the outlying areas of Jaipur—Man-
sarovar, Raja Park, Jawahar Nagar and Shastri Nagar are now almost
exclusively Hindu and identified as BJP bastions. The walled city is
not only Hindu but also upper-caste dominated. Such communally
homogeneous neighbourhoods *do* give people a sense of security, but
they also reduce the everyday interactions that at one time were a
long-term safeguard against stereotypy.

The gemstone industry, traditionally a meeting ground of people
from different faiths, is also being affected by the changing political
culture of Rajasthan. Some Bania and Jain traders are training Hindu
craftsmen to take the place of the Muslims.

The emerging 'master' narrative is also shaped by the inter-genera-
tional contradictions within the communities. During the riot itself
there was conflict between younger leaders of the Mochis and the
biradari's elders. As for the Muslims, earlier the Muslim League in
Jaipur barely managed to get enough votes in elections to save its
security deposit, but the fanaticism of the Bajrang Dal youth is now
sought to be matched by the Students Islamic Movement of India
(SIMI) and the Students Islamic Organization of India (SIO), the
youth wing of the Jamaat-i-Islami which has gained a foothold in
areas like Topkhana Huzuri. The master narrative, if one ignores its
community-specific contents and focuses on its demonology, is finding new adherents among the Muslims, too.

Mutuality and Survival

Two issues remain to be discussed. The first of them can be posed
in the form of a question. Does the term 'communal riot', which we
have ourselves used throughout this book, describe adequately what
happened at Jaipur on 24 and 25 October? The media play up the
violence in their reports on death, arson, and aggressive assertion of
ethnic barriers. But a closer scrutiny of the violence itself reveals the
riot to be an omnibus expression for a variety of conflicts, not all of
them communal. In Jaipur, the violence served as a rubric under
which many diverse motives could find place. These motives ranged
from the eagerness to settle personal scores or oust one's tenants to
open greed and plunder. (The frankness with which some of the
rioters confessed that they had been motivated by the prospect of a
good loot surprised at least one of us during the fieldwork.) To

categorize such a riot as 'communal' only strengthens the popular middle-class belief in India that there are inexorable divides among communities and that religious identities, especially when brought into public life, are a constant source of conflict.[66]

Second, obscured by the dominant narrative and its authors in Rajasthan, there *is* the mutuality between persons who helped, re-assured, protected each other, and shared the moments of immense fear and anxiety. That mutuality was not based on modern, secular ideologies but on values derived from the same 'primordial' religious sentiments that were mobilized to sanctify the violence of the riots. In neighbourhood after neighbourhood one heard of people risking their life and their own well-being for the sake of others. At Koliyon ki Kothi the women reported how their Muslim neighbours protected them, saying 'We are between you and the attackers; nothing will happen [to you]'; near the Pahadganj park a Muslim boy saved an old Hindu woman who would have otherwise died, from mob fury. From Rishi Ghalav Nagar three orphaned children came to the Shamins for shelter; a Dalit family had taken care of them till it was safe to move out.[67] Shanti, whose brother had been killed (presumably by a Muslim) found it safest to stay with Baba Mohammed Sahab for four to five days. An unknown Hindu *tongawala* helped Moham-mad Naimuddin to escape after a crowd shouting '*Jai Shri Ram*' had caught hold of his cycle and beaten his friend Siraj to death with sticks and iron rods. Later Naimuddin was able to bring the police to the Galta crossing where Siraj's body was lying.[68]

Most of the survivors of Rishi Ghalav Nagar received help and protection from members of the other community. Hammu, whose wife and brother-in-law were killed, found shelter at the home of a Sikh; Hammu's children were brought to the safety of a relative's place by one Raju Pandit.[69] Darbar Ali's daughter, Tahira, was saved even as his son was killed and he was brutally assaulted; Shabuddin's aunt was killed as he himself would have been had it not been for

[66]As for the 'fundamental' communal divide, the fact remains that barely three weeks before the Rath Yatra, using the same strategy of political mobi-lization, the upper castes had sought to divide the Hindus to protect their privileges against affirmative action by the state in favour of the lower castes. Only with the court's stay order on the issue could the time become opportune for using the idiom of Hindu unity.

[67]Interview of Ms Shamin by Mamta Jaithly, 6 November 1990.

[68]FIR 456/1990, 24 October 1990, Ramganj Police Station.

[69]FIR 480/1990 of Shabuddin, 24 October 1990, Ramganj Police Station.

two Khatiks who hid him and then misdirected the rioters. At Abdul Hakim's house, Hakim himself and several persons belonging to a Pinnara family lay dead but his children were sheltered by a Dalit woman who worked for the family; her daughter suckled Hakim's child even though her own son was on the rampage with the rioters. This was not the only case; in some other instances too, help and shelter came even from persons and families responsible for the violence. Gupta, the local BJP leader had tacitly supported the violence, but he also locked in his neighbours, Ali Sher Khan and his family, to protect them from the rioters.[70] And Khan's family was rehabilitated with the help of Deepak Purohit, gemstone dealer and employer of Khan's son. 'He was an angel (*farishtā*) for us,' says Khan.

Adjacent to Rishi Ghalav Nagar is the colony's extension where families belonging to different faiths had been living together for a longer period; many of them had been shifted from the Surya Nagar slum, following the floods of 1981. Here the rioters were not even allowed to enter the neighbourhood. Many Muslims of the area vivid-ly remember the efforts of their neighbours to protect them. One such survivor is Yusuf Ali. He recalls that Ram Narayan, a local tough belonging to the Khatik caste, almost single-handedly confronted a crowd of some 200 rioters who came to the neighbourhood. 'Go away,' he shouted at them, 'all houses are ours; no one will do any-thing.' Ram Narayan, Ali adds, was a feared 'history sheeter', a man with a criminal record. He ran a taxi, lived in a hut near Ali's house and often came to take water from Ali. His attitude mattered. Together with Lalchand, a Khatik meat seller, and a Punjabi called Harishji, he refused to allow rioting in their area.

There are other instances, too, where a little personal courage paid rich dividends, as if the mobs were unable to handle resistance and waited to be hoodwinked or defied. When a mob banged on the door of Shafiquddin and shouted, 'We will burn you alive if you don't open up,' he opened the door to find a large number of armed men. His neighbours who were with the crowd whispered to him, 'Just do as we say. Say Ram Ram.' He did so. They took him with them around the corner. After a while, the neighbours told him 'Now you

[70]In the course of an interview on 16 July 1992, Ali Sher Khan remem-bered: '[Gupta said], "*Chacha*, you sit here quietly. Nothing will happen to you." ... There had been *mohabbat* (affection) between us. When I was doing my tailoring, I would supervise the construction of his house. Gupta and Dhan Singh were my good friends till the issue of the mosque arose in the colony.'

fall behind and slip away. We shall do the explaining.' They apparently told the leaders of the mob later that though he was a Muslim he was a good man. When the rioters went to the next person's house he ran back.

Razia's account re-lives that night of terror for her three children and extended family staying in four houses at Surya Nagar and their survival, made possible by Hindu families in the neighbourhood. At about noon, Razia's family had seen the dense black smoke rising from seven to eight places in the city.

Then we saw between 100 and 150 young, low caste men, between the ages of 18 and 25 years, armed with sticks. I did not recognize them; they were from outside the colony.... at the crossing, they asked which were the Muslim houses. 'No one lives here', our *mohalla* people told them. One was Kajod, who works in the Collectorate, Jai Singh, a tailor master and Babu Lal Bijwala.

All of Razia's family collected in her house. They locked themselves in. An hour later, at about 1.30 PM a child came running to then and said that he had seen the local mosque burning and one person being killed. Razia's younger brother and sister's husband went to see what had happened. They were spotted, but they managed to escape through a lane to Babubhai's house. Then in the evening around 7 PM, Razia needed some milk powder for the children. Her sister's baby was only one year old. Some eight to ten 'boys' standing there recognized her brothers and her sister's husband. They followed them, caught them and asked them their names; Mahesh and Rakesh, they replied. But while replying Razia's brother hesitated. That was a dangerous slip. 'Where do you live?' the boys now asked. At Kajod's, the two answered. The boys did not believe them and so followed them. Razia immediately opened the door and let them in. Let her tell the rest of the story in her own words:

The boys then started banging the door with sticks, yelling 'Muslims come out.' A crowd of about a hundred collected with swords, cycle chains and iron rods. We went to the roof and four of us women jumped over to the Kajods' roof. We hid among the goats but they had seen our shadows and started shouting. We went down to the Kajods' house all of us crying. They made us wear *ghagrā-lugdi* [women's wear more frequently worn by Rajput women in Rajasthan] and said, 'You are with us. Nothing will happen. We shall not allow the heat to touch you–*anch nahin āne denge*.' Then Kajod went and spoke to them and told them, 'Leave them they are good people, else you will have to deal with us.' After that the police jeep came and the rioters ran away. This was at about 8.30 at night.

Later Kajod told us, 'Our house is now unsafe.' He took us to Jai Singh's next door. But the men had seen us and we jumped onto the Sindhi's roof. He locked us inside for the night. They came again at 9.30 PM. All night we heard cries and saw people with torches burning houses. In our colony people sat at the crossing all night so that nothing would happen. No one came that night. At 5.30 AM we left for Pahadganj where my *devar* lives. Jai Singhji and the Sindhi had come to leave us. At the crossing five persons with sticks and *lutiyās* stopped us. They said, '*Bolo Jai Siyā Ram.*' All of us said '*Jai Siyā Ram.*' Then they let us go. We were again stopped at the *mandi* and said '*Jai Siyā Ram.*' A little ahead we told them, 'Now we are in the Muslim area. Go back now.' We stayed two months at Pahadganj, then went to Sanganer, then Tonk for three months. The people of our colony asked us to return but we are afraid. We rented, then bought a house at Van Vihar. Our colony people are very good. They still come to see us on festivals, our children tie *rākhis* on them.[71]

The fate of Jamil, too, was decided by his Hindu neighbours. Pappu, the young son of Chatar Singh, came to know of the presence of a lone Muslim tenant in a neighbouring house. While a crowd was shouting '*Jai Shri Ram*' and banging at his door, Chatar Singh and another neighbour, Babulal Bijwala, leapt across the roof and persuaded Jamil to open the backdoor. 'We dragged Jamilbhai to safety,' Pappu says. For two days Jamil was kept in Babulal's house in his daughter-in-law's room, where she had just delivered a baby. Jamil was shaven clean and presented as her uncle who had come from outside. When he left, Pappu's mother, Premdevi, put a ritual mark of *tilak* on his forehead and tied *kalava* (sacred thread) on his hand, to make him look like a Hindu and, perhaps less intentionally, to protect him by providing him with a 'magical' guard.[72]

We talked to Premdevi, a devout Hindu and naturally confident of the breadth of her piety. It was from her 'low-brow' piety that she drew her public norms.

I follow all Hindu *devatā*s and I also believe in Muslim gods. I believe in Ajmer's Khwaja saheb and Sayyad baba. You find his *sthān*s everywhere; he fulfils all desires and brings peace of mind. I even follow the *isāi devata*s [Christian gods] like Ishāmasih and Guru Nanak. The gods tell us to do one's *karma*. They were men but great men and we must fold our hands. All people who do good work must be worshipped. There are fanatics in all communities, whether Hindu or Muslim. Compassion is within all individuals.

[71]Razia Sultan on 30 April 1992.

[72]Interview with Ismail Khan, landlord of Jamil's house, 30 April 1992. Khan's family, like six other Muslim householders in the same lane, has sold its house.

'Should there be a temple or a mosque at Ayodhya?' we asked. Prem-devi said: 'The best thing will be if both the mandir and the masjid remain. They are god's homes, not made to be destroyed. The *janmabhumi* controversy is a fight for the chair among leaders, and the poor die.'

In the same neighbourhood lived Gangadevi, the wife of Babulal Bijwala. She recounted her family's close relations with the Muslim Manihar family she had been so protective towards:

For 20 years we lived together in the *basti* below in huts. They [the Manihar family] had a hutment and so did we. Then they were allotted a plot. We had very good relations with them, no sense of being Hindu or Muslim. We came here in 1973 and lived together after that. There was affection between us. When I faced a problem—for instance, when my child had an accident on Moharrum—Munna [their eldest son] rushed her to the big hospital. She had come under a truck when she was going with her grandfather to see the *tāzia*. She was saved but her foot was cut; she has an artificial foot. So we shared each other's sorrows and joys.

Like others, Gangadevi was shocked that religious violence had erupted in Jaipur at all. 'This is the first time I've heard of such a thing [the riot]. But nothing happened in our neighbourhood.' She seemed unaware that the violence did not touch her neighbourhood because some like her had taken a position:

When we heard of Jamil, we jumped across and fetched him. We were so scared, we thought someone might kill us.... My elder son had gone to Ayod-hya for *kārsevā*—he ran away ... I had the responsibility of my daughters-in-law and grandchildren. I don't go anywhere, to any temple. My temple is in my home where I worship all gods. For Ram and Rahim I light *agarbattis*, [incense sticks], for Sayyad baba I light an *agarbatti*.

I said to Jamil, 'see son, you are just like this son [of mine] here.' Then I gave him tea and dinner. If anyone asked, I said, 'He is our guest, my daughter-in-law's uncle from Delhi.' The next day my nephew came to sell some newspapers. I told him to leave Jamil at Galta Gate....

After eight or ten days his [Jamil's] relatives and his mother came to thank me. Possibly it is due to their *duā* (blessing) that my son returned from Ayod-hya where so many died. His mother said, 'you have saved my son, your son will also come back safe.' He [the *kārsevak* son] is not in the BJP but went because of his friends; he was only twenty. The police came to leave him in a car. He said, 'I was put in jail.' I said 'good, even better if they'd broken your limbs. Here you come back after twenty-two days, and you knew your wife was going to have a baby.'

... I was going mad. Some strangers would pass by our house saying 'they are coming. Coming in a bus, in a truck.' I said 'let them come. I was so sick of the rumours.' We were all together, the people of this colony. We'd been together for twenty years. But who listens to poor people? Our daughter was killed for dowry. It is now one and a half year; the police don't listen. She was hanged by her husband and in-laws, Agarwals of our own caste. Who bothers? ... our Muslim neighbours left the colony even though we did not want them to. But when our daughter was killed by her in-laws, they all came to share our sorrow.

Such experiences allow one not merely to relive the fear and the trauma that persons or families lived through, but also their survival through their community ties with concerned Hindus. These ties manage to cross even ideological divides—the mother of a *kārsevak* protects his declared 'enemy', and the enemy's relatives in turn come to offer their blessings for the safe return of the *kārsevak* from his mission of destroying the enemy's place of worship. We end this part of our story with the account of an interview with a group of Kolis in mid-1992 that shows the complexity of social relationships that religion *qua* ideology has still not been able to linearize.

'The Muslims killed many,' Dalchand Koli began, 'Eight to ten corpses were found, all after the curfew was lifted. They had been so badly burnt by Muslims they were unidentifiable.'[73] Nathuram, a more elderly Koli, gently corrected him, 'No, two were killed.' Keshav Lal said, 'We learnt that Koli houses had been burnt. My son and his friend went to the park to see what had happened. He saw thousands of Muslims. As he was running away, another group of Muslims surrounded him. He was stabbed. Another was hit by an iron rod.' However, the women of Koli households had a different story. One said, 'Of the two who had gone to investigate and were injured; one was a Hindu, the other a Muslim.' Hemlata remembered that the crowd had come shouting '*Jai Shri Ram*'. She added, 'The Muslim who lives in the house across us, Rais, who does gemstone work, protected us.' Toshibai, her mother, confirmed her account, 'The Muslims did nothing to us. They did not burn my house, break anything. During curfew Rais and Jumma came to our home, sat with us, and helped us.' Keshav Lal, a Koli whose son had been stabbed, was treated by Seraj, the Muslim doctor at what is called the Mahavaton ki Dispensary.[74]

---

[73]Kesar Lal's affidavit is similar. It says that the Muslims set fire to Koli homes so that 'several were burnt alive'. Exhibit B-1, Tibrewal Commission.

[74]Dalchand acknowledged his good work among the poor as he charges only Rs 3 per person irrespective of religion.

At several Koli homes, machines for *bindai* indicate their shift from unskilled labour (*beldāri*), which fetches between 30 and 40 rupees a day, to the gemstone business. They get their work from local Muslim manufacturers. Dalchand refers to his patrons as 'Rajak bhai' and 'Babu bhai'. 'Are they Hindus?', we ask him. 'No they are Muslims.' The Muslims he feels are '*milansar*' (friendly); at least their older folks are.

If we don't go to their weddings and festivals then they send us food.... Its the *Bāman-Baniās* [Brahmans and Banias] who practice *chchuā-chchut* against us.... Now see what a struggle it is to get a *piao* [drinking water kiosk] at Manak Chowk. But the Banias of Jauhari bazar, the *sethlog*, refuse to permit the release of the order [to set up a kiosk].'

We shall return to this theme of community and survival in the next section.

CHAPTER FIVE

IX. The Aftermath and the Ruins—I

On 29 October 1991, we were at Ayodhya again. This time the VHP and the Bajrang Dal, with support from the rest of the RSS family, had planned a 40-day-long sacrificial ritual called Bajrang Rudra Yajna. Since Ayodhya had become the focus of an agitation in 1990, this was the first time that the RSS made its presence known openly and visibly. The Yajna was to be followed, starting 27 November, by a Ram Yajna.[1] A four-day meet was organized as a part of the first Yajna to propagate the cause of the *parivār*. Of these four days, the first (30 October) was designated as *shaurya divas*, the day of valour, and the fourth (2 November) as *shraddhā divas*, day of respect. Both were meant to honour those who had fallen martyrs to the cause of the new Ram Temple at Ayodhya between 30 October and 2 November in 1990. Presumably, keeping in mind the press and other sundry demands of high politics in India, the Gregorian calendar had to be used instead of the Indian for deciding the dates of the yajna.

We listened to five of the speeches and the chairman's frequent brief interventions on the Day of Valour at the newly established Karsevakpuram, a temporary campus or mini-township established at Ayodhya for the participants in the Yajna and for housing the *kārsevaks* from all over India. The township had its own checkposts, passes, including passes for parking space, and even a public relations office. It had two retail booksellers and a separate tent where the yajna was being actually conducted but which seemed to elicit little interest. One of the two booksellers was a Bengali RSS activist from Allahabad, deeply committed to the unification of all Hindus. But her Bengali cultural chauvinism was not dead. Her mournful refrain

---

[1]The Ram Yajna was subsequently cancelled because the organizers feared that it would tire out the *kārsevaks* and other outsiders who had been in the city already for 40 days.

during our chat was the 'backwardness' of the Uttar Pradeshis, specially the Uttar Pradeshi women, and their lack of knowledge as well as interest in the 'unhappy' situation of the Hindus.

The pandal where the meeting was held and the speeches delivered was a large one, with sitting space for roughly 12,000 people. On the Day of Valour it was about one-fourth full and, though the crowd was sometimes enthusiastic, it could hardly be called frenzied or even forbiddingly aggressive. The speeches, however, made up for the absence of fanatic listeners; they were fiery in the old oratorial style. Unfortunately for the press and outside visitors, they were also variations on a single set of arguments and soon became tiresome.

Two or three recurrent themes characterized them. All the speakers emphasized the intrinsic tolerance of Hinduism and the Hindus and, predictably, some of the speakers used that to 'prove' Hinduism's intrinsic superiority over other religions. Most speakers reminded the audience of the VHP's claim that, while historically speaking 3,000 Hindu temples had been destroyed or desecrated by Muslims, the VHP was demanding the return of only three. The sole variation on this theme was in the speech of a non-resident Indian from Britain, one Mr Khanna, who was introduced as a functionary of the VHP in England. He said that if non-violence did not work, the movement would have to take to violence. He claimed that 20,000 temples were due to the Hindus from the Muslims, but they were claiming only three of them. And if the three were not returned, 20,000 mosques would have to be destroyed. Probably, being an expatriate, Mr Khanna was not that well-informed about the changing currents of Indian politics. He said things which the more hard-boiled political kinds avoided. We shall come back to this.

A second important theme was Mulayam Singh Yadav. He was repeatedly described as a Ravan who had insulted and humiliated all Hindus by organizing state repression of the *kārsevak*s at Ayodhya the previous year. Virtually all speakers claimed that the Day of Valour would go down in the history of India as a day as important as Vijaya Dashami, the final day of the Durga puja as well as a day that celebrates the triumph of Ram over Ravan. This was because a demon as dangerous as Mulayam Singh had been defeated on that day by Ram himself. And his demonic pride, that had led him to say that not even a bird in flight could get near enough the disputed structure to touch it, lay shattered.[2] The same fate had befallen his minister Azam Khan (also a member of the Babri Masjid Action

Committee) who had declared that any eye raised at the mosque (presumably with the intention of demolishing it) would be pulled out; when the day of reckoning came, not merely were thousands of eyes raised at the mosque but saffron flags were flown atop it.

There were some wild exaggerations in this context, too. Two of the speakers mentioned the hundreds of thousands of *kārsevaks* who had descended upon and fought at Ayodhya in October 1990.

Strangely, some of the strongest attacks and epithets were reserved for Vishwanath Pratap Singh, the erstwhile prime minister. Though Mulayam Singh and Vishwanath Pratap had already fallen apart politically and were now in opposite camps, they were usually clubbed together. The latter was depicted as the political twin of Mulayam Singh and as a dedicated enemy of Hindu nationalism. He was sometimes referred to as *Bhi Bhi Singh* (cowardly lion, a pun on his name), *paidāishi andhā* (congenitally blind) and *dāsiyon kā dās* (a servant of maid-servants) and ridiculed as a lover of Muslims, a protagonist of minorityism, and as the authentic progeny of Babar. One speaker, Shakti Swarupji Maharaj from Gujarat, accused him of implementing the Mandal Commission Report to divide the Hindus. (The Maharaj was introduced to the audiences as the rightful inheritor of Vallabbhai Patel's legacy, as he was now repeatedly doing in the rest of Gujarat what Patel had done at Somnath; namely, the Maharaj was trying to rebuild temples destroyed by medieval Muslim invaders from outside India.)

Comparatively, the Congress-I party and the Muslims were attacked or ridiculed much less: The reasons for this were not very clear. Perhaps, it was easier to attack someone with a strong ideological posture, rather than a political party that seemed to have a diffused ideological commitment. As for the Muslims, at that point in time they probably appeared less dangerous than the 'hidden internal' enemy. The attack on V. P. Singh was particularly vicious because

[2]On the day the results of the state elections in UP were declared in 1991 and the BJP was declared the winner, the party's president as well as some of its major functionaries were interviewed on camera for the television by anchorman Pranay Roy's team presenting the election results. All the BJP leaders openly admitted that Mulayam Singh Yadav had served as the greatest benefactor of the BJP by his unthinking, crudely provocative stance and total dependence on the coercive power of the law-enforcing machinery of the state.

he perhaps posed, in the eyes of the Sangh family, a greater electoral threat than Mulayam Singh at that point of time. Also, the family probably perceived Mulayam as a local, short-term threat, Vishwanath Pratap as a long-term, country-wide threat. The latter after all was the supremo of a party in alliance with the 'pseudo-secularist' Left parties (in turn seen as particularly dedicated enemies of the family) and seemed to command the allegiance of a majority of the Muslims.

It is even possible that Vishwanath Pratap was seen as an immediate political threat, given his protest against the demolition of some temples in the annexe of the Ramjanmabhumi.[3] That this particular act of protest by the former prime minister had struck home became obvious when one speaker wondered why Singh had not gone to Kashmir till then to agitate against the destruction of thousands of temples there? Was it because he knew that if he did that, the same Muslims whom he loved so dearly would chop his body into little pieces and throw them into the river Jhelum? Was that why, the '*singh*' became a '*gidadh*' (jackal) at the very thought of such an intervention in Kashmir? Whatever the reason, V. P. Singh was the constant butt of the black humour of the speakers and all of them called upon the audience to teach a lesson, presumably electorally, to the two Singhs, sons of Babar.[4]

[3] By the time we undertook this visit, the VHP and its allies had acquired and demolished a few of the adjoining old temples and acquired the land for constructing the proposed Ram temple, to the chagrin of many *pujāris* and residents of Ayodhya, especially Chetram Das of Sankatmochan temple. The Janata Dal threatened to start a counter-*kārsevā* and some priests went to the press on the issue. See for example 'JD to start Karseva', *The Times of India*, 21 October 1991; and 'No Sign of Yagna in Ayodhya', *The Hindu*, 25 October 1991.

About five months later, on 22 March 1992, four old temples were razed to the ground to make place for VHP's grandiose scheme: Sankatmochan mandir, Sumitra bhavan, Lomesh Rishi Ashram mandir, and Dwarkadas mandir. *The Pioneer*, 23 March 1992; and Radhika Ramaseshan, 'On a Demolition Spree', *The Pioneer*, 24 March 1992.

[4] Girilal Jain ('The Challenge for the BJP', *Sunday Mail*, 3 November 1991), no lover of Singh or the Janata Dal, was the only political analyst to sense that 'V. P. Singh has ... helped focus attention sharply on the fact that the Ramjanmabhumi–Babri masjid dispute is as much an intra-Hindu one as a Hindu–Muslim one, if not more [so].'

Third, following the long-standing RSS practice, almost all the speakers bewailed the absence of unity among Hindus and the presence of internal enemies among them. The only variation was provided by one rather shrill demagogue from Rajasthan, Shiva Saraswati, who lamented the lack of proper religious 'capitals' in Hinduism of the kind Muslims and Christians had—such as Mecca, Medina and the Vatican. She expected the Ramjanmabhumi to perform that function in the future. The enemies of Hinduism were the ones, she suggested, who sought to subvert this project.[5]

Finally, every speech pointed out that if the people could hand out a humiliating electoral defeat to the Mulayam Singh government, they could throw out P. V. Narsimha Rao's government in Delhi the same way, if it stood in the way of the construction of the Ram temple. This was followed, in two speeches, by direct pleas to the listeners to ensure the victory of the BJP in the next general elections. However, some speakers also made it clear that if the BJP dragged its feet over the construction of the temple, its government in the state would be pulled down. One of them decried the fact that despite a government of Ram-worshippers at Lucknow, no action had yet been taken against the officials who had been responsible for the deaths of the *kārsevak*s on 30 October and 2 November the previous year.

We heard four speeches at the Ramjanmabhumi at a memorial meeting that started around 12 noon. The meeting attracted an audience of between 1,000 and 1,200 people—a remarkably small number, considering the preparations that had gone into it. The number was a source of embarrassment to some of the organizers, too.

The meeting was held next to the Babri mosque, near about the place where the foundation-laying ceremony of the future Ram temple had been performed by the Sangh family and where the pilgrims offered their donations, many of them mechanically, under the impression that the structure belonged to the temple complex. The VHP showroom that provided the backdrop for the stage from which the Hindu religious and political leaders spoke looked rather bare in comparison to its old self just a few months ago. The posters and large portraits had been taken down. A new addition was a fairly

---

[5]This theme of territorialization of the sacred and mimicry of faiths reportedly enjoying more this-worldly power were to recur more and more frequently over the next eighteen months.

large sticker pasted on one of the walls. It read, paradoxically invoking Islamic imagery: Ayodhya, crushed by oppression, do not be sad. We will pass your way again, carrying with us our own *kafan*s (shrouds used by Muslims for covering dead bodies).[6]

The speeches were delivered by Swami Avaidyanath, Nrityagopal Das, Uma Bharati, Vinay Katiyar and Saakshiji Maharaj. All were in continuity with the speeches at Karsevakpuram, but for a slightly more aggressive tone. However, there was now an additional element in the speeches which did not entirely fit in with the tone. Despite the aggressiveness—Nrityagopal Das even prophesied the total destruction of the families and lineages, *vamshanāsh*, of the enemies of the Ram temple—all the speakers took care to avoid provoking the listeners to attack the mosque and Muslims. It was very skilled tightrope-walking.

The most skilful turned out to be Uma Bharati, ostensibly a world-renouncer (*sanyāsini*) but actually a tough politician and a BJP member of Parliament. She had a somewhat rough, masculine voice and compensated for it by her conspicuously feminine, elegant attire and smart, contemporary make-up and hair-do. The temple would have to be built on the basis of strength, not anybody's kindness or charity, she affirmed. Bharati went so far as to specifically request the audience not to call their 'Muslim brethren' *Babar ki aulād* (children of Babar). She said that the real progeny of Babar were those Hindus who were trying to protect the mosque. 'Our opponents are not Muslims', but 'eunuchs' like V. P. Singh and Mulayam Singh. In this connection, she also compared the strong reaction to the mention of Maulana Azad as a 'show boy' over Indian television to the feeble reaction to the comment of Rajnath Sonkar Shastri, Janata Dal MP from Uttar Pradesh, that Ram was a *durāchāri* (one who flouts codes of conduct). 'Such persons should be burnt alive', she thundered.

Bharati attacked the Muslims for putting their religion before their country, for thinking of themselves as 'Muslim Indians' and not 'Indian Muslims'. But she did so in the guise of a tale about a Buddhist monk in Thailand who was asked what he would offer Lord Buddha, if they ever came face to face. The young monk replied that he would cut his head off with a sword and offer it to Buddha. Whereupon he was asked what he would do if Lord Buddha came to conquer his land at the head of an army. The monk replied, without any hesitation,

---

[6]'*Daman se kuchli hui Ayodhya, tu udās nā ho. Ham apne kafan sāth le phir wohin se guzrenge.*'

that he would use the same sword on Buddha, because the country came first, even before religion and God. As at Karsevakpuram, all four speeches at Ramjanmabhumi made a fervent plea to the audience to vote for the BJP and not to allow the demon Mulayam Singh to stage a comeback to the Assembly. In the process, the speakers once again ridiculed V. P. Singh and his party. Uma Bharati borrowed a few lines from a famous Urdu couplet, even as she apologized to the crowd for making use of that language, to abuse V. P. Singh: '*Inki tārif kyā punch rahé ho, inki umrā to gunāhon mein guzri.*' (Why do you ask who he is, his whole life has been spent in sin.) The speakers also urged the listeners to work towards a BJP government at the Centre.

At exactly 12.07 PM three saffron flags were hoisted. Which means three flagpoles with flags were brought in and held up in front of the audience. The hoisting—that is, the unfurling by hand—was done by Swami Avaidyanath, Ramchandra Paramhans and Nrityagopal Das. In the course of the speeches it was said that these flags symbolized the three flags hoisted by the *kārsevak*s on top of the Babri masjid in 1990. Two speakers added that the flags symbolized the three flags that would one day fly at Ayodhya, Kashi and Mathura. According to Saakshiji Maharaj, the BJP MP from Mathura, the saffron flag that had fallen from the hands of the Hindus in the Battle of Panipat had been at long last picked up again, on the day it was unfurled on the dome of the Babri mosque the previous year. However, the speakers also made explicit that they would not like any adventurous or precipitate action by the *kārsevak*s. The speeches, like the ones delivered at Karsevakpuram, contained hints that the organizers did not want the temple right then, but would probably prefer the work to begin some time before the next national elections, so that it could be electorally encashed. They seemed afraid that the people might lose interest in the Ramjanmabhumi movement as quickly as the people of Ayodhya had already seemed to have done.

One thing was very clear. The leadership of the BJP, the VHP and the Bajrang Dal were trying to check their over-enthusiastic followers. They did not want any trouble. The followers, mostly teenagers and young adults from the lower-middle class, were not that easy to control—they appeared keen to mount an attack or a movement for the demolition of the Babri masjid right then. The leadership, on the other hand, seemed to know the risk that such a step would constitute for the survival of the BJP government in UP. In fact, some of them in their speeches emphasized the need not only for valour, but also for discipline as a vital principle of their movement. They obviously failed to make an adequate impression on the *kārsevaks*, for the next day a restless mob of young men attacked the Babri masjid once again and caused some damage to it, besides planting the mandatory saffron flags on the domes of the mosque.

In sum, two impressions remained vivid in the minds of the observers. First, one got the feeling that the conciliatory behaviour underlying the non-conciliatory posture and idiom was not merely an attempt to placate the sizeable national and international press, but probably represented a political design. Second, the speeches were obviously campaign speeches. Altogether, the meeting had the flavour of a small, roadside election meeting of the BJP.

Otherwise too, Ayodhya seemed to be returning to 'normal'. All around there were signs that the Ramjanmabhumi movement was being accommodated within the normal culture of Indian politics.

The claim of many that the people of Ayodhya were mostly not interested in the movement and were in fact hostile to it—till the ham-handedness of Mulayam Singh Yadav pushed them into the lap of the movement—seemed to have a certain face validity. We hardly saw anybody from Ayodhya taking interest in the happenings around the Ramjanmabhumi temple or in the Karsevakpuram that housed the *kārsevaks*. Even the children of Ayodhya, as a priest pointed out, were not interested in the fun any more. They lived their life as if the Bajrang Rudra Yajna was being held in some other city.

Nor did the people of Ayodhya seem to take interest in the fiery speeches and in the coverage of the movement in the local newspapers. Probably the stand taken by some of the priests against the movement had influenced them. Probably they had read between the lines of the speeches made on the Day of Valour at Karsevakpuram and Ramjanmabhumi and felt that the leadership of the movement was more interested in politics than in the temple.

Even the visiting journalists of the national papers were gradually getting sucked into the normal politics that the movement had now come to represent. Some complained to us that they were being forced to listen to standard election speeches. A few journalists left Ayodhya, claiming that nothing much was happening there and it was getting boring. Many of them were overtly pessimistic or had total contempt for and fear of the movement. One of them, working for an international news agency, even confided to us that he was tired and demoralized by his experiences at Ayodhya and would ask the agency for a different assignment on his return to Delhi. One other journalist had coined a slogan as a spoof on a VHP slogan which went: '*Ramlallā ab āyengé, mandir wohi banāyengé* (Dear Ram will now come, and make the temple himself).'

There had already grown a flourishing market relating to the movement—to serve the visitors, journalists, *kārsevaks*, and the simply curious. The two respectable Faizabad hotels were packed with journalists; it was impossible for any newcomer to get a place in them. There were also a few Shri Ram fast-food outlets. A number of shops sold cassettes of fiery speeches about the temple movement—mostly by Uma Bharati and Ritambhara, the two *sanyāsinis* who neither spoke nor dressed like world renouncers. The shops also sold aggressive political-religious *bhajans*, usually set to the tunes of popular commercial film songs, including disco numbers. We found a *bhajan* that sang the praises of Lord Krishna in the tune of the film song that was a great hit of 1990—*Jummā chummā de de* (Jumma, give a kiss). Two of the fire-eating cassettes of *bhajans* had a Muslim, Sayed Ali, as the director of the orchestral arrangements for the songs. For the small shopkeepers who sold these cassettes, it was business as usual.

Even the *kārsevaks*, though always looking for excitement and sometimes for trouble, seemed mainly in search of some entertainment. Many contingents of visiting *kārsevaks*, who were supposed to depart after a few days to make way for new batches of volunteers (there being insufficient space at Karsevakpuram), refused to call it a day and hung around the city. They had come on a free trip and apparently wanted to make the most of it.

It was also obvious that the leaders of the movement were looking for respectability and were unwilling to precipitate a crisis. We got involved in a fracas that exemplified this unwillingness neatly. An elderly Muslim was caught, allegedly stealing a curtain from a temple. He was wearing a tattered *dhoti* and looked both hungry and mentally disturbed. Some of the Dal activists, at last finding an opportunity to satisfy their blood lust, were about to lynch him. The police were helpless or, rather, said they were so. They certainly did not want to take on the Bajrang Dal. The thief was badly beaten in front of the policemen and was being accused of being a spy of Syed

Shahabuddin and others of his ilk.[7] There were demands from the Bajrang Dal boys that the thief be handed over to them for disposal of the case. The police seemed to agree quite readily. Guessing what such disposal would mean, we rushed back to inform Vinay Katiyar, the MP for Faizabad, and the founder-head of Bajrang Dal, whose house was just a few steps away in the same lane where the event was taking place. A tense Katiyar immediately rushed to the spot with his security guards in a jeep and embarked on what can only be called a one-man *lathi*-charge to disperse the crowd. After that he told the police, loudly and publicly and probably for our benefit too, to maintain law and order strictly. The 'thief' was then taken to the police station. We have no further clue as to his subsequent fate.

The Bajrang Dal boys were very angry that Katiyar had used force on them. They felt betrayed and said so. But it was patent that Katiyar did not want an incident under the eyes of the national and international press and he did not want to embarrass the BJP government of UP.

Within a few days even the newspapers caught on to the game. Though their editorial positions and middle-class morality forced their staff to continue either with their partisan pro-BJP stand or with their sanitized, by-now anaemic slogans of secularism, they also sensed the declining interest in the movement and the re-emergence of unheroic politics. Though some of them continued to talk of the fanaticism of the BJP and the VHP, this talk no longer had the touch of panic it previously had;[8] exactly as some of their other colleagues did not sound that enthusiastic when talking of the beauties of *kārseva*.

Even the BJP, its all-India political ambitions now aroused and trying to behave like a responsible future government in waiting, knew that the political returns from the Ram Mandir issue were

[7]The alleged thief's *dhoti* seemed to have been subtly provocative to northern and western Indian *kārsevaks*. They were unaccustomed to see Muslims in *dhotis* worn in the 'Hindu' way and yet that happens to be the dress of a majority of the Muslims in many parts of Uttar Pradesh. Especially to the Gujarati *kārsevaks* with whom we talked, the 'culprit' seemed to be in disguise.

[8]For example, Bhaskar Roy, 'Confusion in the Ranks', and Coomi Kapoor, 'The BJP's Dilemma', *Indian Express*, 15 September 1991; Sumit Mitra, 'Softening Stance, Friendly Overtures', *Indian Express*, 10 November 1991; and Saroj Nagi, 'BJP Does the Balancing Act', *The Illustrated Weekly of India*, 12 October 1991, p. 16.

diminishing. Jaswant Singh, the suave BJP Member of Parliament, virtually gave the game away when he said, 'You cannot make political soufflé rise twice from the same recipe.'[9] Bhausaheb Deoras, younger brother of Sarsanghchalak Balasaheb Deoras, was even more direct when he came to the next phase of politics. Claiming that he was speaking in his personal capacity—unheard-of liberty in a cadre-based, disciplined party—he pleaded for parliamentary support to the minority Indian National Congress government and talked of the indisciplined nature of the Bajrang Dal (brought about, he felt, by the absence of RSS training for the rank and file of the Dal).[10]

Apparently, competitive, democratic politics has its own logic. In another few weeks, most of the major members of the RSS family were shyly learning to sing a new tune. The VHP was trying to soften its language and stand; the RSS seemed willing to shelve temporarily even its core ideology of Hindutva. It was now talking of the *svadeshi* (the indigenous), with its strong Gandhian associations, and of social justice, with its clear social democratic connotations.[11]

The BJP, being a political party, could afford to go further. It ventured into a new programme, an Ekta Yatra or pilgrimage of unity. Starting from Kanyakumari on 26 December, the Yatra was supposed to end at Srinagar in separatist, violence-ridden Kashmir, on India's Republic Day, 26 January. As many as 20,000 BJP volunteers from all over India were to join the flag-hoisting ceremony at Lal Chowk, Srinagar. The party probably felt that this would be a reasonably good distraction from its pussyfooting on the Ayodhya front. This time it was not starting a religious movement but a nationalist movement, for its overt aim was to raise the national flag which the Sangh family had previously refused to own as its own. It expected to get a good press and good public support.

[9]Jaswant Singh, in *India Today*, quoted in The *Times of India*, 1 December 1991, p. 24.

[10]Prasun Sonwalkar, 'RSS Leader for BJP–Cong Tie-Up', *The Times of India*, 26 November 1991.

[11]Swaminathan S. Anklesaria Aiyer, 'Views on Ekta Yatra—I', *The Times of India*, 19 December 1991; '"Hindutva" Fades from RSS Ideology', *The Times of India*, 14 March 1992. Also Rajni K Bajaj, 'BJP Changes Horses Mid-Stream', *Current*, 14 March 1992, who says at one place: '... People like firebrand MP from Madhya Pradesh Uma Bharati have started shunning the press completely since her only constituency so far has been her battle for the construction of Ram Temple at Ayodhya.'

As it happened, at the end of the Yatra, the BJP had to raise the flag under the auspices of the Indian army and under the patronage of the Congress government at New Delhi, to the embarrassment of its supporters. For the flag-hoisting, a token contingent of BJP leaders had to be flown in and out by the army. The BJP leadership were taken to the venue in government vehicles; previously they had been put up by the government around the headquarters of the Border Security Force. The flagpost had to be provided by the Central Reserve Police Force and even the flag had to be borrowed from the army because the one that the BJP leaders were carrying got torn in the mêlée.[12] Judging by the video footage obtained by the news agencies on the scene, it was, by all criteria, a pathetic and comical performance. And this time the media, that had played such a significant role in playing up the Ayodhya episode, was unwilling to play footsie.

The party, however, had other logs in the fire. It was systematically but without any fanfare trying to build bridges with the newly elected Congress regime at Delhi. So much so that, to some journalists covering the budget session of Parliament, the BJP's opposition to the party in power looked like part of a pre-arranged game.[13]

Otherwise too, 'normal' politics was catching up with the BJP. Within it, there were now the squabbles usual in a large party trying to represent a highly diverse society. By the end of March 1992, the temple issue itself had factionalized the party. One group wanted to commence work on it straightway; the other, politically more alert and with larger pan-Indian ambitions, wanted to put it on the back-burner.[14]

There were other more serious forms of factional battles, too, within the party. In April 1992, party functionary Uma Bharati accused the BJP government of Madhya Pradesh of harassing not merely her but also her family for factional reasons. She herself had been

[12]Venkitesh Ramkrishnan, 'A Caravan to Kashmir: The End of the Ekta Yatra', *Frontline*, 14 February 1992, pp. 4–18; see pp. 4–5; Chidananda Rajghatta and Prema Viswanathan, 'BJP: Unflagging Tempo', and Sunil Narula, 'The Fold that was Left out in the Cold', *The Times of India*, 2 February 1992; 'A Pyrrhic Victory for the BJP', *The Pioneer*, 28 January 1992.

[13]See for instance, Praful Bidwai, 'Congress Identity in Peril: Playing Footsie with BJP', *The Times of India*, 2 February 1992; Sunil Saxena, 'I Don't Want a Tiff with the Centre: Kalyan', *The Pioneer*, 9 February 1992; and Ajay Bose, 'It's only a Charade', *The Pioneer*, 9 March 1992.

[14]Diwakar and Rajiv Saxena, 'BJP Leaders Split over Temple Deadline', *The Sunday Observer*, 5 April 1992.

accused, falsely she claimed, of being sexually involved with a general secretary of the party (Govindacharya, the party theoretician and the party's main link with the Indian literati). In addition, false and fictitious criminal cases had been slapped on her brother, she alleged. Though she had managed to get these cases cleared through the intervention of the central leadership of the party, she had to 'pay a high price' for it and had to 'go through hell'. This 'mental torture', she said, had resulted in a nervous breakdown and she had even tried to commit suicide because of the torment. She expressed her desire to resign from the party to go back to the life of an ascetic.[15]

To cap it all, a crude opinion poll conducted at Delhi and Lucknow revealed that, in both cities, roughly three-fourths of the Hindu respondents were against the demolition of the small temples at Ayodhya (to make way for the large Ram temple) and were hurt by it. They felt that such demolitions were not in the best tradition of the Hindu religion (Table 15). It was not very happy news for the party functionaries at a time when some of them were already saying privately that, in case of a snap poll in UP, the party would lose decisively.

TABLE 15
SUMMARY OF OPINION POLL AT DELHI AND LUCKNOW,
APRIL 1992[16] (ALL FIGURES IN PERCENTAGES)

Questions	Yes	No	Don't know/ Can't say
Is it justified to demolish small temples to build a larger Ram temple?	24	74	2
As a Hindu, have the demolitions of temples in Ayodhya hurt your sentiments?	76	20	4
Is the demolition of temples in the best tradition of Hindu religion?	73	20	7

[15]'Uma Bharati Seeks Sanyas', *The Pioneer*, 8 April 1992; Also Prasun Sonwalkar, 'Uma Bharati Threatens to Quit BJP', *The Times of India*, 8 April 1992; 'Bharati's Move Shows up Fissures in BJP Ranks', *The Pioneer*, 10 April 1992.

[16]For further details of the poll see 'Most Hindus Oppose Temple Demolitions', *The Pioneer*, 5 April 1992. Also Kanchan Gupta, 'Can the BJP Hold Out?', *The Pioneer*, 7 April 1992.

X. THE AFTERMATH AND THE RUINS—II

We were in Ayodhya again at the end of February 1992. By this time Mother India seemed to have swallowed up the Ramjanmabhumi movement even more decisively. A few told us that the political situation had not changed, but everyone insisted that the social situation had certainly done so.[17]

Some of the changes were not obvious. Others were. The litigation between the Hindus and the Muslims over the Babri masjid went on, but the litigants, who had to travel between Faizabad–Ayodhya and Lucknow for the hearings of the court cases, travelled together in the same car. They were old friends and petrol was expensive, we were informed. In the Ramjanmabhumi complex, the place where the foundation of the Ram temple had been laid and the VHP showroom that had aroused so much of ire and anxiety in activists, scholars and journalists, now looked desolate, lifeless, and terribly shabby. The heat and the dust of India had caught up with them.

When two of us walked into the showroom, we constituted a majority, for there was only one other apathetic, elderly visitor strolling around the place, apart from the caretaker. In the temple annexe there were still a number of metal detectors, but none of the police personnel manned them carefully, not even to ensure that everyone walked through them. When one of us walked around one of the detectors deliberately, no one even noticed. The number of pilgrims visiting the place was small. Probably the history of violence kept many of them away, more so given that there were other quieter and less controversial temples associated with Lord Ram's birth in the same area. The two Faizabad hotels where journalists used to vie for accommodation were now busy with marriage parties; and it was with much difficulty that we could discover a few of the fiery tapes that had been selling like hot cakes in November 1991.

The fate of a movement provides only a partial guide to the fate of the lifestyle into which the movement is supposed to be an intervention. Ayodhya, the timeless, sacred city and the chosen site of the secular battle for the political allegiance of Indians, also seemed to

---

[17]Mahant Laldas in his interview in Patwardhan's film, *Ram ka Nam* had already compared the events of 1990 with a storm that fells large trees and houses but none the less has some time or the other to pass; and with a bad trip that ends when the effects of the intoxicant wear off.

be following its own trajectory, partly independent of the concerns of outsiders and their game plans.

In February 1992, we met two prominent Muslims, one said to be a moderate, the other recommended to us as a hard-liner by local journalists. They, we thought, might provide clues to the mind of a community that, according to some, comprised the ultimate victims and, according to others, the ultimate aggressors in inter-religious strife in India.

We first met Munnu Mia, also known as Munnubabu. His formal name is Ilias Ansar Hussain. A prominent Shia of Ayodhya and a devout Muslim, he is also the builder and manager of a Ram temple called Sundar Bhavan. It is a small temple close to the better-known Kanak Bhavan. The Hindu estate owner who financed the temple came to know of Munnu Mia when the latter helped him get timber supplies. When work on the temple began in 1949, Munnu Mia was appointed the person in charge. The temple was completed in 1951 and he has been its manager ever since. Munnu Mia is proud of his temple. Though the financier had the major say in the design of the temple, Munnu Mia claims to have introduced into the design elements of 'English' style', whatever that might mean.

Munnu Mia's family has stayed in Ayodhya for approximately 450 years. They came with the Mughal Emperor Humayun (1507–56). The family has always owned land, but the family finances improved after one of Munnu Mia's forefathers safely handed over to the British garrison at Kanpur seven white women stranded at Lucknow during the Sepoy Mutiny of 1857. As a reward, he was given a land grant of seven villages. Munnu Mia's father remained a landlord till the Zamindari Abolition Act was passed. After that the elder Hussain became a compounder in a hospital and started a business in tobacco.

Munnu Mia was born in 1907 or 1908—he does not know for sure. However, he might have been born one or two years earlier for he claims to be 87 or 88. Though more than 85, he is in good health and looks seventyish. For much of his life, he was in the Indian Forest Service. After retirement, he has become a timber merchant. His son Sabir Ali works for the Uttar Pradesh Electricity Board. He was present during part of the interview.

In his long life, Munnu Mia says, he has seen only two riots in Ayodhya, one in 1912, the other in 1934. The first one was over the killing of cows which the Bairagis opposed. The killing of cows in Ayodhya was finally stopped and the Muslims switched to buffaloes.

Subsequently, all butchery was banned within the municipal area of Ayodhya. Meat now comes to Ayodhya from Faizabad. Munnu Mia's son hinted that, given these restrictions, even some of the *baba*s, belonging mainly perhaps to sects that permit meat-eating, visit Muslim households nowadays to secretly eat meat.

The riot of 1934 was over the Janmabhumi temple and it was partly instigated by outsiders. The Hindus wanted the temple to be opened. The riot ended without any clear-cut decision on the subject.

With only these two riots during a period of more than 80 years, communal relations in Ayodhya had always been good, Munnu Mia says. He remembers saying *namāz* at Babri masjid for many years, without any problem. When they used to go to the masjid, the priests were friendly and hospitable to the *namāzi*s. Shoes had to be taken off at the insistence of the Bairagis, but the latter used to look after the shoes and also give *prasād*, offerings, to the Muslim devotees when they came to collect their shoes after saying *namāz*.

This tradition of amity, Munnu Mia feels, is not dead. During the recent curfews, every Muslim household was supplied with food by the Hindus. Otherwise, too, the social relationships and cultural bonds remain intact. Even today the gold and silver embroidery work on the dress of the icons is done by both Muslims and Hindus (previously it used to be the monopoly of Muslims); the dresses and crowns of the gods are still stitched by Muslim tailors and Muslim craftsmen. The only thing the Muslims do not do is to sell sweets, for the sweets are often used as offerings to the gods. Even today, when Muslims take out a *tāzia*, Hindus throw rice and money on it and walk under it, for a *tāzia* is supposed to be auspicious.

Nothing—Munnu Mia emphasizes the word 'nothing'—has changed in the relationship between the two communities. 'The recent riots have had no effect on us', he says, because 'the resident and the educated Hindus do not want the masjid to be demolished.' 'Only the goondas want that', he adds in English.

Ayodhya is sacred to both Hindus and Muslims, Munnu Mia avers. To the Hindus for obvious reasons. To the Muslims because it is associated with Hazrat Shis (apparently Noah of the ark fame) who is buried at the Shis Parvat at Ayodhya. The Hindus know the same hillock as Mani Parvat; they view it as the discarded part of Gandhamādan Parvat that Hanuman brought for Lakshman in the days of the Ramayana, to get hold of the life-saving herb, *vishalyakaranī*.

The presence of Hazrat Shis makes Ayodhya doubly sacred. Contrary to the popular belief, Munnu Mia says, Babar never visited Ayodhya; nor did he construct a mosque there. His general Mir Baqi constructed the mosque 'with the consent of the *babas*'. That is why the residents of Ayodhya have no animus towards the masjid and do not want it levelled. Till now, in trying to demolish the masjid, the outsiders have only managed to demolish some mandirs.

Even today, Munnu Mia says, irrespective of whether one is a Hindu or a Muslim, the standard greeting of Ayodhya remains *Jai Siya Ram* or, if the other party happens to be a priest, *Babaji dandavat*. In this respect, things have not changed since the nineteenth century, Munnu Mia insists. All communal frictions at Ayodhya have been instigated by outsiders motivated mainly by money. The local Hindus know this. That is why the *babas* stood guard for ten days without sleeping in front of Muslim homes during the recent riots. 'There has been no effect on us of the riots,' he repeats.

He recognizes, though, that in recent years, some things have tended to interfere with the placid rhythm of Ayodhya. Becoming a priest at Ayodhya is now occasionally a means of avoiding detection as a criminal. Many *babas* now come from Bihar and it has become easy for a Bihari with a shady past to become a disciple of a *baba* to avoid the police.

Also Advani has reportedly collected 470 million rupees and that money is having its impact. Munnu Mia implies that some of the money has gone to the pro-VHP priests. However, Munnu Mia has a soft corner for even Ramchandra Paramhans, the fiery leader of the Ramjanambhumi movement and one of the small minority of pro-BJP priests left in Ayodhya at the time. Ramchandra is Munnu Mia's childhood friend, *'langotiā yār'*, and is apparently seen by the latter as a lovable rogue whose angry rhetoric is mainly a political ploy. Now that Ramchandra has made a lot of money after joining the BJP and the VHP, he sends sweets to Munnu Mia and helps him with money. Munnu Mia calls him a competent person (*kābil ādmi*), a good orator, and a 'very good man'. Ramchandra always joins his friend's family on religious festivals and special occasions. He came to dine at Munnu Mia's place at the time of the marriage of his son Sabir. 'When you had money', Munnu Mia quotes Ramchandra as saying, 'You gave me money and food; now that I have money, you also deserve this.'

We also met Haji Mohammad Kalim Shamshi, the administrator of Tatshah mosque. He also looks after a *madrasā* or traditional Islamic school, an *idgāh*, and a *musāfirkhānā* or travellers' lodge. The *madrasā* and the *musāfirkhānā* are both under the Tatshah mosque. Shamshi himself has been educated in the Tatshah *madrasā*. He also has a private business. Shamshi is the one who was described as an orthodox and aggressive Sunni leader.

The interview took place in the austere *musāfirkhānā*, inhabited by poor, itinerant lodgers and small-time traders such as a seller of grass mats from Bihar. Shamshi turned out to be a well-preserved man of 73, with a powerful voice and a self-assured manner. He told us that for the last hundred years his family has been living in Ayodhya. He himself, though, was born at Ujjain and brought up at Etawa. The Shamshis originally belonged to Multan and are, therefore, Punjabis. They were Khatris before being converted to Islam.

Like Munnu Mia and many others in Ayodhya—and for that matter in the whole of Avadh—Shamshi spoke elegant, somewhat Sanskritized Urdu, generously sprinkled with both Urdu couplets and Avadhi sayings. Shamshi told us that the relationship between the Hindus and the Muslims had not been destroyed by the events of 1990–91. In fact, the relationship had reverted to its older form. For the ordinary people had already seen through the games of the politicians. As a result, inter-religious relationships were again becoming what they had been over the centuries. When specifically asked, he said that his shop, which had predominantly Hindu clients, did not lose any business. The temporary aberration during 1990–91 was brought about by the love that some politicians had for power and money.

In other words, rightly or wrongly, Shamshi blames greedy politicians entirely for what happened in Ayodhya during 1990–91. 'We do not want to fight among ourselves, neither the Hindus nor the Muslims.' Outsiders have instigated the quarrel and they might still manage to damage the good relations between the two communities. Some of the politicians have amassed massive fortunes; they might still precipitate some crisis or other; just as in the late 1940s, one Mr Nayyar spoilt the cordial atmosphere by introducing icons of gods into the Babri masjid, and as, in 1984, Rajiv Gandhi aggravated the conflict by unlocking the masjid.

Shamshi seems convinced that the issue of the Babri masjid has been wrongly posed. 'In our faith, you cannot read *namāz* at a masjid built on forcibly occupied land.' Though doubtful of the wisdom of the courts, Shamshi claims that the Muslims were willing to abide by the decision of the court. He, however, adds: 'We are capable of offering major sacrifices; we are also capable of giving enormous amounts of love.' Islam does not teach blood-letting; it teaches one to live in peace with one another. '*Ātmā sāf, paramātmā pās*' (If the heart is clean, God is close).

Ayodhya is '*pavitra*' (sacred) for both Hindus and Muslims. Muslims have 1,24,000 prophets. Hazrat Shis was one of them. He is buried at Ayodhya. 'Let God give understanding to both us and them.' This is not the kind of understanding the politicians arrive at, Shamshi adds. For them the basis of any understanding is: 'You worship money; we also worship money.'

The bitterness between the Hindus and the Muslims has also grown, Shamshi feels, because of the use of abusive terms such as *katuā*. But something of the older relationship survives. It survives because people now know that the conflict about the Babri masjid is actually a struggle for power. It is a battle for 'votes and notes'. The leaders' seats of power are seats studded with nails.

When asked how his own Hindu friends have reacted to the turmoil of the last two years, a tinge of sorrow creeps into Shamshi's voice. Referring to his own age, he says, 'Hindu friends of mine who were humane are now mostly dead; a new crop has taken their place. This crop consists of *pujāris* (worshippers) of *dharma*, not of *insāf* (justice).' So they have not been always articulate on this issue. If and when some have been so, those in power have tried to make sure that such voices do not find public expression. The latter do not want the local Hindus and Muslims to settle the issue through negotiations among themselves. 'If we were given a chance', Shamshi says, 'we would have solved the problem long ago. Either we would have taken away the temple or given away the mosque. Or both would have been there and *pujā* and *namāz* would have gone on as usual.' But the public figures make statements elsewhere (presumably at political centres like Lucknow and Delhi) which again 'ignite' emotions. This is compounded by the unthinking, partisan behaviour of the newspapers. When the newspapers start to write the truth, the condition of Hindustan will improve.

At Ayodhya itself, even today, whatever might be in the hearts of the people, they come and talk nicely and smilingly to each other, Shamshi adds. 'Even when the Rajah of Ayodhya comes to me, he touches my feet in respect, and calls me chāchā (uncle).'

The evening prayers are announced and Shamshi politely seeks our permission to go back to his mosque. It also begins to get dark and we, too, begin to think of returning to our hotels and, then, after a decent interval, to our known world at Delhi. Despite our long, intense conversations, we sense that both Munnu Mia and Haji Shamshi live in a world mostly unknown to us. Along with their fellow Muslims, Hindu neighbours and friends, they are part of an Ayodhya to which we will remain as much strangers as the members of the *Sangh parivār* with their high-pitched nationalism and use of faith as a political ideology. And that Ayodhya, we also sense, is once again trying to return to its normal rhythms of community life.

But does that Ayodhya have any chance of survival? Are its residents living in an unreal world of which the social and political support-base has already collapsed? Is the cultural geography of Ayodhya an exception within a modernizing, developing, secularizing India? Do those who are a part of that psychological landscape have any future? Was the trust of the Muslims of Ayodhya in their Hindu neighbours a self-destructive romanticization and a pathetic self-delusion?

We felt that we might get a part-answer in Colonelgunj. There had been a riot in the town the previous year, the closest that communal rioting had come to the sacred town of Ayodhya.

Colonelganj

Colonelganj is a small town in the Gonda district of east UP, some three hours journey by road from Ayodhya. From 30 September to 2 October 1990, the town and a number of small rural hamlets around it saw Hindu–Muslim clashes which left, according to official figures, 41 dead—five in Colonelganj and the rest in the villages—and scores injured. Unofficial estimates put the toll at over 200 dead. None of the affected areas had ever seen a communal riot before.

The trouble, we were told, started at around 2 PM on 30 September when the annual Durga procession was subjected to brickbatting as it wound its way through the narrow lanes of Kasaibadi, a Muslim dominated area of the town. One press report said that the provocation was a rumour that a Muslim boy had been beaten up by some Hindus.[18] Another said that some of the young men leading the procession were giving a display of their skill with *lāthis* when one of them was accidentally injured. As he was being rushed to a hospital, a cry of 'he has been killed' went up. In the ensuing confusion, stones and bombs began to be thrown from the rooftops of an orphanage and a mosque.[19] In any case, the procession had been all along shouting inflammatory slogans, as if its aim was to provoke violence.[20] Those who threw stones and bombs from rooftops were also probably waiting for an opportunity to do so.

Those marching in the procession lost no time in retaliating. They were not unprepared for the attack; in fact, they had come well armed. They hit back with bricks and bombs.

The situation in the town itself was brought under control by nightfall following an afternoon of intense violence. But in whichever direction the processionists scattered after being attacked, they wreaked havoc on the property and lives of any Muslims they could lay their hands on. For instance, a large mob assembled outside the police station on the main Gonda road and torched the huts of some Muslims located right opposite it, besides spearing to death four men who could not escape in time with the rest. The policemen present there did nothing to prevent the killings. The fall out of the riots in the adjoining rural areas in the coming days was to prove equally brutal.

Since Colonelganj was placed under curfew soon after the violence erupted, people from neighbouring villages who had come to participate in, or simply see, the procession, could not return to their homes. It took little effort and even less time, for some political activists to spread the rumour that thousands of Muslims had in a pre-planned move swooped down on the villagers who had gone to Colonelganj and massacred them. Women and children had been specially singled out.[21] By mid-morning on 1 October, the looting and burning of Muslim homes in the rural areas surrounding Colonelganj

[18]Rajiv Saxena, '200 Die in Gonda Carnage', *The Sunday Observer*, 7 October 1990.

[19]'*Gonda me Dangā: Tanāv Gāon me Pasār Rahā hai*', *Navbharat Times*, Lucknow, 5 October 1990.

[20]*The Times of India*, 7 October 1990.

[21]'*Indian People's Front Jānch Dal ki Report*' (Report of the investigative team of the Indian People's Front), mimeo.

had begun. And when the villagers still did not come back that night, on the following day, 2 October, the slaughter of the Muslims got underway.

We went to a village where such killings had taken place. According to Ram Raj Singh alias Nangu Singh, the son of the *grām pradhān* or village chief of Chatrauli, there were only ten Muslim families in his village. They had been settled there by his forefathers on land which still belongs to his family. On 1 October, around noon, some 500-odd men attacked the Muslims in the village and killed eight of them, including a three-month-old child whom they drowned in a well after beating his mother unconscious. When Nangu Singh tried to save the Muslims, the mob turned on him. Unarmed, he ran and took refuge with the family of one Bhole Singh. In no time, the latter's house was surrounded by hundreds of rioters howling for Nangu Singh's blood. But they did not give him up, allowing him instead to slip out of the backdoor to safety.

Why had he risked his life to save the Muslims from being killed? Nangu Singh had a simple answer. He said that since he was the son of the village *pradhān*, it was his duty to protect his people, irrespective of their caste or religion. He had a responsibility towards them which had to have priority over everything else. But the real tragedy, felt Nangu Singh, was that the bloodthirsty mob of looters and murderers was not made up of unknown outsiders but of those who knew their victims well and who were equally well-known to them. 'They were not all *lakhiārās*' (local toughs); they were from adjoining villages, many of them people from whom such violence was totally unexpected. And, said Nangu Singh, they were led by a local landlord, who had a hand in most of the crimes in the area but had never been arrested.

Now there were no Muslim families left in his village. The few who survived the carnage had shifted to areas where there were larger concentrations of Muslims.

Bhole Singh is a painfully shy man in his early twenties. Only after a great deal of persuasion did he haltingly tell his story. He was sitting on the roof of his house, when he saw some people forcibly dragging a girl away. He recognized her as belonging to a Muslim family from the village. On seeing him, she screamed for help. Bhole Singh somehow managed to rescue her from her abductors—he has only one arm—and then locked her up in his house. Later, they came back and demanded that he hand her over to them, but he refused. Then some men from the PAC came for her, saying that the girl's brother had sent them. Bhole Singh told them to bring the brother along because he did not trust the police. 'It was only after he came, that I let the girl out of the locked house.' Bhole Singh's act of chivalry did not go down well with the criminals-turned-fanatics in the village, specially since they were already sore with his family over another matter concerning a Muslim neighbour.

According to Bhole Singh, his family wanted to purchase a plot of land behind their house which belonged to a Muslim. After he had agreed to sell, they made him an advance payment of Rs 25,000 pending registration. This angered the Hindu landlords of the area. Not that they wanted the land for themselves or that they did not want Bhole Singh's family to have it. What was the need, they asked, to pay anything to a Muslim, when his land could have been easily acquired for free with the use of just a little force? The family refused to backtrack despite their threats. Furious, the landlords took advantage of the communal frenzy sweeping the area and murdered the Muslim landowner. Subsequently, one of them turned up in court and produced a forged will in which the Muslim had gifted away his entire land to him. 'Now, why would he do that', asks Bhole Singh, 'when he had a wife, two children and a third one on the way?'

Bhole Singh was visibly agitated when we suggested that some might accuse him of being a bad Hindu.

In which Ramayan does it say that Muslims should be killed? I have also read it. Ram made so many sacrifices in his life, and now look what they are doing in his name. Why is it that there is no difference between Hindus and Muslims when we work alongside in the fields or when they come to thatch our roofs, but when there is a riot they suddenly become our enemies fit to be killed?

Bhole Singh said that he and his family were being continually harassed since the riot, but they did not have a moment's regret for what they had done.

The social situation of Jaiswal, a medical doctor in private practice, was better. The doctor stays close to the centre of the town of Colonelganj in an old-style, semi-colonial mansion surrounded by land in which he grows mainly vegetables. We went to him because some Muslim informants had mentioned his name as a person who had saved a number of Muslims, both individuals and families, from certain death. We visited him at his home with two other social activists and one of his Muslim admirers whose family he had saved.

The doctor looked an ordinary general practitioner with some land, cattle and a large house. The whole episode now seemed to his family, his wife casually remarked, a strange aberration in their otherwise placid life. We found the doctor a quiet family man who did not dramatize his exploits. Nor did he try to turn the targets of his good work into 'pure' victims. He told one of us, who had stayed back a few minutes at his home after the others had taken their leave, that he had not mentioned in front of all the visitors that some of the Muslims he had saved or tried to save, including the person who was accompanying us and was obviously an admirer of the doctor, were also aggressive persons. They had given a good fight to the Hindu mobs and the police. But he felt that they did not deserve to die because some of their violence was counter-violence. The doctor presumably did not operate on the basis of any romantic concept of amity when he had ordered one of his sons to stand with a gun to protect the Muslims, telling him, 'Son, you must protect them even if you have to sacrifice your life.'

Perhaps a part of Jaiswal's concern for the Muslims derived from the fact that the labourers working on his farm were mostly Muslim. The activists accompanying us, members of the Indian People's Front and all given to various versions of Maoism, were also quick to point out to us that the Muslims constituted an economic investment for the doctor; that his kindness had a hard 'material' basis. It could be so, but the family did not seem to be particularly aware that their self-interest also was tied up with the fate of the Muslim families in their neighbourhood. The doctor seemed to trace his concern for his Muslim neighbours to his family's three-generation-long exposure to Muslim friends, colleagues and their culture. One of the Jaiswals had learnt Persian and many others knew excellent Urdu and studied through it. The Muslims were not strangers to them, the doctor seemed to suggest.

Mrs Jaiswal, who joined our conversation, spoke admiringly of her husband's courage and seemed proud of him. She felt that he had done his duty and conformed to his true *dharma*. She was obviously touched by the fact that the Muslims had mentioned the Jaiswal family as their benefactors and had sent us to their place. In fact, she seemed surprised that we had taken the trouble to come to her home to ask about the family's experiences.

We did not get any clear answers to the questions with which we had gone to Colonelgunj, but when we left the town at dusk, we carried back memories of the inner resilience of those who refused to be swept off their feet by the atmosphere of hate and violence. Once again we had found the willingness to resist in places where community life and community obligations were not distant memories and where the traditional codes of conduct had not weakened through processes of social change and massification.

Perhaps the answers we sought lay not in objective history but in the fate of the shared traditions and moral universe of the residents of Ayodhya, Hindus *and* Muslims, and in the ability of that universe to evoke a response in the rest of the society. That response and its contours constitute the ending of our story of Ayodhya in the next chapter.

CHAPTER 6

XI. The Final Assault

True to Indian practices, the problem at Ramjanmabhumi did not die out or get resolved once and for all. It again began to simmer towards the middle of 1992. What had once looked like the resolution of a crisis began to look like the end of a cycle and the beginning of another. And this time, neither the traditional cultural, economic and social ties of the Muslims of Ayodhya with their Hindu neighbours nor their three-century-old integration into the lifestyle, cultural concerns and manners of the pilgrim town could protect them from the larger political and social forces buffeting South Asia.

On 5 July 1992, more than a year-and-a-half after the symbolic *kārsevā* was first performed in Ayodhya, *kārsevak*s from various parts of the country, including a sizeable number of priests and holy men began to construct 'a part' of the projected Ram temple just east of the Babri masjid. The construction began with the *singhadvar* (lion gate)—a 138 foot long, 116 foot wide and 6 foot deep foundational structure. The place had been taken over by the BJP government of UP in the name of building tourist facilities. This was also the place, the reader may remember, where some temples had been demolished earlier to make way for the Ram temple.

The reasons for this sudden spurt of activity were not impossible to guess. The BJP regime in UP felt it was not doing particularly well. The party had come close to ensuring a riot-free state—there had been only one major flare-up at Varanasi during its rule—but it was itself acquiring the standardized form and flabbiness of the governments by other parties that had ruled the state. The logic of Indian politics was catching up with it. Riddled with charges of corruption and bad governance, true and false, the party sensed that, to retain its support and come back to power in the next elections, it had to provide some spectacular diversion from everyday politics. The Ram temple promised in the party's manifesto must have looked an easy way out, especially as the party was under pressure on this score from the VHP and the Bajrang Dal.

No fully reliable clue to the public mood during the period is available, but one opinion survey was conducted at Lucknow and a few nearby villages (N= 413) at the time. It showed that while the BJP was not in the doghouse as far as public opinion went, there would have been wide public support if the Central government had handled the *parivar* firmly at that stage. (Tables 16–18. As the survey had a disproportionately high number of urban respondants, the table also gives figures adjusted for rural–urban differences in UP.)

The mood of the *kārsevaks*, who were this time carefully chosen and then directed to Ayodhya by their local VHP or Bajrang Dal leaders, was one of defiance. It was turning so even before the Allahabad High Court had ordered, on 28 November 1992, that all construction activity at the Ramjanmabhumi had to cease at the borders of the disputed site. The Bajrang Dal chief, Vinay Katiyar, had already warned the Central Government that if force was used against the *kārsevaks*, the streets would be strewn with their dead bodies. This gave weight to rumours that a few of the more fanatic elements amongst the *kārsevaks* had been organized into *balidāni jathās* or suicide squads, and some were armed with plastic bombs and other such explosives.

TABLE 16

ESTIMATES OF PUBLIC OPINION IN UP ON THE EVE OF
6 DECEMBER 1992

Questions	Yes	No	Other	Total
Should the UP govt. prevent the proposed *karseva* on the disputed area?	59.0	36.5	4.5	100.0
	56.5	37.0	6.5	100.0
If the UP govt. allows the *karseva* to take place, should the Centre dismiss it?	48.5	41.0	10.5	100.0
	50.5	37.5	12.0	100.0

SOURCE: MRAS-Burke Survey, *The Pioneer*, 29 November 1992.

NOTE: Shaded figures are adjusted for actual rural–urban differences in UP.

TABLE 17

ESTIMATES OF PUBLIC OPINION IN UP ON THE EVE OF
6 DECEMBER 1992

Question	Good or better	Fair	Poor	Don't know	Total
How would you rate the overall performance of the UP govt?	66	25.5	8.5	1	101
	63	24.5	10.5	1.5	99.5

SOURCE and NOTE, as in Table 16.

TABLE 18

ESTIMATES OF PUBLIC OPINION IN UP ON THE EVE OF
6 DECEMBER 1992

Question	Cong-I	BJP	JD/ SJP	Others	DK/Cannot say
If the Centre dismisses the UP govt. for allowing *karseva* against the court orders and Assembly elections are held, which party would you vote for?	41.5	26	7	1	24.5
	39.5	23.5	10.5	1	25.5

SOURCE and NOTE, as in Table 16.

The mood of the *kārsevaks* was matched by some grandiloquent statements from their leaders. The politician-*sadhu* Ramchandra Paramhans asked, rhetorically, 'If we could perform *kārsevā* during the rule of Mulayam Singh Yadav, who can stop us now?' Swami Parmanand declared, more dramatically, 'Now, even if Ramlalla himself comes down from the heavens and asks us to stop *kārsevā*, we will not listen to him.' Ashok Singhal threatened the Central Government that if it made any attempt to interfere, *kārsevā* would immediately begin from the *garbha griha* (sanctum sanctorum) itself; that is, the mosque would be destroyed. Later, upon seeing one of the thousands of monkeys of Ayodhya climb on to a dome of the Babri masjid, he said that since Hanumanji himself had come and blessed them, there could not be a better omen.

Initially the number of people engaged in *kārsevā* ran into a few hundreds. Gradually, the number swelled but, according to intelligence reports, did not cross 8,000. The VHP maintained that more than 50,000 *kārsevaks* were present at any given time in Ayodhya during the entire period. A number of MLAs of the BJP arrived with their supporters and constituents to perform *kārsevā*. Among them was Badshah Singh, MLA from Hamirpur, who brought along with him 40 Muslims for the purpose.

Matters came to a head when the construction activity continued, violating the orders of the High Court. Singhal issued a statement asking *kārsevaks* from all over the country to rush to Ayodhya for a possible confrontation with the authorities. When the District Magistrate of Faizabad, Ravindranath Shrivastava, along with the Senior Superintendent of Police, D. B. Roy, went to the site to try and implement the orders of the Court, unaccompanied by any police contingent, angry *kārsevaks* chanting '*Jai Shri Ram*' surrounded them. Singhal had to intervene before the crowd would release them. Onkar Bhave and Paramhans were also present at the spot. The magistrate's appeal to the *sants* to obey court orders angered them, and it was only after he and the SSP touched their feet and begged forgiveness that the *sants* were mollified.[1]

Effigies of the High Court judges, two Hindus and a Muslim, who gave the order, were burnt at Ayodhya, and it was announced that 20 July would be observed as anti-judiciary day. The day after the order was passed, lawyers of the the Bar Association of Faizabad arrived in Ayodhya to perform *kārsevā*.

This time the local Muslims did not remain quiet. About a hundred of them staged a protest march to the disputed shrine and courted arrest. This was the first time since the temple movement had been launched that they took to the streets in Ayodhya. Earlier, they had expressed fear, anger, despair; this time they talked the language of confrontation. In a meeting of the Babri Masjid Action Committee held in Faizabad during the time, Muslim leaders announced that if within ten days all building activity near the disputed structure was not stopped, they would lead others of their faith to Ayodhya and physically force the *kārsevaks* to stop. But despite this brave talk, the Muslim shopkeepers of Ayodhya, fearing a backlash, downed their shutters on hearing the Court judgement.[2]

[1]*Jansatta*, 18 July, 1992.
[2]*Jansatta*, 16 July 1992.

Muslims in some other parts of India were less constrained. At a few places they took to the streets, provoking inevitable organized reaction. Communal riots broke out in Malegaon in Maharashtra, and Thiruvananthapuram in Kerala, where members of the Islamic Sevak Sangh (ISS), a militant Muslim outfit, attacked Hindus participating in an RSS drill. The ISS, as its name suggests, is modelled on, of all things, the RSS. The rioting lasted over two days and left at least six people dead. Elsewhere in the state, thousands of Muslims demonstrated, demanding protection for the Babri Masjid.

Just when it began to look as if the dismissal of the state government for its failure to implement court orders and a clash between the Central government and the *kārsevaks* would take the crisis to its logical end, the newly elected Prime Minister, P. V. Narasimha Rao, bought himself a four-month reprieve. He promised to solve the problem at Ayodhya if he could be given time and the *kārsevaks* were withdrawn from the construction site. An agreement between the government and the movement, including the activist *sadhus* and *sants*, was signed, and the VHP ordered the *kārsevaks* to shift construction work to an undisputed site nearby where a Lakshman temple was supposed to come up. (At the time the VHP razed to the ground a number of small temples in the vicinity of the disputed structure, a temple where the mythic king of the serpents, Sheshnag, used to be worshipped was also torn down. As many believed this to be inauspicious, they now hastily turned their energy to building a temple to Ram's brother, since Lakshman was an incarnation of Sheshnag.)

From the beginning of September to almost the end of November, over 90 meetings were held between Hindu and Muslim delegations, but other than bringing leaders of the Babri Masjid Action Committee and the VHP to the negotiating table little else was achieved by the government. (Privately however, the Prime Minister was said to be in touch with Rajendra Singh, the most important of the RSS general secretaries. Singh reportedly urged Rao more than once to pressurize the Allahabad High Court to give its judgement, so that some solution could be found on the basis of the judgement, whatever be its nature. He probably felt that the *parivār* could hold the *kārsevaks* in check taking advantage of the verdict. It seems that there was no response from Narsimha Rao to Singh's plea.[3])

[3]By 4 December, Singh's patience was to wear thin. He was to say to one of the mediators that those who had betrayed the *parivār* thus would certainly

The VHP maintained all along that they would not extend the deadline any further. In the meanwhile, to keep the issue alive they launched yet another of their mass contact programmes, the Ram Charan Paduka Pujan. The Pujan involved consecrating at Nandigram in Faizabad on 22 September some 12,000 *khadau*s or wooden slippers, a huge number of them built by local Muslim artisans. Local myth has it that it was at Nandigram that Bharat worshipped the *khadau*s of Lord Ram, when the latter was in exile. After consecration, the *khadau*s were sent out to all corners of the country and prayers were offered to them at local temples. The campaign, however, failed to elicit much popular response.

Even as its talks with the government were going on, the VHP announced on 31 October that *kārsevā* would resume at Ayodhya on 6 December. Later, when the negotiations failed, it appeared that the government was thinking of taking over the 2.77 acres of disputed land and dismissing the BJP ministry in UP, so that there could be no defiance of the Allahabad High Court's order staying building activities at the disputed site. But on the evening of 28 November, the Supreme Court accepted a four-point affidavit of the UP Government which promised that the *kārsevā* would be symbolic, there would be no construction activity, no court order would be violated, and the security of the disputed structure would be ensured. Later events suggest the BJP's submission had been a ploy to allow the unhindered flow of *kārsevak*s and party leaders into Ayodhya.

By the end of November, more than 20,000 *kārsevak*s had reached the city, and as their numbers continued to rise with the approach of 6 December, it became clear that the entire show was, probably for the first time, being orchestrated by the RSS. Never before in the history of the temple movement had the BJP-VHP-Bajrang Dal combine managed to collect such large crowds at Ayodhya on their own. At the final count, an estimated 2,00,000 persons came from all the states of India barring those in the north-east, a large proportion of them drawn from the RSS cadres. Everyone could not join the *kārsevak*s; severe controls and preliminary screening were introduced by the RSS.[4] It was not a purely spontaneous show put up by the faithful but a tightly organized, fully planned political exercise.

---

be taught a lesson. Singh's feelings were communicated to the RSS leaders camping at Ayodhya, who took it as the final nod they had been waiting for.

[4]Sanjay Kaw, 'A *Karsevak* for Three Days', *The Statesman*, 4 December 1992; and 'Fanaticism in Uniform', ibid., 5 December 1992. Kaw, a freelance

The largest representations were from Maharashtra, Andhra Pradesh, Gujarat, Karnataka and UP. And this time round, the composition of the *kārsevak*s differed from that of the earlier gatherings at Ayodhya. There was a heavy turnout of women, Dalits, and tribals and the 'backward' castes. Besides, a large number of *kārsevak*s were drawn from the rural areas.[5]

The high level of motivation of the *kārsevak*s was evident from the testimony of Kaw. Continuously exposed to the VHP's massive propaganda, many of them believed that only they were the true Hindus; the rest were traitors.[6] Their faith infected many ordinary citizens and even the paramilitary arm of the government. Talking of the traditionally anti-Muslim Provincial Armed Constabulary, Kaw mentions how the *kārsevak*s were 'treated with respect, even deference' by the guardians of law and order. As a PAC man told a group of *kārsevak*s that included Kaw, 'Don't worry about us, we are solidly behind you.' Subsequently the PAC invited some of the *kārsevak*s to their camp for breakfast.

Meanwhile, the BJP sent Lal Krishna Advani and Murli Manohar Joshi on separate *yātrā*s to mobilize *kārsevak*s for Ayodhya. The tempo was building up. Though towards the end of November Advani had advised party MPs to stay away from Ayodhya, within 36 hours he was to change his mind. Now he himself was going to offer *kārseva*, presumably to convince the supporters of his party that he was not backtracking on the promise to build a temple at the place of the Babri mosque.[7] Carried away by his new-found enthusiasm,

---

journalist, who with great difficulty managed to enlist as a *kārsevak*, describes the strict control exercised on them by the RSS. His testimony vividly captures the centralized, heavily organized, orchestrated nature of the events of 6 December. The organization included liaison with the security apparatus of the government as well as surveillance on journalists and the *kārsevak*s themselves.

[5]In chapter 5, especially in the context of Gujarat, we have already hinted at the political processes contributing to the changing composition of the activists going to Ayodhya.

[6]Ibid.

[7]Ajoy Bose, 'Caught in a Dilemma', *The Pioneer*, 1 December 1992. Bose also notes that Advani was no longer his normal self, 'convincing and forthright'; he was 'tense and irritable'. This ambivalence, Bose adds, 'characterized the entire BJP leadership then.'

Advani in a public meeting at Azamgarh, UP, assured the crowds on 2 December that the *kārsevā* would be 'physical, with bricks and shovels,' a remark he was later to deny making.[8] Vinay Katiyar had been less circumspect. He had already declared on 30 Novemebr:

There is nothing called symbolic *kārseva*. ... This country is not run by court orders. It is run by society. ... [The] judiciary has no authority to pass any orders regarding the Ram mandir. ... If there is any *sangharsh* we are ready for it. ... *Kuch bigādne par hi kuch bantā hai* (Only when something is destroyed, something is born).[9]

Atal Behari Vajpayee was subtler when speaking to one of us on the morning of December 5 at Lucknow. Asked if, given the large gathering of *kārsevak*s at Ayodhya, he thought the Babri masjid would remain safe on 6 December, Vajpayee said, '*Āshā hai, aur āshankā bhi*' (There are hopes, but also doubts).[10] On 6 December, minutes before the Babri masjid was attacked by the *kārsevak*s, Sadhvi Ritambhara in a brief conversation at the site used a similar 'double entendre'. Asked if she thought that the Allahabad High Court order would be violated that day, she replied, '*Kārsevā* will be performed like *kārsevā*. Whether there will be any violation or not, you will see later.' She added 'All the tasks that are carried out before the construction [of the temple] begins will be performed. We will do *kārsevā* only in the mandir.' What did she mean by *kārseva*,

---

Why did Advani, expected to reach Ayodhya on the morning of 6 December along with journalists who had accompanied him in his *yātrā*, change his schedule to reach Ayodhya the previous evening? Apparently, he joined a closed-door meeting that same evening and another one the next morning at Katiyar's home. Others in the meetings were Moreshwar Save of the Shiv Sena, K. S. Sudarshan and H. V. Sheshadri of the RSS, Pramod Mahajan of the BJP, Katiyar and Singhal. Some reports claim that Advani left the meeting 'grim-faced'. Citizens' Tribunal on Ayodhya, *Report of the Enquiry Commission* (New Delhi: Citizens Tribunal on Ayodhya, 1993). Others say that some of the more aggressive *kārsevak*s gathered outside Katiyar's house to raise slogans against Advani.

[8]Amit Prakash, 'Advani Denies Making "Shovel and Bricks" Statement', *The Pioneer*, 9 December 1992.

[9]Kanchan Gupta, '"Karseva Can't be Symbolic", Says Katiyar', *The Pioneer*, 1 December 1992.

[10]When asked in the BJP's first press conference after 6 December why he did not offer *kārsevā* despite being at Lucknow on 5 December, Vajpayee made what in retrospect was to look like a tell-tale slip. He had to manage the aftermath at Delhi, he said.

as opposed to the official VHP announcement? 'Now look,' she replied, 'We can calm ourselves, but we cannot calm lakhs of people by making them pour some water around. Everyone knows this well. So we are not going to leave this place after only washing and cleaning it.' Did that mean they were going to pull the mosque down? 'What we want to say is that, today, we do not want to break the structure, and it will not survive either.'

One of us reached Ayodhya in the early afternoon of 5 December, in time to hear some of the most important leaders of the *parivār* addressing the thousands of assembled *kārsevak*s on the sprawling grounds of the Ram Katha Kunj, adjoining the disputed plot of 2.77 acres. The lectures continued till late in the evening, with speaker after speaker assuring the crowd that they would return home completely satisfied. Paramhans told the *kārsevak*s, 'What is in your mind is in ours as well; do not think that you will be unable to finish the task you have come here to perform.'

In the midst of these speeches, the VHP's Marg Darshak Mandal after hours of deliberation communicated to its impatient flock the nature of the *kārsevā* that was to be performed the following day. Acharya Dharmendra, one of its prominent members, and Katiyar, President of the Bajrang Dal, announced that symbolic *kārsevā* would be initiated by the *sant*s at four locations simultaneously at 12.15 PM.

This symbolic *kārsevā* would include fetching water from the river Saryu to wash and clean the *chabutrā* (platform), constructed the previous July (according to one of the *sant*s, this was essential because politicians visiting the site had made it impure); the filling of the *shilānyās* pit next to the platform with sand from the river bed, followed by the sprinkling of holy water over the entire disputed plot; the levelling of the low-lying area around the Sheshavatar temple; and the laying of bricks at an undisclosed place. It appeared at the time that the VHP had decided to continue with symbolic *kārsevā* till the Allahabad High Court gave its judgement in the land acquisition case on 11 December.

But by the day-end there were signs that Vajpayee's misgivings about the *kārsevak*s would be proved right and the *kārsevā* would not be restricted to hymn-singing on the disputed site, as Kalyan Singh had claimed in his affidavit before the Supreme Court. In the evening, angry *kārsevak*s confronted Nrityagopal Das and Paramhans and abused them for agreeing to a symbolic *kārsevā*. Hundreds more roughed up Katiyar, when he went to Karsevakpuram to pacify the already highly charged and motivated *kārsevaks*. They made it clear that they had come to Ayodhya to demolish the mosque and would not settle for less. The plan to have carefully selected, highly indoctrinated *kārsevaks* was now paying dividends.

If there were pressures from large sections of the *kārsevaks*, subjected to intense propaganda for months if not years, the intentions of a section of the leadership of the *parivar*, too, had become suspect by this time. Journalists were barred entry into the Ram Katha Kunj and the surrounding areas adjoining the disputed 2.77 acre plot where, it was widely believed, selected groups of *kārsevaks* were being trained to demolish the masjid. A photograph of *kārsevaks* pulling a huge boulder with ropes at a practice session at the Ram Katha Kunj on 5 December was published the following day in the *Indian Express*. The same day a journalist from Lucknow, who managed to get into the forbidden premises, was detained for several hours, and allowed to go only after her captors were sure that she would not file any copy for her newspaper on what she had witnessed.

Shortly before midnight, we found near the mosque, Katiyar deep in discussion with a youngish man called Champat Rai, a relatively unknown and non-descript RSS leader posted at Ayodhya who headed the Sangh's activities in the Avadh region and, thus, was automatically in charge of the *kārsevā* scheduled for the following day. The two men surveyed more than once the area that lay between the makeshift gate that was the only way open to the mosque and a pit that had been the *shilānyās sthal* (before being demolished earlier in the year). It seemed that they were deciding upon the spot where *kārsevā* would be performed the following day, especially since the area they were marking out was not on the disputed plot. By the next morning, a saffron flag, too had been planted at the spot. As later events showed, it was through this very place that hundreds of *kārsevaks* were allowed to force their way in, after breaking down the bamboo fence enclosing the disputed plot, and attack the mosque.

By about 7 AM on 6 December, the entire area surrounding the Babri masjid had been cleared of ordinary *kārsevaks* and was under the control of small teams of RSS men. One of them contained about fifteen men from Maharashtra; its task was to ensure an orderly *kārsevā*. But apart from that, they were unwilling to reveal anything about themselves, which may or may not have been under instructions. But a group of teenagers, also from Maharashtra, who were being hustled out of the grounds along with an elderly man by the RSS volunteers and two policemen were more vocal. '*Jab hum idhar se* finally *jāyenge nā, to idhar kuch nahin bachnekā*' (When we finally leave this place, nothing here will survive), they declared confidently, amidst much laughter in which the RSS workers and the police joined. The elderly man, obviously not one of them, chided the boys for their disobedience and urged them to follow the directive of the Marg Darshak Mandal. 'I am also a *kārsevak*,' he told them, 'but I believe that our *kārsevā* should be as disciplined as Gandhiji's satyagraha.' The boys jeered at him for taking Gandhi's name with respect, '*Are tum use Gandhiji bolte ho, par hum to use sālā buddha, harami bolte hain*' (You call him Gandhiji, but we call him a bloody old bastard), they said, leaving the old man staring after them.

By mid-morning, the area surrounding the disputed site was overflowing with *kārsevaks* straining at the barricades. Their mood was belligerent. They were being held back by RSS volunteers and a handful of policemen. Some of them who managed to break the cordon from time to time and rush into the grounds looked almost possessed; they broke down when they were dragged out.[11] Assorted *sadhus*, including the better known ones—such as Paramhans in a canary yellow sweater, his normally unkempt beard and hair neatly combed out—bustled about importantly, airing their views. Sadhu Vishwas Bapu of Junagadh, who said he had been a paratrooper in the Indian army before renouncing the world, was one of them. According to his not terribly cogent argument, if the government and the secularists wanted the people to believe that the disputed structure was indeed a mosque and not a temple, they would first have to say that Godse, Beant Singh and Sivaresan (assassins of M. K. Gandhi, Indira Gandhi and Rajiv Gandhi respectively) were the heroes and Gandhiji, Indira and Rajiv the offenders. 'If they agree, so will we',

---

[11]At least one newspaper mentioned psychiatric problems that broke out in a number of *kārsevaks* who had to be hospitalized after 7 December. Biswajeet Banerjee, 'Sevaks Found to be Mentally Ill', *The Pioneer*, 24 December 1992. According to the psychiatrist treating them, who refused to be identified, the patients reportedly suffered from, among other things, auditory hallucinations, paranoia, insomnia and aggressiveness. Poverty, unemployment and illiteracy may have contributed to their illness, he said, and the absence of proper treatment had pushed them towards religion. Bagfuls of letters, mostly incoherent, were recovered from the patients, a majority of them addressed to the President, the Prime Minister and the Chief Minister of UP.

concluded Vishwas Babu in fluent English, before wandering off in search of a new audience.

As the appointed hour came closer, a last minute change was made in the scheduled programme. *Kārsevaks* were now not required to form human chains from the banks of the Saryu some distance away to the site of the *kārsevā* to supply the sand needed for the cleaning operation. Sushil Modi, the BJP MLA from Patna, said that this would now be done the following morning at 8.30 AM He rushed away when we asked, 'What use will the sand be tomorrow, when it is needed for today's ceremony.'

From 11 AM onwards, the top leaders of the *parivār* including Advani, Joshi, Singhal, Sheshadri, Sudarshan, Katiyar, Bharati and Avaidyanath began arriving at the disputed site. They did not go anywhere near the spot where they were going to perform *kārsevā* in less than an hour, but moved around aimlessly and left as hurriedly as they had come, surrounded by security men and small groups of *kārsevaks*. By 11.45 AM all the leaders had left. The last to be seen was Singhal who was trying to push some *kārsevaks* away from the fence surrounding the mosque.[12]

At about the time Singhal was spotted near the mosque, the posse of the Provincial Armed Constabulary posted inside it inexplicably began to move out. Senior police officials drinking tea on the terrace of the control room did not stop them as they strolled past below, as if the PAC had orders to quit its post. At about the same time, two *kārsevaks* could be seen climbing the boundary wall of the mosque from the back before quickly disappearing from sight.[13]

Soon after the bigwigs of the *parivār* had left, at about 11.45 AM, a group of not more than twenty boys suddenly rushed into the fenced ground, ostensibly to help the RSS men evict some of the *kārsevaks* who had earlier broken the police cordon at the temporary gate. This group was not wearing the usual saffron headband with *Jai Shri Ram* written on it, but lemon yellow bands that could be clearly seen from a distance because of the brightness of the colour. No one quite remembered seeing headbands of this colour before.

---

[12]At least one news report says that Advani made some half-hearted efforts to stop the *kārsevaks* but soon gave up and was, by some accounts, close to tears. Singhal did try to stop the 'frenzied' *kārsevaks* who tried to disrobe him. *The Pioneer*, 10 December 1992.

[13]These events have been captured in the video-newsmagazine *Newstrack*, January 1993.

The yellow-banded group moved towards the gate where the police was perfunctorily trying to control a rapidly swelling crowd which outnumbered them hopelessly. This could have been a signal, for no sooner had these boys been sighted by the *kārsevak*s straining at the barrier, than there was an announcement on the public address system asking the boys to withdraw from there immediately. As the boys left, followed by the RSS men who had been positioned there since the morning, the crowd of *kārsevak*s broke through and rushed to the mosque armed with hammers, iron rods, pickaxes, crowbars, bamboos and shovels. Simultaneously, hordes of *kārsevak*s appeared on top of the outer wall of the mosque from the sides and back, pelting the police with stones and bricks. As the forces ran for safety, D. B. Rai, Senior Superintendent of Police, Faizabad, could be seen shouting at them to return. They chose not to obey him and, instead, stood around watching from the sidelines.[14]

As some of the *kārsevak*s started to break down the mosque with their bare hands, an RSS functionary stood on the watchtower in front of the mosque, directing them, and frequently blowing a whistle and waving a flag, as if he was directing a work squad or athletic team. Small groups of women collected on the rooftops of adjoining buildings, and threw *gulal* at the *kārsevak*s. They sang and clapped, even as a few others began to uproot telephone wires.

Did the leaders know beforehand what was going to happen that afternoon? There can be no final answer to that question. Perhaps some did, others did not. Certainly one answer seems to emerge from our narrative, another from the likes of Chandan Mitra.[15] Not that the leadership of the *parivār* comes off any better from Mitra's graphic description of their behaviour during that crucial period when the attack on the mosque was mounted—the giggling political *sanyāsin*s, Uma Bharati and Ritambhara; Joshi overcome by the size of the mammoth crowd; Singhal, convinced that the *kārsevā* would go along expected lines and giving precise orders, to a crowd that could not care less, about how to wipe and clean the site of the projected temple; the moment of reckoning when the crowd goes berserk on seeing two *kārsevak*s on the top of the domes of the mosque

[14]After the events of 6 December, Rai was suspended. He later publicly expressed his desire to contest the State Assembly elections on a BJP ticket.

[15]Chandan Mitra, 'Control Room that had no Control', *The Hindustan Times*, 8 December 1992.

while the high command sat, 'tense', 'sombre-faced', 'hopelessly
sullen', with faces like 'grim death'; the lament of Rajendra Singh,
the *de facto* supremo of the RSS, 'the ministry is gone'; and finally
the pathetic and belated attempts to calm down the crowd by the
leaders taking turn in appealing to the *kārsevaks*, while others like
Acharya Dharmendra tried to interest an uninterested crowd in a
bhajan.[16] The high command recovered soon enough, but for Advani
who, perhaps sensing the long-term implications of what was happening, wore a 'worried, faraway expression on his face'.[17]

At about 12.30 PM some half an hour after the mosque had been
stormed, water began to be pumped into a small, crude, tank-like,
brick-and-mud structure a little distance away from the mosque, just
below Manas Bhawan. This was to mix the cement that was later
used to build the platform and wall of the temple on the rubble of
the mosque. VHP ambulances stood ready in all the nearby lanes to
cart away injured *kārsevaks* to the civil hospital in Faizabad where
the former health minister in the BJP government in UP, Harish
Chandra Shrivastava, was said to be in command.[18]

Soon after the *kārsevaks* started tearing the mosque down, journalists and cameramen covering the events came under a well-
orchestrated attack. It was not difficult to single them out for this
purpose, since all media persons present wore prominent pink identity
badges issued to them by the VHP the day before. Most cameramen
and photographers had their equipment smashed to pieces. Journalists
were beaten up, in some cases seriously, their notebooks were torn

[16]Ibid.
[17]Ibid.
[18]How much commitment to a cause the temple movement elicited can be
gauged from the police reports which say that 869 *kārsevaks* were injured
that day. *Citizens' Tribunal on Ayodhya: Report of the Enquiry Commission*
(New Delhi: Citizens' Tribunal on Ayodhya, 1993), p. 155. Though in this
description of events, we have adduced evidence of prior planning and even
a conspiracy, the element of ideological fervour and moral passion in some
of the young *kārsevaks* and the simple faith of some of the older ones should
not be under-estimated. Certainly the prior planning was not very efficient
and the conspiracy not widespread, for most of the injuries were easily
avoidable. Many were due to the angry, spontaneous attempts by the younger
volunteers to break the mosque by their own efforts, often with their bare
hands. The passions that were often conspicuous by their absence in the
leaders, were all too obvious in some of the followers.

and tape recorders broken. At least in one instance, there was an attempt to kill a young woman journalist.[19]

One group of *kārsevak*s blocked all entry points into Ayodhya to keep out central security forces, while another began to loot and burn the homes of the Muslims of the city and destroy masjids and idgahs.

The low, continuous chant of '*Jai Shri Ram*,' coming over the loudspeakers since dawn, suddenly became more aggressive in both tone and content:

Jai Shri Ram, bolo Jai Shri Ram,
Jinnah bolo Jai Shri Ram,
Gandhi bolo Jai Shri Ram,
Mullah bolo Jai Shri Ram...

Initially, there were some hurried, panicky pleas to the *kārsevak*s over the public address system to maintain discipline. These were followed by expressions of concern for their safety, as the 500 year old mosque began to come apart slowly. After a while the *kārsevak*s received only guidance and encouragement from the BJP leaders and the *sant*s of the VHP's Marg Darshak Mandal assembled at the Ram Katha Kunj. Singhal grandly announced that the dawn of Hindu rebellion had arrived, while Vijaya Raje Scindia declared that she could now die without any regret, for she had seen her dream come true. Kedarnath Sahani's short speech was a warning to the Muslims.

> Those who do not even want to say *Vande Mataram*, those who want to see the flag of Pakistan flutter in Kashmir, the process of showing them their right place has begun.

It was, however, the triumvirate of Uma Bharati, Ritambhara and Dharmendra who dominated the 'show'. Bharati in her several turns at the microphone gave the crowds two slogans, '*Ram nām satya hai, Babri Masjid dhvasth hai*,' (True is the name of Ram; Babri masjid has been demolished) and '*Ek dhakka aur do, Babri masjid tod do*' (Give one more push, and break the Babri Masjid). Both, along with the old favourite '*Jai Shri Ram*', rent the air for hours afterwards. She also introduced to the crowd one Shiv Kumari Prachchanya of Meerut as 'the first woman ever to have climbed the dome of that

---

[19]See for example Saroj Nagi and Vrinda Gopinath, 'Media Attacked to Stop Demolition Photos', *The Pioneer*, 14 December 1992.; and 'President Hears Media's Horrific Tales', *The Pioneer*, 10 December 1992. On 5 December, too, a German television crew had been beaten up by the *kārsevak*s at Ayodhya.

structure,' and the parents of Sharad and Ram Kumar Kothari, two brothers killed in police firing on 2 November 1990, while trying to attack the mosque. 'There were tears in the eyes of their mother'. Bharati told her audience, 'as she for the first time felt that her sons had not sacrificed their lives in vain, and that their murder at the hands of those *nar pishāch*s (blood-sucking monsters), Mulayam and V. P. Singh, had been avenged.'

As the day wore on, Ritambhara took over. She asked the *kārsevak*s to immerse themselves totally in this auspicious and holy task, specially since the administration was lending them its full support by remaining mute. The *sadhvi* instructed them to leave the site only if they had been hurt or were feeling unwell. Ritambhara made several speeches and followed them up by what appeared to be a VHP version of the traditional *'ārti'* to the goddess Durga in which the crowds lustily joined:

Mil ke bolo, jai mātā di
Ma tere bete, tujhe bulāte
tu niche ājā,
hum shish katā dein, tujhe chadhā dein
tu khappar lā de, hum khun bahā dein
tu binti meri, puri kar de
tujhse māngun, mannat meri puri kar de
mujhko chāhiye,
Ayodhya chāhiye, Mathura chāhiye, Kashi chāhiye
tu puri kar de, jai mātā di.

(Let us together praise Mother Durga,
Mother your sons are calling you,
Come down
We shall cut our heads off and offer them to you
Bring your drinking bowl and we will fill it with blood,
Listen to my pleas,
Fulfil my wishes,
Give me Ayodhya, give me Mathura, give me Kashi.)

By the time the last of the domes of the Babri masjid came crashing down at 5.45 PM, scattered spirals of smoke could be seen at a distance. Realizing that Muslim houses in the city were being attacked by the *kārsevak*s, Ritambhara quickly began to urge the authorities on the public address system to stop the 'Mussalmans from burning their own homes'. She was joined by Dharmendra, who shouted that some 'outlaws' were setting fire to their own huts to make a fast buck and give the innocent *kārsevak*s a bad name. Later, he changed his tune and said to the press that this was the only way in which Ayodhya could become a Vatican for the Hindus.

XII. AYODHYA'S 'FIRST' RIOT

The two earlier riots at Ayodhya had become distant memories for the residents of the town. Moreover, in retrospect they had reworked the memories to read the riots as aberrant behaviour produced by transient passions to which a neighbourhood could sometimes be prone. More so as the seven-year-old movement run by the *parivār* had failed to polarize the community. The community's moment of reckoning had now come.

Between nightfall on 6 December and mid-afternoon the next day, rampaging mobs of *kārsevaks* killed and then burnt 13 men and children in Ayodhya. While nearly all the Muslims of the town had left their homes before 6 December for safer spots, many others fled on hearing the news that the Babri masjid had fallen. Those who died were the ones who could not escape in time.

Simultaneously, as if to spite the VHP's claim that the Hindus had never destroyed places of worship of other faiths and that it was the most tolerant of faiths, scores of places of worship at Ayodhya were systematically destroyed by the *kārsevaks*. Table 19 gives the estimates made by three agencies.

For nearly twelve hours after the resignation of Kalyan Singh's government and after governer's rule had been imposed in the state,

TABLE 19
ESTIMATES OF DAMAGED RELIGIOUS PLACES AND TOMBS BY
DIFFERENT AGENCIES

Agency	Mosque	Mazar	Idgah	Madrasa	Temple
District Administration	19	9	0	2	0
District Police	14	5	3	0	1
Relief Council	23	11	0	0	0

SOURCE: Kamala Prasad, Dinesh Mohan, Kamal A. Mitra Chenoy, Kirti Singh, Sagari Chhabra, S. C. Shukla, *Report of the Inquiry Commission, Submitted to Citizens' Tribunal on Ayodhya* (New Delhi: Citizens' Tribunal on Ayodhya, 1993), p. 154.

mobs roamed the streets of the temple town, shouting '*Jai Shri Ram*' and plundering and torching Muslim homes and business establishments in broad daylight and without resistance. It was Ayodhya's first proper Hindu–Muslim riot and it turned out to be quite impressive in scale; in all 134 houses were destroyed.

The destruction had a pattern. First the *kārsevaks* looted the valuables and currency. Most *kārsevaks* who participated in the sacking of the Muslim localities of Ayodhya were from South and West India; they found jewellery and cash particularly attractive because they could carry them back with them unobtrusively. Then they smashed to pieces all the things inside the houses and what they could not break with their bare hands or sticks—from furniture to motorcycles to books and clothes—they made into bonfires. In some cases, the *kārsevaks* distributed what they could not carry away among a few favoured local Hindus. A few houses were not set on fire bcause they were too close to Hindu homes; the rest were systematically burnt. Any mosque they could find was a bonus. Within the day, barring two, all the masjids and idgahs of Ayodhya were either destroyed or damaged.

In this systematic destruction, the *kārsevaks* received some useful help from a majority of the UP police, the PAC and, for the first time, a few of the local Hindus. While some locals identified Muslim property for the *kārsevaks*, the police did its bit by either actively participating in the looting or considerably turning a blind eye to what was happening around them. For instance, on the morning of 7 December, in the heavily policed Ramkot area, just behind the disputed site, some *kārsevaks* set fire to Lala Tailors, a shop owned by a Muslim. The PAC men on duty there, instead of interfering, urged the arsonists to throw out the odd pieces of wooden furniture lying inside; the agents of the law then used the wood to make a fire in the middle of the road to ward off the winter chill.

Ten days later, many localities of Ayodhya still bore the scars of the victory march of Hindu nationalism.[20] Everything had been left as it was; the 24 hour curfew was still in force, making it impossible for those who had run away to come back. Only a handful of Muslims

---

[20]We need hardly tell the reader that the victory march touched many places other than Ayodhya. For a random sample, see '15 Kashmiri Students Thrown off Running Train', *The Times of India*, 13 December 1992.

could be found in Ayodhya, those who had either been saved by their neighbours or had successfully evaded the *kārsevaks*.

Fifty-year-old Beechu was one of them. His house, overlooking a rather beautiful garden, was in the *basti* of Mirapur Bulandi, on a stretch of road called Rajghat. It was attacked by about a hundred men at 11 AM on 7 December. Within half-an-hour, the other seven Muslim houses in the *mohallā* met the same fate. There were no casualties, for most of the families had left well in advance. Beechu, who owns a cycle shop, was saved by two of his Hindu neighbours, Sarju Yadav and Subhash, who tied a Bajrang Dal band on his head and passed him off as a *kārsevak*. 'It was very difficult,' says Yadav, because the men who came here, did not speak any Hindi, only Telugu. 'I somehow managed to convince them in the little English I know.' Subhash did not think that any Hindu from their *basti* was involved in the attack; on the other hand, he was convinced that the *kārsevaks* had prior knowledge about the location of Muslim households in the area. Where were the police at the time? Yadav and Subhash replied, almost in unison, 'We only saw one man in uniform, and he was leading the *kārsevaks*.'

Around the time Mirapur Bulandi was being overrun, the neighbouring locality of Machwana situated on Kaushalya Ghat was under siege. An embittered Abdul Sattar pointed out what used to be his house. 'I am a very poor man, and so I also had very little. But now even that has gone.' He had not yet lodged an FIR with the police, preferring to wait for some local Muslim leader to accompany him to the police station. 'The police are pressurizing us to sign statements they have prepared. I am not educated; who knows what they have written,' he said.

All the seven or eight Muslim homes in Machwana and a similar number in adjoining Shikwana were, when we visited them, little more than burnt-out shells. Sattar, who was hiding in a flower bed nearby, when the *kārsevaks* were ransacking the place, swears that he saw Hindus from his own locality as well as some from the neighbouring ones egging the outsiders on. The inhabitants of Shikwana agree. They say that the *kārsevaks* were brought back to their locality three times to break down the house of the local landlord, Nawab Tahir Husain Sahib. They succeeded the third time and reduced to ashes most things in the house, including the 75-year-old Tahir Husain himself. He was torched at his front door, and a few bones were all that were found of the aristocrat whose family had lived in Ayodhya for more than three hundred years.

Stepping inside the ruins of what must once have been a grand house, we saw a frail woman of about 70 years, wearing a shabby sari and high-powered glasses standing with her hands folded and tears rolling down her cheeks. She was looking very vulnerable in front of two uniformed policemen. She was pleading with them to let her testify as one of the witnesses to the murder of her husband. The police refused. She was not present inside the house when the *kārsevaks* descended on it and, as far as they were concerned, she was of no use to them. She tried to argue with them through her tears: 'It is true that I didn't see anything, but I could hear them shouting, *"māro, kāto, luto, phunk-do, phunk-do"* (Kill him, cut him into pieces, loot, burn, burn), as I hid in the bushes under the window at the back of the house. I also heard Husain Sahib begging the *kārsevaks* to spare his life—*"mujhe mat māro, mujhe mat māro"* (Don't kill me, don't kill me), he had screamed.'

The police were unmoved; they wandered off to round up other witnesses for the inquiry, unconvinced even about Tahir Husain's death. 'The *mohallā* people say that the bones are his, but what is the proof? Nobody actually saw him being killed; he might have run away.' 'That is untrue,' wailed Aliya Begum after them. 'I will swear on anything you say, the Qur'an, the Ramayana.' No one paid much heed, as she stood alone in the courtyard of her house surrounded by spilt grain, broken china, burnt beds and chairs, torn photographs, and bits and pieces of other personal belongings, awaiting the return of her sons, their wives and children who had managed to escape in time.

Outside the two policemen continued with their investigations. Why did they wait for ten days before starting them, we tried to find out. 'We only heard what had happened here yesterday, ' said one of them, slightly affronted. The police *chowki* to which they were attached, we soon found out, was less them a five-minute walk from the house of Tahir Husain.

Husain's neighbour, Ali Ramzan's cycle shop was located at the same crossing as the Katra police *chowki*. 'When a mob began destroying my shop, the police encouraged them by shouting, "loot it, loot it"; and now they want me to lodge an FIR with them.' Ramzan, however is not complaining too much. His 6-year-old son, Zubair Ahmed, is still alive. Zubair was trying to slip out of the back of his house, when he was caught by the *kārsevaks* attacking it, who then tried to throw him into the bonfire they had made of the things taken from his house. Zubair was saved by a Hindu friend of his father's, who claimed Zubair was his son.

Further down the road, across from Ashrafi Bhavan are the *mohallā*s of Mughalpura and Begumpura. A few Muslim houses here survived the *kārsevā*. According to Mohammed Amin and Abdul Hafiz of Mughalpura, around 8 AM on 7 December, minutes after the PAC guard posted in their *basti* went off duty, an army of *kārsevaks* overran their houses. While Amin hid in some tall grass behind his house, Hafiz slipped into a freshly dug grave. Too scared to go back to their homes even after a couple of hours had passed, Amin, Hafiz and the others who had fled with them, decided to seek refuge in the Katra police *chowki*. 'They refused to let us in,' says Amin; so they went running to a PAC camp at a nearby school.

The situation there was even worse. The police accused us of being murderers. They said we must have knifed some people and were running away from being caught, and that in order to hide our crime we were bringing in the story about the *kārsevaks*. They threatened to kill us and had their command-ing officer not turned up, we don't know what would have happened to us.

Except for the wife of their zamindar, no other neighbour came out to help them. 'Many of us were also terrified,' says Sheetal, a young man who lives in Begumpura, 'because if we pleaded with the mob to stop the looting and burning, they were quite ready to turn on us.' Despite which, Sheetal personally saved the lives of a number of people of his neighbourhood and was dubbed a 'traitor' for his ef-forts by his Hindu friends.

Unlike many other towns and cities, there are no Muslim ghettos in Ayodhya. Muslim and Hindu houses stand side by side in most localities. But there are a few, very small, predominantly Muslim pockets like Alamganj Katra and Society. These neighbourhoods were still totally deserted; they had been completely destroyed, especially Society, with its 20 odd Muslim houses reduced to rubble and the minarets of its tiny mosque strewn about on the grass. Most of the bricks from the house were dated 1924. The hungry street dogs of the localities moved around with us hoping for some food and, per-haps, happy to see some signs of life again.

In the Tehdi Bazar *mohallā* just behind the disputed site, adjacent to a vacant plot of land where many of the *kārsevaks* had camped

during their stay in the city, 13-year-old Tony and his father Shaukat
were first attacked and then burnt in the courtyard of their house.
Shreds of their blood-stained clothes still lay at the spot where they
had been lynched. The Muslims of the *basti* had not yet returned;
three of their Hindu neighbours, all women, told the story.

Tehdi Bazar was the first neighbourhood to be attacked at around
4 AM, on 7 December, by a mob of 'thousands' carrying guns and
swords. The ten to twelve Muslim houses were ransacked and then
set on fire. Apart from Shaukat and his son, two brothers Salim and
Nadir were killed. They were two of the three sons of the last imam
of the Babri masjid. The remaining brother was spared because the
*kārsevak*s thought he was insane. 'We hid some of them in our houses
for three days, the others took refuge in the Ramjanmabhumi police
station,' said one of the women.

Tehdi Bazar was the place from where the Ayodhya riots really
began, and Hindus of the town blame Haji Mehboob, the local head
of the Babri Masjid Action Committee, for it. Mehboob's house, located on the outskirts of the *basti*, overlooks one of the main roads
leading up to the disputed site, which was constantly used by the
*kārsevak*s. According to those who hold him responsible for starting
the violence, and they include local journalists and a number of
*mahant*s, Mehboob fired a gun—some say he threw a bomb—on a
procession of *kārsevak*s on the evening of 6 December. As a result
one person—some say five—died. The *kārsevak*s were enraged and
swore vengeance. The rest of the events at Ayodhya followed from
Mehboob's folly, it is said. The two prominent VHP *mahant*s of Ayodhya, Ramchandra Paramhans and Nrityagopal Das, disagree. They
insist that the Muslims, taking advantage of the prevailing situation,
set fire to their own houses to claim compensation from the government.

The Muslims are reluctant to accept the more popular theory, although they do not deny it outright either. Says Nasir Husain, the
administrator of the Shahi mosque in Faizabad,

I don't know whether he fired the shot, but if he did, it must have been in
self-defence. Only a fool could have been aggressive at that point in time,
with lakhs of *kārsevak*s milling around the place, and Haji Mehboob is no
fool.

Others cite the curious behaviour on that day of Station House
Officer Shukla of the Ramjanmabhumi police *thana*. It was well

known that the SHO intensely disliked Mehboob. In fact, just a few weeks earlier Shukla had arrested him on what many think was a trumped-up charge. Yet, not only did Shukla save the lives of Mehboob and his family by locking them up in jail till the danger was over, but also let Mehboob walk away scot-free afterwards. The Muslims say that, given the enmity between the two, Shukla would not have let Mehboob escape had there been any truth in the popular story.

When the conversation veered round to Mehboob, one of the Hindu women in Tehdi Bazar had also murmured under her breath: 'He had to save his own life after all.'

The fact that Muslims and their property were rather systematically attacked this time, as if the *kārsevak*s had gone around with a voter's list in their hands, has for the first time clearly divided the city along religious lines. What eight years of propaganda could not do, the first riot of the city has done. The reader might remember that earlier both communities held outsiders responsible for the large-scale violence at Ayodhya and often proudly insisted that they would survive *kārsevā* after *kārsevā* together. This time there has been no such talk. Ayodhya as a community—and as a sacred city where both the Hindus and the Muslims, with their interlocking myths, legends, lifestyles and shared experiences of co-survival have a place, perhaps even a sanctified place—might not yet be defeated but it is certainly in decline. The community at Ayodhya was always an imperfect one but it was a community all the same, whereas it has become now a place haunted by the private demons of two separated groups, fearful, suspicious and on guard. Hindu nationalism and its foot-soldiers have done their job.

Though virtually in every locality we discovered some Hindus who had protected their Muslim neighbours, often at great risk to themselves, and though all the Muslims we met, with one exception, acknowledged this handsomely, there was a clear decline in the casual approach many locals had to the political '*tamāshā*s' or 'spectacles' organized by outsiders which gave some local residents access to money and power. We have already suggested that many Muslims of Ayodhya used to see the temple movement in instrumental terms but, now, the thousands of pairs of footwear Muslims made for the Paduka Pujan movement, the character certificate that Munnu Mia gave to Paramhans, and even the participation of some Muslims in the *kārsevā* on 6 December seemed to belong to another age. When one local Muslim *kārsevak* was killed by the other *kārsevaks*, we were told that his neighbours refused to participate in his funeral or read the *namāz e janazā*.

The Muslims of Ayodhya see the events of 6-7 December as part of a continuing process of this new divide. They are afraid and angry, and many of them feel let down by the local Hindus. They are now convinced that, in at least some cases, their neighbours have been willing partners in the atrocities committed against them. It is this sense of betrayal rather than the death of more than a thousand people in riots all over India after December 6 that seems to occupy their mind. Abdul Sattar has made up his mind to move to Bombay, where his son has a tailoring establishment. Abdul Hafiz is waiting for the curfew to lift and for the others to return before leaving.

A group of small boys, roughly eight to ten years old, are equally determined to stay on. Said one of them, who saw the destruction of his *mohallā* from a nearby garden where he had hidden, 'We will learn how to use guns and fight like the Palestinians.' What did he know of them, we asked. 'I know that many powerful people have been trying to wipe out all traces of the Palestinians for many years but have failed. Because they have aswered back bravely with the gun. We shall do the same.' The other children nodded in agreement.

Sehanawa

A few miles outside Faizabad, on the road to Sultanpur, lies the village of Sehanawa. It is a village with roughly the same number of Hindus and Muslims. The majority of them earn their living from agriculture or related occupations. On the face of it, there is nothing that marks out Sehanawa from the countless other sleepy villages of eastern UP. As it happened, prior to the first assault on the Babri masjid by *kārsevaks* in 1990, one of us had accidentally gone to Sehanawa, while travelling with a documentary film crew, to get some random insights into the mood of Muslim villagers in rural Faizabad and near Ayodhya. But the nondescript village had been clean forgotten by its casual visitor though, as we later found out, the villagers had not forgotten the visit.

The reader may also remember that Nrityagopal Das had, in the course of a conversation, mentioned that the Babri mosque could have been taken to Sehanawa, since the local Shias had themselves

offered to shift the mosque to the village as a solution to the conflict
at Ayodhya. According to him, Mir Baqi, the builder of the mosque
in 1528, was buried in the village and his descendants still lived
there. Ramchandra Paramhans, too, had once said more or less the
same thing.

Towards the end of one of our last visits to Ayodhya, on a sudden
impulse we decided to visit Sehanawa, merely to see how the descendants of Baqi—that formidable medieval warhorse and ultimate
'Hindu-baiter'—had reacted to the trauma of Ayodhya. We thought
that visit might help us to round off our story.

We reached Sehanawa after sunset, and asked one of the villagers
to take us to the house of Baqi's descendants. The man, obviously a
Muslim, readily—in fact enthusiastically—agreed, for he remembered the earlier visit of one of us. He jumped into our car and led
us to a house on the outskirts of the village and went in to talk to
the family. Soon a bare cot was taken out of the house for us to sit
on. After a few minutes, a quiet, elderly man—tall, fair and blue-
eyed—emerged from the house to greet us in the local dialect. He
did not look like a grandee in disguise but a very dignified peasant.
We were sure that he was the householder and the main person to
whom we were going to be introduced.

We had barely asked him whether what we had heard in Ayodhya
about Sehanawa and the family of Baqi was true when, before our
host could respond, a large number of men, some returning from the
fields and some from a mosque nearby gathered around us. A couple
of elders in the crowd shouted that all this talk about the descendants
of Baqi was rubbish. 'We have nothing to do with Mir Baqi. He
never came here and he certainly did not die here. If he had, would
there not be a tomb or something to mark the grave of such an important person?' asked one of the elders firmly. 'Now you will go
and write all these things and there would be attacks on the village.
We want to be left alone,' he added. The others nodded in agreement,
urging us to disbelieve the lies that the local VHP leaders were
spreading so that the visiting *kārsevak*s could direct their wrath
towards Sehanawa and destroy the entire village. They said they had
already organized vigilance bodies for 24-hour guard duty and the
entire Muslim community in the village lived in constant panic,
fearing an attack at any time from outsiders. They produced before
us the two young gandsons of the last *imam* of the Babri mosque
whose parents had been killed in the riots of 7 December; both

of them looked traumatized and had swollen, red eyes, obviously from weeping.

.We sat for a while with the group and one of us promised to send the villagers a video cassette of the documentary that had been partly shot in the village. But it was obvious that any further attempt to trace the family of Baqi and their response to the chain of events at Ayodhya would be futile. As we prepared to leave, one of the local shopkeepers, the most articulate of the lot, took us aside. He told us that a couple of years ago, the Hindi magazine *Maya* had carried a story on Mir Baqi's association with Sehanawa based on conversations its correspondent had with some villagers. According to the shopkeeper these men just wanted to feel important; the fact that they would feature in a popular magazine led them to say many things that were false. 'It is because of their lies that we are suffering today,' he added. Obviously we were not the only ones who had come to Sehanawa, chasing the legend of Mir Baqi. The villagers also told us that several Indian and foreign journalists, television producers and even an American university professor had visited them. 'We told them all the same thing.'

It was already dusk. As we were leaving the village the thought struck us that, whatever Mir Baqi might have been, his descendants were not a part of any aristocracy sired by a conquering general but were part of the ordinary peasantry of Avadh in an ordinary village of eastern UP, sharing the fears and anxieties of a besieged community.

INDEX